# Palgrave Studies in the History of the Media

Series Editors
Professor Bill Bell
Cardiff University, UK

Dr Chandrika Kaul
University of St Andrews
UK

Professor Kenneth Osgood
Colorado School of
Mines, USA

Dr Alexander S. Wilkinson
University College Dublin
Ireland

Palgrave Studies in the History of the Media publishes original, high-quality research into the cultures of communication from the middle ages to the present day. The series explores the variety of subjects and disciplinary approaches that characterize this vibrant field of enquiry. The series will help shape current interpretations not only of the media, in all its forms, but also of the powerful relationship between the media and politics, society, and the economy.

Advisory Board: Professor Carlos Barrera (University of Navarra, Spain), Professor Peter Burke (Emmanuel College, Cambridge), Professor Denis Cryle (Central Queensland University, Australia), Professor David Culbert (Louisiana State University, Baton Rouge), Professor Nicholas Cull (Center on Public Diplomacy, University of Southern California), Professor Tom O'Malley (Centre for Media History, University of Wales, Aberystwyth), Professor Chester Pach (Ohio University).

More information about this series at
http://www.springer.com/series/14578

Jonathan Theodore

# The Modern Cultural Myth of the Decline and Fall of the Roman Empire

palgrave
macmillan

Jonathan Theodore
Manchester
United Kingdom

Palgrave Studies in the History of the Media
ISBN 978-1-137-56996-7 (hardcover)    ISBN 978-1-137-56997-4 (eBook)
ISBN 978-1-349-84893-5 (softcover)
DOI 10.1057/978-1-137-56997-4

Library of Congress Control Number: 2016949423

© The Editor(s) (if applicable) and The Author(s) 2016, First softcover printing 2018
The author(s) has/have asserted their right(s) to be identified as the author(s) of this work in accordance with the Copyright, Designs and Patents Act 1988.
This work is subject to copyright. All rights are solely and exclusively licensed by the Publisher, whether the whole or part of the material is concerned, specifically the rights of translation, reprinting, reuse of illustrations, recitation, broadcasting, reproduction on microfilms or in any other physical way, and transmission or information storage and retrieval, electronic adaptation, computer software, or by similar or dissimilar methodology now known or hereafter developed.
The use of general descriptive names, registered names, trademarks, service marks, etc. in this publication does not imply, even in the absence of a specific statement, that such names are exempt from the relevant protective laws and regulations and therefore free for general use.
The publisher, the authors and the editors are safe to assume that the advice and information in this book are believed to be true and accurate at the date of publication. Neither the publisher nor the authors or the editors give a warranty, express or implied, with respect to the material contained herein or for any errors or omissions that may have been made.

Cover illustration: © Sergey Borisov / Alamy Stock Photo

Printed on acid-free paper

This Palgrave Macmillan imprint is published by Springer Nature
The registered company is Macmillan Publishers Ltd. London

# ABSTRACT

For this study, I am investigating the "decline and fall" of Rome, as represented in British and US culture and thought, from the late nineteenth through the early twenty-first centuries. It is my argument that the decline and fall of Rome is no straightforward historical fact, but a "myth" in the terms coined by Claude Lévi-Strauss, meaning not a "falsehood" but a complex social and ideological construct. It represents the fears of European and US thinkers as they confront the perceived instability and pitfalls of the civilization to which they have belonged. The material I have gathered illustrates the value of the decline and fall as a spatiotemporal *concept*, rather than a *historical* event—even when most of its popular and intellectual representations characterise it as such. I am therefore inquiring into the ways in which writers, filmmakers and the media have conceptualized this "decline"; and the parallels they have drawn, deliberately or unconsciously, with their contemporary world. My work fits into a broader collection of studies examining the continuing impact of the Greco-Roman heritage on our cultural and ideological horizons. However, though the representation of antiquity is a fast-growing field of scholarly inquiry, the theme of this project has been little examined. I am critical of the standard model of the "sociology of representation" in history, which holds that such media are almost exclusively a vehicle to articulate contemporary concerns, and which omits the recurring role of deeper, historical and cultural narratives. When I consider the "decline and fall," it instead becomes apparent how the present is adapted to fit the enduring tropes of the past.

# ACKNOWLEDGEMENTS

It would be all too easy to spread the net of debt and gratitude as wide as possible, but I will keep this short and sincere. First and foremost I would like to thank my former PhD supervisor Richard Howells, for his constant and invaluable guidance and assistance in formulating and drafting my ideas. He has been everything a research supervisor could be.

I am also extremely grateful to David Gwynn for his kind and constructive thoughts on this book as it developed. Furthermore, I would like to thank both him and Brian Young for stimulating my interest in history and culture many years ago as an undergraduate.

I would also like to thank my parents for their emotional support and all-round sensible advice on this project.

# CONTENTS

| | | |
|---|---|---|
| 1 | **Introduction** | 1 |
| | *Representation and Myth* | 1 |
| | *Hermeneutics and Historical Consciousness* | 4 |
| | *Antiquity, Past and Present* | 8 |
| | *Methodology* | 13 |
| | | |
| 2 | **Historiography, Myth and Visual Culture** | 21 |
| | *The Fall of the Western Roman Empire and Its Modern Historiography* | 21 |
| | *The Decline and Fall as an Atypical Model of Myth* | 34 |
| | *Myth as Interdisciplinary Study* | 39 |
| | *Theories of Myth* | 41 |
| | *Historiography, Myth and Literature* | 51 |
| | *Historical "Consciousness" and Narrative* | 52 |
| | *Classics and the Vernacular* | 57 |
| | *Film and a Consciousness of Antiquity* | 63 |
| | *Truth and Accuracy in Historical Cinema* | 65 |
| | | |
| 3 | **The Fall of Rome and Ideas of Decline** | 83 |
| | *The Tradition of Decline* | 83 |
| | *Gibbon's Decline and Fall* | 90 |
| | *Gibbon and Concepts of Decadence* | 100 |

4 Roman Decline and the West in the Modern Age 113
  Rome and Reflections on Twentieth-Century Society 113
  Roman Narratives and the Cold War 121
  Mann, Hollywood, and Historical "Truth" 126
  The Fall and Contemporary Discourses of Empire 139

5 Decadence, Imperialism, and Decline from the Late
  Twentieth Century 151
  Mass Culture and Its Critics 151
  Gladiator, Rome, and the USA in AD 2000 161
  9/11 and Critics of Empire 170
  Cinema and the Decline and Fall in the New Millennium 177
  Rome, Civilization, and the Modern Age 184

6 Conclusion 195

Bibliography 201

Index 223

CHAPTER 1

# Introduction

### REPRESENTATION AND MYTH

For this book, I am investigating the "decline and fall" of Rome, as perceived and imagined in aspects of British and US culture and thought, from the late nineteenth through the early twenty-first centuries. It is an interdisciplinary study of these representations and their cultural functions. I am inquiring into the ways in which writers,[1] filmmakers and the media have conceptualized this "decline"; and the parallels they have drawn, deliberately or unconsciously, to their contemporary world. My work fits within a broader collection of studies examining the continuing impact of the Greco-Roman heritage on our present cultural and ideological horizons. However, though the representation of various areas of antiquity is a fast-growing field of scholarly inquiry, the theme of this project has been little examined in this context.

By "representation" I refer to the ways in which material has been transmitted, rewritten, adapted and reimagined. The re-presentation of past eras in new cultural forms is a complex activity, one that is bound up in a much broader set of social and historical processes. The *reception* of classical and medieval culture has a rich and meaningful history of its own. These successive interpretations of the past can prove to be far removed from the events or ideas they describe. And yet one can never fully understand the history of the post-classical world without some measure of direct reference to the ancient cultures against which it has never ceased to define itself, by varying methods and means.

By looking through the prism of the sociology of representation, however, it becomes possible to emphasize the subject's value in a rather different light: as "illuminating textual manifestations of the *mentalities* of the societies from which they arose."[2] The standard model of the cultural "representation" of history theorizes that these media are primarily a vehicle to articulate contemporary concerns. While this approach is at least partly correct, it sometimes misses out the recurring constancy in the value of older historical and cultural narratives, of which our topic in question is a prominent one. Expanding on this approach by incorporating such narratives and traditions helps us understand that the "decline and fall of Rome" is no simple unfiltered "fact," but a "myth" in the academic sense coined by Claude Lévi-Strauss, meaning not a falsehood but a complex social and ideological construct.[3] This is a predominantly secular mythology; though it incorporates a moral and eschatological dimension, one which is partly borne of its theological roots. It represents the fears of European and US thinkers as they confront the perceived instability and pitfalls of the civilization to which they belong. It is a paradigm with a currency stretching back hundreds of years, but which still finds a powerful and influential presence in its mediation through the era of celluloid and mass media.

The material I gather in this study illustrates the value of the decline and fall as a spatiotemporal *concept*, rather than a *historical* event—even when most of its popular and intellectual representations characterizes and classify it as such. Divisions such as the "Middle Ages," "Renaissance" and "Modernity" create value-laden demarcation lines out of the past; imposed epochs of time that can overlook the existence of "Modern" characteristics in the Middle Ages, and "Medieval" characteristics in more modern times. The invocation of such categories and processes provides powerful conceptual markers for other social and political narratives, and a cultural presence that continues to wield influence in contemporary times. In this light, the theme of the decline and fall of Rome functions as a conceptual invention, layered with the additional beliefs and purposes of successive generations. Indeed, contemporary historiography on Late Antiquity and the fall of the Western Roman Empire has challenged the strict historical veracity of this idea itself; namely the notion that, in any meaningful historical sense, we can talk seriously about a "fall" in the fifth century AD, much less the notion of a gradual decline in the centuries before that. The whole concept has little remaining value in strict historical, academic analysis of the fourth and fifth centuries. However, it functions as a meaningful narrative and myth that has been appropriated and reinvented by authors, knowingly or unconsciously, with a significance rendered particular and personal to their own time.

Using well-established theories of the sociology of representation, metahistory, and Straussian myth, I can illustrate the value of the decline and fall as a spatiotemporal concept, or historicizing paradigm. It has featured substantially, in overt or latent ways, in the popular culture of the twentieth and twenty-first centuries. In particular, it serves as a metaphor for the concerns cultural authors in Britain, Europe and the US have with the possibility of a similar "decline" in present times, and therefore functions as a vehicle for contemporary concerns and critiques. Despite a long-standing interest in the influence of ancient culture on the modern world, the archetype of the decline and fall of Rome in Western culture and thought has received little direct consideration. While there are many areas of academic writing that touch on the subject—for instance, a large body of literature analysing the representation of the classical world on film—very few have as their primary frame the specific thematic conception of the decline and fall.[4] Much of this omission can be explained by the fact that most scholarship on antiquity and its reception has been taken up by traditional classicists, whose academic background and consequent area of focus are on the depiction of what falls more strictly within the realm of "Classics"—outside of which exists the subject of the decline and fall of Rome.[5] This study is partly, therefore, a revision of existing attitudes—especially with respect to prominently discussed media, such as notable texts and films—and partly a focus on new material that is little studied.[6]

The approach here contradicts somewhat the contention of the ancient historian Glen Bowersock, who in *The Vanishing Paradigm of the Fall of Rome* (1996) writes that, "The fall of Rome is no longer needed, and like the writing on a faded papyrus, it no longer speaks to us," and that the purpose of the obsession with this fall has become to "deny its existence altogether."[7] Instead, I can contend that not only has the decline and fall of Rome survived and persisted as a cultural and intellectual paradigm, but that it has acquired a prominent and particular relevance in the tradition of British and US political, cultural, and historical thought that compares the rise of Rome with one or both of these nations as the respective superpowers of their age.

This role as a regular component of discourse survives to the present day—enhanced, if anything, by the geopolitical developments since the turn of the twenty-first century. It is a myth as much about the present day, as it is about the ancient world; for an essential property of the decline and fall is that it possesses a universal significance, as a moral tale for the modern world. It appeals to deep-rooted anxieties about the structures of order that surround and support us.

A critical analysis of the forms, and the reception, of the decline and fall addresses a key notion; that myths, and their formulation in popular beliefs, act as an essential mediator in the making and remaking of historical consciousness. Following on from that idea, this book will demonstrate how these examples help challenge the still oft-held notion that, when it comes to the transmission of ideas about the classical past, popular culture exists in a largely distinct, even inferior, realm to the literary and intellectual world. Access to the classical or medieval imaginary is provided not only through academic histories, and canonical literature, but through the popular literature, cinema, and other media examined here. They exist within the same continuum of iconographic representation. I am outlining the form the decline and fall of Rome takes as a mythology, not only as a technical description of its structure, but because it can pervade all levels of public consciousness; from the scholarly and intellectual, to popular culture and the mass media. Myth should be recognized as myth, whether it comes from mass media or from their intellectual critics. Different media can carry the same message, encoded and translated using different tools. Representations of the decline and fall of Rome embrace a wide spectrum of cultural output, and possess common underlying themes. Uncovering them helps us to reconceptualize the relationship between mythic, historical, and fictional narratives. Through this approach, I can build on the ideas of Hayden White, particularly his *Metahistory*, to demonstrate the union of popular and elite texts as a broader expression of historical consciousness.[8] One can treat these different media as expressions of a singular myth.

## HERMENEUTICS AND HISTORICAL CONSCIOUSNESS

In this study I seek to answer the question: What, within our time-frame of the late nineteenth century to the present day, does the representation of the decline and fall of Rome tell us about the societies that produced these cultural texts? The fullest answer to this question requires a *hermeneutic* approach: an interpretative, textual analysis of a collection of films, books, and works of professional "history," with some appropriate examples from the media. This combination of the vernacular and intellectual will demonstrate that, rather than being opposed to each other, they combine as components of a wider *cultural* discourse with that past that frames our relationship to it. A cross-comparative approach demonstrates that these texts betray intimate connections with one another; some overt and deliberate, and others wholly unintended, yet clear and evident upon close analysis.

A second and somewhat deeper question I hope to answer is: Are these representations of decline transient and unique to their specific period, or do they possess universal, archetypal qualities? Here a discussion of the theories of myth found, in particular, in the writings of Lévi-Strauss and Clifford Geertz, becomes very appropriate.[9] This book represents a historical study in which the object of historical inquiry here is shifted towards the historiography itself, or rather a *cultural historiography*, where academic or intellectual authorship interacts with a wider popular and cultural consciousness. Arguably it is this form of "historiography," to slightly reposition the word, that plays a much greater role in the formation of common human thinking and learning, and more specifically for us, the mediation of historical ideas such as the "decline and fall" of Rome. This is precisely because it inhabits this whole array of widely experienced cultural artefacts—literature, art, film, scholarship, journalism, propaganda, stretching across what might traditionally be constituted as both "higher" and "lower" cultural forms. Artists and dramatists map out the mental structure and moral character of an age. Culture can get co-opted into political discourse. And, inevitably, these diverse representations constitute a blend of both the real and the imaginary. Just as popular re-presentations of events contain a value "truth" of their own, so historical writing is framed by its own subjectivities. Looking into this range of historical representation opens up not one but two avenues of inquiry—the study of contemporary society through the representation of the past, and, less overtly, the study of the modern transmission of historical consciousness; much or most of which occurs outside strict academic fields.

Although there have been changes in the cinematic, as well as other popular and academic, conceptions of this period over the past century, and previous to that, our focus is on those continuities which bind together these texts. The chronological range is therefore necessarily broad. Academic work on the reception of this period, or history in general, often articulates its own special place, and its relevance to contemporary debates, by proclaiming a "current wave" of films, literature, and other writing; and proffers explanations for the renewed, or growing, relevance of the subject under discussion by focusing on recent historical examples, with some classical examples thrown in for wider context. A prime example of this has been the renewed attention on the USA as an "empire," and an empire seen as potentially threatened with decline, in the wake of the 9/11 attacks. Yet the focus of this kind of study is not on a specific set of material, but on picking up persistent patterns. A strong case can be made for a recent surge of interest in questions concerning the "fall of empires"—particularly the comparison with Ancient Rome and the perceived ills of the contemporary USA—but this, while important, is not the primary focus of this book, nor will it be a justification for its value.

This project must necessarily include an examination of relevant historical writing. Much of this can be easily considered to fall within the subjective criteria described above. Historiography is itself intimately connected to a wider set of discourses. Supposed "historical" descriptions of the past are, to varying degrees, a recursive narrative about the present, and can easily fall victim to anachronism and ideology. All history is informed by what Walter Benjamin calls the "presence of the now,"[10] meaning that any interpretation of a past culture is refracted through the prism of our own thought worlds.[11] When we unravel the layers of preconceptions associated with a historical archetype, we see that it can be understood not just as the factual descriptor of a period of time, nor even as an "arbitrary" historiographical construct. Rather it is a whole ideological framework for comprehending the past, and a discourse manifest across the cultural spectrum.

Consequently, this book explores territory where history dilutes into this cultural historiography; and, at a deeper level, the more anthropological realm of myth. The latter term will be used often and needs to be carefully defined for our purposes. A myth in this sense denotes neither a fact nor a falsehood, but a cultural and societal narrative. Myths are tools that codify abstract ideas into concrete form (Bible stories, such as those contained in Genesis, being a good example).[12] They are complex social and cultural creations, rather than accurate representations of historical truth: they take mutable forms, and embody shifting meanings over time.

Whether the "myth" is accurate or not in any strict factual sense is in some ways just a coincidence. Such accuracy is not the reason for its emergence; rather, the reason lies in a myth's capacity to provide a source of narrative and meaning. This does not mean that myths have little or nothing to do with the historical record, as is pertinent to my considerations here. Myths and traditions use distorted and invented history, but this does not mean they have nothing to do with historical fact. They inhabit a world built on both fact and fictions.[13]

If myths help define our thinking, then they can be as important as any "factual" truth.[14] At the heart of our perception of the world are the stories we weave into it. Much of what is commonly considered "truth" is the narrative product of human need. When it comes to the treatment of the past, beliefs, intentions, and human imagination, are as much a part of history as actual "History" in the more formal sense is.[15] The significance of historical events, in this context, is approached from the position of society's views on them, not the events themselves—value is instead generated from the *impression* of what occurred, and why, and the forms in which that impression survives as a cultural imprint. Within the push and pull of social and cultural forces, the meaning and accorded value of any historical event becomes contingent and liable to change. Siegfried Kracauer contended that "society is full of events that defy control …. [I]t swallows up ideas fed into it and, in adapting them to its inarticulate needs, often completely distorts their original meanings."[16] Far-fetched ideas or interpretations that seem to have a limited initial bearing on "reality" can acquire a powerful significance of their own, forming their own presence in the "real." Hence the assertion by Richard Howells that the "unsinkable" nature of the Titanic has become one of the most important, and discussed, ingredients of the story, from history classes to popular representations—despite it being demonstrably factually inaccurate, and an invention *after* the event.[17]

Much the same can be said about the idea of a Roman decline and fall. One could infer that there is a disjunction between the "truth" and "falsehood" surrounding a past event—whatever their respective importance to its representation—but the line cannot be so easily drawn. Truth is a consequence not so much of data, but of narrative and the search for meaning. While the story of the decline and fall of the Roman Empire purports, in its various forms, to be a representation of some essential human and historical "truth," it is better described as something akin to a myth or moral tale; one broadly constant, and yet appropriated for a range of different purposes by its authors. In this way, these creative, artistic, and (what might otherwise be deemed) "unhistorical" qualities can directly lead to the formation of a historical consciousness, a paradigm that embraces the popular as much as it does academic or intellectual domains. The close association of history and art provides a means by which myth can permeate, in the conjunction between the two. Such is clearly evident in the ideal of the decline and fall—a historicizing paradigm with a currency stretching back hundreds of years, but which still finds a powerful and influential presence in its mediation through the era of celluloid and mass culture.

## ANTIQUITY, PAST AND PRESENT

My focus on the theme of the decline and fall of Rome requires a clear awareness of the overall historical background to this period. "Late Antiquity" (c. AD 300–600) is a term used by historians to describe the transitional centuries in Europe and the Mediterranean from "Classical" Antiquity to the Middle Ages. It is normally treated as beginning with the reorganization of the Empire under Diocletian, at the end of the third century, and ending with the upheavals of the Islamic conquests in the seventh. In this time, the Roman Empire underwent a wholesale political, cultural and social transformation, starting with the reforms of Diocletian and the adoption of Christianity as the official—and eventually exclusive—religion of the Empire, and culminating in Western Europe with the destruction of Roman rule by a wave of Germanic migrations. Late Antiquity was consequently a period of enormous and far-reaching change. In particular, the fusion of Greco-Roman, Christian and Germanic traditions after Rome's "fall"—meaning, in strict historical terms, the end of the Western Roman Empire as a political unit from AD 476—laid the cultural, political and ideological foundations of what we have since commonly defined as "Western Europe."

In contrast with the long-cherished field of classical scholarship, Late Antiquity has only comparatively recently been the beneficiary of a thriving body of research. This movement was largely initiated by Peter Brown, whose seminal survey *The World of Late Antiquity* (1971) challenged the "Gibbonian" contention that the Christianized Roman world was sapped of its vitality and wallowing in decadence, weakening to the point that it withered under the onslaught of the Germanic hordes. The entire notion of late antiquity is in part a corrective to a previous bias, which assumed that the entire Roman world fell apart in the fifth century, just because this is what happened to some degree in the Western Roman Empire. For this reason, Peter Brown relocated the cultural centre of gravity of the world to the Near East and the Levant Brown and later scholars have instead emphasized the vigour and vitality of the later Roman world, especially in its capacity for cultural creativity and innovation. Consequently, the collapse of the empire in the West is more attributed to contingent and external factors than morally clouded concepts of creeping enervation and decay. As Glen Bowersock argues, "a new generation of historians of antiquity would rewrite the decline of the classical world as the rise of late antiquity."[18]

The significance of the questions explored in this book is borne out by the fact that "antiquity" has such a powerful latent presence on our cultural horizons. The Greco-Roman heritage is a cornerstone of our cultural traditions: the decline in classical studies is not mirrored by falling interest in the ancient world. With a boundless opportunity for interpretation, Rome has been remade and refashioned countless times, and embodied most conceivable archetypes of triumph and tragedy. Its rooted presence in our heritage makes it an extraordinarily fertile paradigm for generating and subverting meaning.

The consequence of this substantive cultural record is that, over the centuries, questions about history, culture, and society have both been brought to and derived from ancient history and texts. These often involve subjects far removed from the Hellenic and Roman world, but which still owe some origin to the ancient world and its literature.[19] Americans and Europeans have long used Rome to define themselves and their place in human history, and to measure their political, cultural and spiritual achievements. The legacy of the ancient world has been both grounds for assurance and optimism, and a testament to decline and decay. Attitudes to the empire have varied between anything from the guiding light of civilization to the whore of Babylon.[20] It could be a potent symbol of oppressive power or a revolutionary alternative to the existing order. The French Revolution viewed itself as Rome reincarnated—and with some modifications, the same principles are found in the political rhetoric of the Founding Fathers.[21] For the theologically-inclined writers of Medieval and Renaissance times, the later Roman Empire, and especially the city of Rome, could represent the union and concord of humanity under an undivided Christian faith—or a cautionary tale of decadence and corruption. Similarly, the USA's quest for identity drew itself to this repository of historical suggestion. Classical Antiquity endowed the USA with the legitimacy of a cultural, moral, and intellectual tradition linking the New World to Athenian Democracy. Consequently the Roman past has for a long time served as a precedent, an ideal and a warning to US political and cultural commentators. It has been used to tackle questions of history, politics, society and identity.[22]

A somewhat overlooked aspect of this tradition, the idea of a "decline and fall" has deep-rooted origins in the cultural milieu of medieval and modern times. The adjective "Roman" evokes the idea of "ruin" as easily as it does that of "empire."[23] A post-Enlightenment idea of the decadence and decay of Roman power, culture, and civilization was immortalized by Edward Gibbon's six-volume *The History of the Decline and Fall of the Roman Empire* (1776–89).[24] But it had much earlier precedents. Ideas of decline are embodied in a tradition of thought as old as any cultural record. The medieval preoccupation with Rome was endless: Bede, Dante and the like were captivated by its tales. The very ruins of the city provoked awe and admiration—"the old myth of Rome's eternity," a veneration for the past that also transformed it.[25] Fascinated and appalled by the Roman example, writers, commentators, and later filmmakers have constructed narratives of decadence and decline, tracing a progressive fall from cultural and spiritual heights to a nadir of ruin in the fifth century; or, in the East, the exotic, Orientalist repression of "Byzantium." Within this model, decadence and corruption have often been a traditional element of explanations of Roman moral and imperial decline. As these ideas matured further, imperial effeminacy fitted nicely with the modern idea of "conspicuous consumption," and old concepts of *luxuria* morphed into puritanical vitriol against sloth and luxury, and both moral and Marxist tirades against the ostentation of the bourgeoisie.[26]

The repertoire of concepts, images and ideas surrounding the decline and fall of Rome—and the archetype of "decline" in general—have been assembled and mediated over many centuries. They have foundations in intertwining traditions of "classical" and "Christian."[27] Historians, theologians, philosophers, writers, dramatists—and more recently filmmakers—have all contributed to the common stock.[28] Gibbon took the moral evaluations of Tacitus and Sallust and expanded them to fit a vast new casual framework for the emergence of Medieval and Enlightened Europe. Cecil B. DeMille's depictions of the pagan city of Rome as a cesspit of vice and decadence owe themselves to the patristic injunctions of Augustine and Jerome. Voltaire reapplied the classical schemata of four world empires to the four great ages of the arts. Contemporary cultural "mediators" have been heir to this growing treasury of schemata on decline. The film *Gladiator* (Dreamworks 2000) belongs as much to this ongoing process of appropriation as does the sixth-century Gothic propagandist Jordanes.

This tradition—one that conjoins disciplines of thought and methods of representation—is a long one with deep roots. It is a conceptual map that historians, writers, intellectuals and the like have consciously or unconsciously drawn on, and the shape of its influence can be discerned in the contours of our cultural terrain. It helps reveal the interpenetration of the modern and medieval worlds, the universalities in narrative human thought, and the interplay of history and myth. It is not a strictly historiographical tradition, but involves a considerable amount of historical or pseudo-historical writing.

Inevitably, the topic at hand could be treated as extremely broad. The "modern" archetype of a decline and fall can be roughly conceived as stretching from the writings of Edward Gibbon, and extending to the present day. It has intensified in the years since 9/11, with renewed consideration of the place of the USA as an "empire"—a discussion that was similarly very much evident in the USA and Great Britain at the turn of the twentieth century. However, inevitable constraints of length require that some stricter, coherent parameters are defined. This study is concerned primarily with covering the late nineteenth to the early twenty-first centuries because there has been an active interchange between academic and imaginative meanings from the nineteenth century into the twentieth and after. This period saw the emergence of so-called "professional histories"—but those histories are conditioned by earlier rhetoric, poetic and mythic traditions, and ideologies couched as objective truth.[29]

These representations were not cultivated in isolation from an exclusively "intellectual" sphere of scholarship, but emerged through an active engagement with it. In 1874, Theodor Mommsen, one of the most prominent nineteenth-century historians of Ancient Rome, went so far as to observe: "The historian has perhaps greater affinity with the artist than with the scholar."[30] Film itself follows long-standing literary traditions,[31] and cinema's representations of Rome have their roots in both the "histories" of the nineteenth century, and literary portrayals of antiquity and its "fall." Indeed, knowledge of Rome is increasingly a consequence of its presentation in moving images: classicist and film historian Maria Wyke contends that historical films are worth examining for creating "a consciousness of history far exceeding that of historical scholarship in its range and impact."[32]

An awareness of the relationship between history and these other cultural forms leads us to constitute the principle here of an *imaginative historiography*, a dialogue with the past that also belongs to its own recursive tradition, one that shapes a society's historical capital. This, in turn, can be seen as part of a larger concept of history; one that stretches beyond simply the knowledge and attempted understanding of the past, and represents the web of connections to the past that holds a culture together and encodes its identity. As David Morgan argues, "Language and vision, word and image, text and picture are in fact deeply enmeshed and collaborate powerfully in assembling our sense of the real."[33] The representations examined here are part of the meta-historical framework by which the present interfaces with the past, and conceives a sense of its heritage. The decline and fall of Rome has been constituted and reconstituted as a "mythic" narrative; in religion, history and politics, as much as literature and the visual arts.

This emphasis on a firm historical context contradicts the approach of many representational studies, which focus merely on the *present* significance of depictions of the past: forging a tight recursive horizon in which the formal historical content is almost a coincidence, or inconvenience. I will demonstrate that Rome is *not* simply an arbitrary enabling device. Instead, I am emphasizing that the transmission of these ideas exists within a *tradition* in which new meanings have been gradually layered over time. Writers, filmmakers and artists position themselves, deliberately or unconsciously, in relation to their predecessors. Popular authors and creative artists often do not directly acknowledge their inspirations and sources, and may not possess a conscious awareness of the influences that shape their creative impulses.[34]

The classical and post-classical world is a particularly powerful source of these archetypes: such as the one under investigation in this book. Yet these sources can be appropriated and reimagined in new and novel ways. Rome was not described solely through the language of inertia, but by the assimilation of new events and ideas, and the experiences of its collective contributors as mediated through their interpretations. As with any living intellectual tradition, these ideas have not been static and mechanical, but are involved in active and engaged response with the contemporary world. Representations "have ceaselessly shifted in structure and meaning."[35] There is no single, universal conception of "antiquity" or "decline and fall"—rather, these terms denote a plurality of uses and appropriations. Ideas could be developed in whole new ways. Subsequent generations have added to or distorted the meaning of events and ideas, as a form of cultural "Chinese whispers." This book therefore considers the ever-evolving nature of interface of classical and modern cultural forms, and consequently the value of a productive exchange between scholarship on classical (and medieval) culture and cultural theories of the popular.

## Methodology

The nexus of this study is on historical forms of representations of decline, and their mutual relationship. The questions posed here require an interdisciplinary methodological framework. I need to consider what constitutes "myth," and thereby delve into social anthropology; the nature of symbolic and metaphorical representation, as described in semiotics and cultural theory; and historiography for the ideas and writings of historians. This multi-disciplinary approach was championed by Clifford Geertz, who referred to the need to have an "intellectual armoury" of concepts at hand when delving into the root of meaning.[36] The value of interdisciplinary work was also praised by Terry Eagleton, who stated that, "much of the interesting work on the humanities" now being carried out is "constantly transgressing the frontiers between traditional subject areas."[37] Similarly, historical scholarship now involves a wide synthesis of varying fields—anthropology, psychology, sociology, and quantitative studies.[38]

The range of possible approaches that can and are used in studies such as this are extremely broad. It includes: taking particular examples (such as in films, plays, books, art) to elicit generalized patterns and trends; examining the impact of reception in shaping our entire view of a work; charting the specific history of a text, style, idea, or discourse; or emphasizing the formal and transhistorical qualities of a text in its mediated representations.

All of these approaches throw up obvious questions and criticisms. Extrapolating trends draws charges of selectivity and positivism; prioritizing textual "reception" carries the danger or charge of cultural materialism (and very commonly a Marxian approach); while favouring supposedly enduring qualities could be judged as veneration, particularly in relation to the "classics" and their perceived cultural authority.

The theories explored and utilized here are therefore guides to inform and underpin the research, rather than a rigid set of rules. In this study I am employing a *hermeneutic* methodology in my analysis. This is an interpretative approach that emphasizes the subjective qualities of appraisal, over scientific or social-scientific analysis. The importance of hermeneutics in the study of culture was outlined by the anthropologist Clifford Geertz, who famously stated that "man is an animal suspended in webs of significance that he himself has spun," and that "those webs are what we call culture." That culture itself is "an assemblage of texts"—a story people tell themselves, about themselves.[39] The hermeneutic or interpretative methodology is akin to "penetrating a literary text," through the "close reading" of its cultural equivalents.[40] For Geertz, the analysis of culture, and cultural history, is "not an experimental science in search of law, but an interpretive one in search of meaning"[41]—in the context of this project, the meaning embedded in the traditions of the decline and fall. In contrast to the rigid and quasi-scientific structuralism of Strauss and Saussure, the anthropologist Geertz championed the use of a multidisciplinary and hermeneutic approach, providing a range of concepts and theories to unravel meaning.[42] He declared opposition to "increasingly hollow" general theories of cultural interpretation, arguing that one shouldn't try and explain social phenomena by "weaving them into grand textures" or "arranging abstracted entities into unified patterns."[43] Instead, he stated a desire to replace "an experimental science in search of law to an interpretative one in search of meaning,"[44] making his methodology particularly relevant to the approach in this book.

"Anthropological" approaches to myth in a cultural context have typically veered between empirical field work and comparative study. The former prioritizes the collection and comprehension of the myths, rituals, and practices of a particular people, in their specific context. Comparative approaches, conversely, are more concerned with the *ontology* of myth, and seek to unravel and expose common properties in their content, usage and themes. Comparative *theories*, therefore, hold that myths have strikingly similar features, even when widely separated in time and space. It is the comparative tradition, in both the cultural and the social anthropology of myth, which is of greater interest and value to this study.

Much scholarship on media, culture and society has seen a strong tradition of "scientific" or content-based examination, usually quantitative in kind. The danger with this this kind of content analysis is that it only touches the surface, and misses the deeper, sometimes buried meaning.[45] Objective social sciences try to render ambivalence into clear and precise meaning—thereby imposing their *own*, potentially quite subjective, order and narrative on the subject. Conversely, hermeneutics recognizes the ambiguities of its art, and thrives on it.

However, though certain conceptual tools, appropriated from fields such as cultural anthropology, are used in the aid of this study, this method of inquiry still falls firmly within the umbrella of "history"—as the history of ideas, and their manifold methods of expression, are simply another prism through which we view and analyse the past. This book is rooted in traditional social, historical and political theories and approaches. I am not interested in bracketing these topics within the more novel structures of cultural studies or media theory—though some of the ideas in these theories are undoubtedly very important. Instead, this book simply stresses the coherent links between past and present, and the process by which meaning is mediated from a text.

As part of this book's backdrop, I need to discuss how the cultural climates of pre-Modern Europe influenced the macroscopic perspective of several historians and intellectuals, notably Gibbon. This is for three reasons. Firstly, I wish to demonstrate the importance of social, cultural and political context on historiography and its tradition, especially the historiography of a remote and intellectually "pliable" period; secondly, because I believe that under such writers, key opinions and images of Roman decline and fall fossilized and have been transmitted through varying cultural media to the present day; and thirdly, because they are a useful comparative element within the myth-based model of "decline" I will argue for and employ.

The "decline and fall of Rome" is considered as an invented cultural narrative, rather than a cogent historical observation. The vast majority of contemporary historiography on the period recognizes the manifold errors and loaded presumptions in its logic; however, the relation between the conceptualization of its defining attributes, and the formations of our basic historical and cultural assumptions, has not been formally studied. In examining this relationship further, it is necessary to abstract what I can of the "framework" of myth in more theoretical terms. In particular, I need to consider what anchors the decline of antiquity as an *emergent cultural concept, not a fixed "historic" event*. The trap of anachronism is a particularly powerful one in studies and representations of the ancient world, for a society such as ancient Rome can present us with both striking similarities in character and drives (which are commonly highlighted for these purposes), and deep, profound differences.

Finally, I must point out that this study is concerned with a largely coherent set of Western responses that can be observed in Gibbon's formulation of the myth of decline (and its earlier precedents). The theme and topic of this study are by their nature already broad, and expanding the remit that much further could affect its clarity of focus. The subject of French, Russian, Italian and other cultural responses to the notion of decline and fall is a vast topic, and to fully do it justice could easily require an additional book in itself. However, I do accept that *some* mention could be made of more notable examples of these responses, to illuminate the more essential similarities and contrasts between responses to the decline and fall in the English-speaking West, and those other nations and cultures that saw themselves as the inheritors of the Roman tradition.

NOTES

1. "Writers" referring to those of both popular and intellectual inclinations in their work, or agents of "high" and "low" culture as they might otherwise be described.
2. Richard Howells, *The Myth of the Titanic* (London: Palgrave Macmillan, 1999), p. 21.
3. Claude Lévi-Strauss, *Structural Anthropology*, trans. Clair Jacobson (London: Penguin, 1968), pp. 203–6.
4. One specific study that is centred on this theme, focusing almost exclusively on a positive critical appraisal of Anthony Mann's *The Fall of the Roman Empire* (Paramount Pictures, 1964), is Martin M. Winkler, "Cinema and the Fall of Rome," *Transactions of the American Philological Association*, CXXI (1995), pp. 135–154.
5. The most definitive influential texts in this regard is Jon Solomon, *The Ancient World and the Cinema* (New York: Yale University Press (ori. Pub. 1978), 2001). See also Derek Elley, *The Epic Film: Myth in History* (London: Routledge Kegan and Paul, 1984), Martin M. Winkler (ed.), *Classics and Cinema* (Lewisburg: Bucknell University Press, 1991), and Maria Wyke, "Ancient Rome and the Traditions of Film History," *Screening the Past*, VI (1999), published online at http://tlweb.latrobe.edu.au/humanities/screeningthepast/firstrelease/fr0499/mwfr6b.htm
6. Alexander Demandt, *Der Fall Roms: Die Auflösung des römischen Reiches im Urteil der Nachwelt* (Munich: Beck, 1984), is the most exhaustive study of the impact of the decline and fall of Rome on Western intellectual history, and produces a famous list of "201" reasons that have been cited for the downfall of the empire, including more comical and absurdist notions—everything from "gluttony" to "lead poisoning" and "lack of seriousness."
7. Glen W. Bowersock, "The Vanishing Paradigm of the Fall of Rome," *Bulletin of the American Academy of Arts and Sciences*," LXIX (1996), pp. 29–43.
8. Hayden White, *Metahistory: The Historical Imagination in Nineteenth-Century Europe* (Baltimore: John Hopkins, 1973).
9. Clifford Geertz, "Notes on a Balinese Cockfight," in Clifford Geertz, *The Interpretation of Cultures* (Basic Books: New York (ori. Pub. 1973), 1993), pp. 412–453. See also Strauss (1968).

10. Walter Benjamin, *On the concept of history*, trans. Dennis Redmond (Frankfurt: Gesammelten Schriften, 1974), XIV.
11. Norman F. Cantor, *Inventing the Middle Ages: The Lives, Works, and Ideas of the Great Medievalists of the Twentieth Century* (New York: William Morrow & Company, 1991), p. 37.
12. Howells (1999), p. 2, p. 11.
13. Op. cit., p. 11.
14. Op. cit., p. 48.
15. Marc Ferro, *Cinema and History*, trans. Naomi Greene (Michigan: Wayne State University Press, 1988), p. 29.
16. Siegfried Kracauer, *History: The Last Things Before the Last* (New York: Marcus Weiner (ori. Pub. 1969), 1995) pp. 24–25.
17. Howells (1999), p. 2. He also cites here Robert Darnton's "Great Cat Massacre" as an example of something invested with cultural value, regardless of whether the event actually took place or not.
18. For a broad summary of these ideas see Peter Brown, *The World of Late Antiquity: from Marcus Aurelius to Muhammad* (AD *150–750*), (London: Thames and Hudson (ori. Pub. 1971), 1989), emphasizing the continuity of Roman culture and civilization beyond the end of the Western Roman Empire in 476, and also Peter Brown, *The Rise of Western Christendom: Triumph and Diversity 200–1000* AD (London: Blackwell, 2003), Averil Cameron, *The Later Roman Empire:* AD *284–430*, (Cambridge: Harvard University Press, 1993), and Stephen Mitchell, *A History of the Later Roman Empire.* AD *284–641* (London: Blackwell, 2006). For the quote, see Bowersock (1996), p. 64.
19. An example would be the comparison between modern mass culture and the oft-cited "bread and circuses" maxim of Juvenal, found in Juvenal, *The Sixteen Satires*, trans. Peter Green (London: Penguin Classics, 1998), IV, 10.81.
20. Kevin J. Pratt, "Rome as Eternal," *Journal of the History of Ideas*, XXVI (1965), p. 32.
21. Benjamin (1974), XIV.
22. On these examples see, William L. Vance, *America's Rome* (New Haven: Yale University Press, 1989), Cullen Murphy, *Are We Rome?* (Boston: Houghton Mifflin Harcourt, 2007), Duncan Kennedy, "A sense of place: Rome, history and empire revisited," in Catherine Edwards (ed.), *Roman presences: receptions of Rome in European culture, 1789–1945* (Cambridge: Cambridge University Press, 1999), pp. 19–34, Peter Bondanella, *The eternal city. Roman images in the modern world* (Chapel Hill: University of North Carolina Press, 1987). Several books published or republished since 2001 on contemporary American politics and history discuss the idea of

"imperial presidency"; see for instance Arthur M. Schlesinger, *The Imperial Presidency* (Boston: Houghton Mifflin (ori. Pub. 1973), 2004).
23. Edwards (1999), p. 247.
24. Edward Gibbon, *The History of the Decline and Fall of the Roman Empire*, 6 vols (London: Everyman Library (ori. Pub. 1776–89) 1993). Any future references to this work will be cited from this version.
25. Charles T. Davis, *Dante and the Idea of Rome* (Oxford: Clarendon Press, 1957), p. 3. Dante in particular tried to universalize the "myth" to embrace both pagan and Christian times. The physical decline of the city into ruin played a direct role in inspiring Gibbon, for "it was at Rome ... as I sat amidst the ruins of the Capital ... that the idea of writing the decline and fall of the city first started in my mind," Gibbon (1993), I, p. lxvii.
26. Edwards, p. 13, pp. 111–2, p. 122.
27. See Augustine, *The City of God*, trans. Henry Bettenson (Harmondsworth: Penguin Books (ori. Pub. 1972), 2003). All future quotations from Augustine will be from this version. See also Davis, p. 3.
28. See also Ernest R. Curtis, *European Literature in the Later Middle Ages* (New Jersey: Princeton University Press (ori. Pub. 1953), 1990), which examines the continuity of European literature from Homer to Goethe, with Medieval and Late Antique literature deemed the prime mediator in this transition.
29. White (1973), pp. xi-xii, and Stephen Bann, *The inventions of history: essays on the representation of the past* (Manchester: Manchester Univ. Press, 1990), pp. 4–5.
30. Gilbert Chase, "The Musicologist as Historian: A Matter of Distinction," *Notes*, XXIX (1972), p. 12. British historian George M. Trevelyan enlarged on this theme in an essay collection called *Clio, a Muse: And Other Essays* (London: Longmans Green (ori. Pub. 1904), 1913).
31. Martin M. Winkler (ed.), *Classics and Cinema* (Lewisburg: Bucknell University Press, 1991), p. 9.
32. Op. cit., p. 13.
33. David Morgan, *Visual Piety: A History and Theory of Popular Religious Images* (London: University of California Press, 1998), p. 9.
34. Martin M. Winkler (ed.), *Classics and Cinema* (Lewisburg: Bucknell University Press, 1991), p. 10.
35. Edwards, p. 74.
36. Geertz (1973), p. 4.
37. As quoted in Howells (1999), p. xiv.
38. Arthur Marwick, *The New Nature of History* (London: Palgrave Macmillan, 2001) provides a summary of these evolving trends and techniques in historical scholarship over the twentieth century.
39. Geertz, p. 448.

40. Op. cit., p. 453.
41. Op. cit., p. 5.
42. Op. cit., p. 4.
43. Op. cit., p. 6, p. 17.
44. Op. cit., p. 5.
45. Howells (1999), p. 7. The distinction between overt and latent content is discussed in p. 11, and pp. 18–20.

CHAPTER 2

# Historiography, Myth and Visual Culture

## THE FALL OF THE WESTERN ROMAN EMPIRE AND ITS MODERN HISTORIOGRAPHY

This book posits the decline and fall as a myth that reflects deeper, enduring, cultural and intellectual trends of reception and representation. For this reason, the very different approach of modern historiographical scholarship to the subject needs to be explored in some detail. This must be done by first examining how the field has diverged from the work of Arnold Hugh Martin (A.H.M) Jones, a prominent historian of the later Roman Empire who wrote a key narrative history of Late Rome and early "Byzantium," namely his 1964 book entitled *The Later Roman Empire, 284–602: A Social, Economic, and Administrative Survey*.[1] This work is of key significance, both to the history of its field and the subject of this book in particular, because it marked the end of the historiographical dominance of the Gibbonian approaches to the period. In a recent study of the historian, Bryan Ward-Perkins considers how "before Jones, the social and economic history (indeed the whole story) of the late Roman empire was predominantly apocalyptic, and almost invariably linked to some Grand Theory of Decline."[2] Peter Brown, writing in 1967 about the impact of Jones on the field, described that tradition in this way:

> There has been a tendency to take for granted, both that the main social and economic developments of the Late Roman period provide the clue to the decline and fall of the Roman Empire, and that the transition between

© The Editor(s) (if applicable) and The Author(s) 2016
J. Theodore, *The Modern Cultural Myth of the Decline and Fall of the Roman Empire*, DOI 10.1057/978-1-137-56997-4_2

the ancient world and the Middle Ages is best understood in terms of the replacement, in this period, of an "ancient" by a "medieval" style of society ... the immediate circumstances of the fall of the Western Empire have been understood in terms of a decline in population, of the barbarization of the Roman army ... the divergent destinies of the Eastern and Western Empires merely ratify our impression of the deep-seated weaknesses of Roman society in the West of the third and fourth centuries AD.[3]

He notes that "Jones, by contrast, takes very little for granted." Consequently, "in the present state of Late Roman studies, this book is like the arrival of a steel-plant in a region that has, of late, been given over to light industries."[4]

Jones helped pave the way for the study of what is now called "Late Antiquity," and staged a revamping away from the old historiographical notions of decline and fall. Unlike his predecessors, Jones did *not* argue that internal problems brought down the empire. In his conclusion to *The Later Roman Empire*, he says that the evidence "suggests that the simple but rather unfashionable view that the barbarians played a considerable part in the decline and fall of the empire may have some truth to it ... [that] barbarian attacks probably played a major part in the fall of the West."[5]

Jones, in many ways, represents the beginning of a new and truly "post-Gibbonian" outlook on the period. Yet he also marks the zenith of the older approach; with regard to both his account of the civic and economic structures of Late Roman society, and in the source analysis he used to derive his position. While he moves far away from the melancholic judgements of his predecessors,[6] Jones's survey of the later empire still carries a strain of pessimism, and some notion of decline. Much of its core analysis has come under extensive criticism by a subsequent generation of scholarship.

Jones examined the social, political and administrative developments of the empire from the reforms of Diocletian and Constantine onwards. His conclusion was that such measures—designed to restore and protect the empire from the crises of the third century—as the expansion of the imperial bureaucracy (at the expense of the old "curial" system of local government) and the legitimization and endowment of the Christian Church produced a new set of "idle mouths" that, coupled with a repressive series of laws and economic slump, pushed the empire into a relative decline from the peak condition of the Principate. Jones put the economic condition of the later empire in these terms:

> The basic economic weakness of the empire was that too few producers supported too many idle mouths. This state of affairs was in part an inheritance from the Principate, in part imposed by increasing barbarian pressure, in part again due to the incompetence of the government, in part finally due to the new religion which the empire adopted.[7]

Jones therefore makes clear that the economic condition of the empire had worsened by later imperial times. In particular, the burden of the state was deemed substantially higher.[8] Extra resources were sucked out of a subsistence economy that, by the standards of "the more prosperous days of the Principate,"[9] was depopulated, unproductive and succumbing to agricultural decline, into new or expanded institutions of church, army and state. The economic burden of empire was increased to a punishing level,[10] which promoted famine, enhanced the oppression of the peasantry or quasi-feudal *coloni*, widened the deserted lands (*agri deserti*), and hurt the landowning classes who had built and sustained the cities, and upon whose support and prosperity Roman rule ultimately depended. The imperial system became dominated by artificial constraints—as evidenced in the series of proscriptive laws compiled in the Theodosian Code—and the resources of the empire were drained by an overstaffed and inefficient bureaucracy; whilst contributing to the tax hike that helped weaken the imperial structure.[11] Such problems were felt more harshly in the poorer, less populous and more institutionally "unhealthy" West.[12]

Jones's assessment has been of great historiographical value to the study of Late Antiquity, and the transformation of the entire field in the past 40 years. Peter Brown in 1967 considered his work "an event of the first importance in the study of the Later Roman Empire," in particular for its rich and detailed account of Late Roman society, and the Christian Church.[13] Ward-Perkins states that "Jones, as far as I was concerned, had constructed a scholarly edifice so solid that there was really no need to look back beyond 1964..." and describes his knowledge of the fourth to sixth centuries as being "built on the firm foundations of the *Later Roman Empire*."[14]

Of greatest significance for this study is the fact that Jones decouples the notion of decline from any real causal consideration in the "fall" of the Western Empire. While he critiques its social systems and administrative structures, the extent of these judgements is muted, and free from the burden of teleological doom. Nowhere is this clearer than in the very last line of the *Later Roman Empire*, where, after summarizing all the evidence, he concludes that "the internal weaknesses of the empire cannot have been the major factor in its decline."[15] This closing statement underscores this vital break in the academic historiography from the tradition of the decline and fall.

However, despite these profoundly important steps towards the world of Late Antiquity, Jones's thesis has been noticeably modified by the succeeding generation of historians. This principle of real, substantial Roman decline is still present in the *Later Roman Empire*—an idea over which the shadow of Gibbon still looms, even if it is void of his conclusions. As Ward-Perkins puts it, "in comparison to this work [Peter Brown' *World of Late Antiquity*], Jones's *Later Roman Empire is* both very institutional, and undeniably bleak, with its overweening bureaucrats and soldiers, and its peasants struggling under fiscal and legal oppression."[16] While his thesis is free of the sweeping moral indictments of Gibbon, he can still offer the observation that, "The most depressing feature of the later empire is the apparent absence of public spirit."[17] Such a statement echoes the notion of qualitative moral and civic decline found in the writings of historical theorists such as Spengler and Toynbee in the generation before him.

Modern historians have moved even further away from Jones's academic predecessors than he did in arguing against the importance, or even the very idea, of institutional and civic decline. Jones's arguments were founded on a detailed study of the literary and epigraphic evidence available to him: but he has very little to say about the archaeological record, or non-literary material in general. Ward-Perkins finds only three examples in the entire 1,500 pages of the *Later Roman Empire*.[18] Averil Cameron states that, "Visual art was not part of Jones's conception of what to include. The use now made by virtually all late antique historians of archaeological and artistic evidence makes a vast change ... one that happened in parallel with the development of the Brownian cultural model of "late antiquity'."[19] Aside from this, his reliance on the bare statements of the literary sources, especially legal codes, has come in for criticism.

Contemporary historians now use a broader base of sources to emphasize the cultural, political and economic vitality of the Late Roman world. In particular, Jones's reliance on literary and epigraphic sources appears to have produced an overly pessimistic assessment of the economy and urban condition of the Later Empire.[20] The boom in Late Antique archaeology since the 1970s has helped revz the view that overtaxation squeezed the economy; suggesting instead that this was a period of economic vitality, not of falling productivity and population numbers, for both halves of the empire.[21] This sits in contrast to Jones's view that the economic condition of the empire had worsened by late imperial times; a process fostered by the new "idle mouths" of the empire, the heavy burden of taxation, and the abandonment of agricultural land. Such an argument was founded on written and primarily legal sources.[22] These are replete with their own inferential problems when viewed in isolation. For example, the term *agri deserti* was coined in fourth-century legal documents to describe land on which no tax was collected, but this does not necessarily mean that tax had previously been collected there, as the law of 422 on which Jones based his argument refers to regions of desert or semi-desert on which it is unlikely agriculture had ever been possible.[23] However, Jones was far from unduly negative on the state of the agricultural economy, stating "the extent of the evil must not be exaggerated," and that it was primarily the approximately 20 per cent of marginal land that was affected.[24] His summary of the state of the empire's agriculture was this: "it must be emphasized that there was no general agricultural decline; land of good and medium quality continued to pay high taxes, yield high rents and command high prices."[25] Similarly, when dealing with the lower classes, he states that "it would be unwise to generalize on the condition of the peasantry under the later Roman empire." He sees evidence that they were not all simply oppressed, exploited, and tied to their land, noting both the existence of free agricultural labourers, and evidence of widespread prosperity amongst the *coloni*.[26]

When it comes to the developments in local government, Jones perceived that the changes in the economic and administrative structures of the Late Roman state brought about a decline in the class of landowning curials. In his eyes, their flight was a symptom (as evident in the *Theodosian Code*) of an overly rigid and repressive state, whose inflexible practices and rising tax burden impoverished and alienated the old landowning class as much as they did the ordinary peasant.[27] Curial decline, however, has come to be recognized not as signifying the decline of local elites, but the evolving nature of Late Roman society. With the decline of secular and pagan building and civic festivals, and the confiscation of *curia* endowments by the state to fund prolonged warfare in the third century, the old town councils lost much of their old wealth, privileges and esteem, whilst having to contend with the greater financial burden imposed by an enlarged army and bureaucracy. Coupled with this were alternatives developing to curial service; entry into the Church, the expanding senatorial class of *honorati*, or service in the enlarged provincial imperial bureaucracy.

But the flight of the curials was not a reflection of the relative decline of the fortunes of the old landowning elite to a new class of idle mouths. Rather it shows the former's reorientation within the new systems of organization and patronage becoming available in the empire.[28] The vast majority of the new imperial bureaucrats were drawn from the old curial classes, rather than new men. They were mostly landlords and former local administrators seeking to replace the increased burdens and reduced prestige of the councils with the opportunities present in these new institutions.[29] The attractiveness of the bureaucracy is show in the repeated laws in the *Theodosian Code* attempting to force councillors back to their cities.[30] In fact, the *Theodosian Code* suggests to us that the state did not want men to shirk their curial duties, and so was to some degree unaware of the extent to which the political relationship between centre and locality had changed. But Jones perceived the restrictive measures described in the law codices as the suggestion of an overly regimented order. As he says, the government used "its powers of coercion to compel the existing workers and property owners to go on performing their essential functions .../ It conformed to the traditional social pattern; the emperors no doubt felt that they were merely preventing deviations from the natural rule."[31] Even here, however, Jones shows a break from his predecessors in moderating his critique, and raised doubts about the totalitarian force of these laws, upon which much of the image of an oppressive Late Roman state relies. As he says, "The theoretical extent and the actual effectiveness of the restrictive legislation have often been exaggerated." In particular, he notes the irony of their imposing nature, for "The laws themselves, by their constant reiteration of the same prohibitions and their frequent condemnation of past offences, show how impossible it was ... to enforce the rules."[32]

The final major element of Jones's "idle mouths" book is the rise of the Christian Church, a body which diverted substantial human and financial resources when an increased fiscal strain made their productive application all the more pressing. As he argues, "the Christian Church imposed a new class of idle mouths on the resources of the empire."[33] Furthermore, he suggests a profound impact of a shift in spiritual values: "Countless earnest Christians, who despaired of saving their souls in the world, flocked to the deserts or crowded into monasteries. Many others ... lived austere and secluded lives of prayer and meditation."[34]

There is no doubt that the official adoption of Christianity brought about a cultural revolution.[35] Churches replaced temples everywhere. The Christian Church acquired huge donations, from the state and private individuals. As it grew as an institution it drew in much of the educated talent of the empire, eventually including even wealthy senators such as Ambrose, and monasticism began to attract substantial numbers of recruits. Along with this came some sweeping ideological changes. Worldly goods became frequently portrayed as a barrier to salvation, in contrast to the pure life of the holy man or ascetic, and prominent aristocrats starting ceding much of their wealth to the Church.[36] This new ideal was a significant contrast to the concept of *otium*, or cultivated leisure, that had been the hallmark of the Greco-Roman aristocracy.

But this does not mean Christian belief was disruptive to Roman rule; rather, it successfully integrated into Roman imperial ideology. Rome had always been accorded a special place in the plans of the gods, and in the principle of *pax deorum* her leaders had recognized the importance of honouring this special relationship. After the adoption of Christianity this relationship could be recast as a divine mission, ordained by the Christian god, of conversion and salvation for all. The emperor was his chosen representative on earth: Rome's power and right to power came from the divine will. In this way, the Christianized Roman Empire lost little of its worldly focus or ideological cohesion. Instead, the Church acted as an extra tool of imperial power. By the end of the fourth century the bulk of the landowning classes had converted to Christianity and, despite some rioting and vocal opposition, most of the apparatus of paganism had been dismantled.[37]

Practically speaking, the Christian Church acquired large financial endowments but pagan religious institutions had also been wealthy and prosperous, and through the fourth century they were progressively stripped.[38] Much of the Church's wealth, land, and buildings were paid for in private endowments; a reflection of the continuing prosperity of landowners, at least at the upper end of the wealth scale, rather than a burden on a drained state. Ecclesiastical writers such as Jerome have given us famous examples of aristocrats who renounced their secular lifestyle and bestowed their worldly wealth on the Church.[39] But this number is tiny compared to those who converted to Christianity but maintained an active service in secular entities such as the imperial bureaucracy. In time, bishops would take on an increasing array of secular duties within the administration of the cities.[40] This somewhat undermines the strength of Jones's "idle mouths" view of the substantial impact of the Christian Church.

The central Gibbonian notion that Christianity fundamentally impaired the functioning of the empire, practically or morally, no longer holds. But such an extreme claim Jones himself made an effort to criticize. David Gwynn points out that the author, characterizing Gibbon as saying that Christianity "sapped the morale of the empire, deadened its intellectual life and … undermined its unity," immediately counters this with the vital observation that, "The East was even more Christian than the West, its theological disputes far more embittered."[41] Yet, of course, the East did not collapse in the fifth century, undermining the entire logic of that argument.

Broadly speaking, modern historiography stresses the success of the Roman Empire to manage its problems, internal and external, until the fifth century AD. The question must therefore be asked: How did a healthy and vital imperial infrastructure collapse in the West in the course of the fifth century? Jones marked a shift towards what he called "the unfashionable view" that the barbarians played the primary role in its downfall.[42] As Ward-Perkins puts it, "Jones's late empire was an austere but powerful structure, brought down only by overwhelming external force."[43] This does not mean that the internal condition of the empire is not important to explain its political collapse in the West, but rather that the language of causation has to be qualified. In this sense, the modern historiography goes further than Jones in downplaying the existence or significance of what he calls its "manifold weaknesses."[44] The trend now is to think rather of *limitations*—many of which are not unique to the state of the empire of the fourth and fifth centuries, but inherent to any sizeable pre-industrial society and state.

These limitations can be briefly outlined. There was the fact of the sheer size of the empire, stretching as it did across half of Europe and North Africa and the Near East. Across such large distances transport and communication were slow—messages from the imperial court to the localities could take weeks to arrive, and moving an army to deal with any sizeable threat took months or longer.[45] An imperial post existed but the speed at which this could transport information was highly erratic, owing to seasonal cycles and prevailing local weather conditions, especially at sea. Lines of communication between the imperial centre and its localities were few and could limit the ability of the court to acquire accurate information: Ammianus' account of the apparent conspiracy at Lepcis Magna, where the coercion of a *comes* and an imperial official kept the emperor in the dark about Berber attacks into Tripolitania for a decade, is a case in point.[46] Furthermore the imperial bureaucracy, though greatly expanded in the era of the "Dominate," was still tiny by the standards of a modern government, its paid officials numbering at most 30,000 and serving a population in the tens of millions.

The result of all this was that the Roman Empire was not "governed" in the modern sense by its imperial centre—there was no budget, no modern civic institutions such as a national health service or police force; nor with the technological limitations of the time could there be. The primary purpose of the imperial regime was to protect the landowning classes of the empire (and therefore the taxpayers and tax collectors) by organizing, supplying, and maintaining the army. What passed for economic policy in the Roman world consisted of ensuring the adequate provision and supply of this entity. And if the goals of the Roman state were limited, its mechanisms of enforcement were even more so. There was no professional "police force" or public prosecution service. And the failure of Diocletian's price edict against Constantine's introduction of the *solidus* shows that, beyond controlling the gold content and therefore the value of the currency, the state had little power to regulate economic activity.[47]

All this meant that, in terms of its day-to-day operation Roman society operated through patronage, upon the informal but extremely important bonds between landowners and their dependents and within the elite. Without the assistance of local elites or patrons, taxes could not be collected and laws could not be enforced. It was the alliance, official and unofficial, between the imperial centre and local elites upon which imperial rule depended, hence the importance in the Late Roman bureaucracy of high officials in a province being drawn from the wealthy members of the landowning class.

In relation to this complex but delicate system, modern historiography focuses on how the barbarian invaders could destroy a (relatively) vigorous and healthy empire by unravelling it; and that, consequently, its downfall was not a necessary process induced by progressive internal failings, but one *contingent* on the circumstances of the fifth century, and the challenges they posed to the structural limitations of imperial rule. Peter Heather argues that "Political limitations ... are directly relevant in another way to the story of Western collapse." This is because the Roman system of patronage that bound the locality to the imperial centre was inherently at risk in a period of turmoil. The process is described thus:

> In return for tax payments, the machinery of the state, military and legal, protected a relatively small landowning class from both outside enemies and internal ones. Because their dominance was based on landowning, these people were vulnerable. They could not up sticks should the imperial centre cease to be able to guarantee their security, so it is hardly surprising that they tended to ingratiate themselves with the rising barbarian powers. This limitation within the system played a considerable role in shaping the nature of the imperial collapse in the old Roman heartlands of central and southern Gaul and Spain.[48]

The empire had a limited capacity to respond to multiple threats. The rise of Sasanian Persia in the third century had already drained much of its slack military capacity and tax revenue, and would occupy the bulk of the attention of the Eastern army until the rise of Islam.[49] From 406 AD the Western Empire was faced both with Alaric's Goths invading Italy and the Vandals, Alans and Suevi crossing the Rhine. These threats exceeded the capacity of the Roman state to resist or manage these threats, and were compounded by further mistakes, failings and ill fortune—perhaps most importantly, the loss of North Africa in 439 to the Vandals and the abortive expedition of 468 to reclaim it.[50]

In the right circumstances, therefore, the link between landowner and government, the whole basis of the Roman administrative structure, was prone to break. It was in the complex circumstances of the late fourth and fifth centuries that these conditions were met. In the wake of invasion and settlement, local elites, whose wealth depended on the land and hence could not be taken with them if they fled, could and would seek accommodation with the invading barbarians, allowing an easy transfer of taxation, manpower, and authority from the Roman state to these new occupiers.[51] This does not mean, however, that the barbarians exploited the manifold internal deficiencies of a crumbling state and social system. As Christopher Wickham outlines, "Rome's violence (whether public or private), corruption and injustice were part of a very stable structure, one which had lasted for centuries and had very few obvious internal flaws." He further observes that while "half the empire … did collapse in the fifth century, the empire survived with no difficulty in the East, however, and arguably reached its peak there in the early sixth century.".[52]

How and why this relationship unravelled is therefore a central question in the fall of the Roman Empire. Without an overriding thesis of decline to occupy historians, its collapse has to be considered contingent on the complex circumstances of the fifth century; what has been described by Bryan Ward-Perkins as a "vicious spiral" of invasion, civil war and barbarian settlement, or by Roger Collins as a domino effect by which the Roman Empire gradually "delegated itself out of existence.."[53]

These views represent poles on a spectrum of debate on the relative violence and turbulence involved in the collapse of the political structures of imperial Roman rule. Nevertheless, it is generally recognized that "The Fall of the Roman Empire in the West" was not the immediate collapse of a civilization: it was, rather, the breaking down of a governmental apparatus that could no longer be sustained in the light of the political, military, and economic conditions of the fifth century AD. Whether this transformation in the fifth century was a hostile and destructive process—a true "assassination"—or a more positive and peaceful accommodation is still to some extent disputed.

Goffart has argued that the barbarian invaders were more or less integrated into the fabric of the Roman world—the fall of the West being an experiment in accommodation gone astray.[54] By contrast, Brian Ward-Perkins has argued for a destructive and dramatic end to the Western Empire, with hostile and bloody invasions incurring such consequences as population decline, urban decay, and the disappearance of much of the comfort and sophistication of the Roman way of life.[55] Such a discussion also leads into the consideration of the long-term and often deleterious consequences for the social organization and cultural traditions of such a civilization once the institutional "prop" of Roman rule was removed, but that is far outside of the time frame normally ascribed to the "decline and fall," and it involves many forces and pressures new to the post-Roman world. Furthermore, whatever decay the post-Roman world saw, it has become accepted that the label of "the Dark Ages" is a very limited and overgeneralized portrait of Western Europe after AD 476, at least outside Britain.

How this idea is mediated profoundly shapes the entire conception of the end of the Western Roman Empire, and its significance. The previous tendency to treat the process as one of the "fall" of a civilization resulted, in its own logic, from an overemphasis of the supposedly "Germanic" nature of the successor states that came into being in the West in the aftermath of the disappearance of the Roman state, and from seeing the interaction of Rome and the so-called Barbarians simply in terms of a mutually existential conflict. Viewed simply as the clash of opposed and asymmetrically advanced cultures, it is not surprising that the issue was wrapped in judgemental language: for how could the beneficiaries of a "higher" civilization fail to triumph over the representatives of a "lower" one? The answer would have to lie in a range of moral or structural possibilities, encoded by the suppositions and predilections of the questioner.

Such imperatives can be witnessed in shifting attitudes to the "Roman–barbarian" dichotomy over the course of the twentieth century. In the 1930s, the English medievalist Eileen Power wrote a very traditional essay about the late Roman Empire and its fall, one which paints a stark contrast between the civilized Germanic world and the barbarism of its successors:

> The battle sagas of the (Germanic) race, which have all but disappeared or have survived only as legends worked up in a later age; the few rude laws which were needed to regulate personal relationships, this was hardly civilization in the Roman sense ... Rome and the barbarians were ... not only protagonists but two different attitudes to life, civilization and barbarism.[56]

She goes on to state that, "The Roman world was a world of schools and universities, writers, and builders. The barbarian world was a world in which mind was in its infancy and its infancy was long." She insists that, "This peaceful infiltration of barbarians which altered the whole character of the society which it invaded would have been impossible, of course, if that society had not been stricken by disease."

Perceptions of the Germanic settlement of Western Europe have changed dramatically since the Second World War, as ideas about the modern position of Germans in Europe have shifted. André Piganiol wrote a book about the fall of the Western Roman Empire that was heavily influenced by the German invasion and occupation of France from 1940–44. Published in 1947, it lays the blame for the destruction of a thriving and prosperous Christian empire at the foot of the "uncivilized" Germanic tribes. Piganiol considers but dismisses any other contributory explanation, including political, economic, or socio-cultural changes. His book finishes with one of the most famous modern statements on the end of the empire: "Roman civilization did not pass peacefully away. It was assassinated."[57] By contrast, Walter Goffart, writing the in 1980s, marked the rehabilitation of the Germanic invaders with his theory of a peaceful "accommodation" and transition from Roman to barbarian rule. As he says, "The more or less orderly garrisoning of Gaul, Spain, Africa and Italy by alien troops gives us no compelling reason to speak of a 'barbarian West.'" His thesis, though a strictly historical one, could be appropriated by scholars with more purely ideological motives: namely to elevate the Germanic people to the status of peaceful collaborators with the Romans, and rightful co-heirs of their legacy.[58]

But a decline *after* the fall or transition of the Western Roman state is a very different field of debate to the tradition of Gibbon, Bury and Rostovtzeff—concerned as it was concerned with a supposed decline *before* any such event. Factors internal to the empire—such as a tendency for civil war—are still cited in modern historiography, but these are better regarded as structural limitations, rather than symptoms of decline. Indeed, Roger Collins cites the continued survival of the East, "despite various modifications, for another thousand years," as the evidence which "effectively undermined the arguments eloquently advanced by Edward Gibbon"; namely, the terminal impact of the rise of Christianity, and the withering of the moral vitality of the empire. This is because "these features ... even without assessing their inherent validity, would have to have been as true of the eastern half of the empire as of the western."[59]

From this, it must ultimately be asked how the East survived—in parts, and in some form, for another thousand years—while the West did not. Jones had a partial answer to this conundrum, saying that, "The Western empire was poorer and less populous, and its social and economic structure more unhealthy. It was thus less able to withstand the tremendous strains imposed by its defensive effort, and the internal weaknesses which it developed." By contrast, the East, "owing to its greater wealth and population ...was better able to carry the burden of defence."[60] Nevertheless, he points out that the East survived even when many of the same conditions applied. As such, his answer is not a complete one. Cameron therefore states that, "Jones did not seriously address the issue of why the eastern empire continued and in what form, and he seems unsure what he thought of it."[61]

While the East was undoubtedly the richer part of the empire, its Western counterpart is no longer seen as being gripped by the ills he extrapolated, so the reasons behind their relative fates have to be more complex. In the West, with its rural economy and aggregated holdings, wealth was concentrated in the hands of a very small number of phenomenally rich senators and aristocrats, unlike the more urbanized and mercantile East. This made it much easier for the Western elite to shield its wealth from the state, and so represented a greater potential limitation on imperial power. This problem came to the fore in the external pressures the Western Empire faced from 406 to its "fall," as it made the problem of its shrinking fiscal base that much more acute.[62] Perhaps most importantly, the East possessed a second line of defence at Constantinople. Its rich Eastern provinces were largely secure from the nomadic and barbarian threats that penetrated the Balkans, and while the Persian menace was formidable it was also stable, the East enjoying a prolonged period of relative peace from 363. In the West, only North Africa, its "breadbasket," benefited from this kind of security, but a series of contingent circumstances brought about its fall to the Vandals in 439.

It should be clear from this historiographical summary just how profound the disjunction is between professional historians on the later Roman Empire and the myth of the decline and fall. The latter is of very little relevance to the modern field of Late Antiquity, and especially the fifth century AD. This has been the case for the past 50 years of academic scholarship. Instead, its meaning lies in the broader realm of myth and *cultural* historiography, and consequently the subject matter of this book.

## THE DECLINE AND FALL AS AN ATYPICAL MODEL OF MYTH

In the above historiographical survey, I note that there is a disjunction between the idea of the "fall of the Western Empire," or "fall of Rome," and that of the "*decline* and fall." It must be asked what the difference is between these two terms, how exactly they cohere in this myth, and whether or not that coherence is necessary and fundamental; meaning, whether it is necessary in the context of this book to talk simultaneously about the decline and fall, rather than just the first or second term.

Clearly, the two ideas have become decoupled in the historical record, because the end of the political and military infrastructure of the Western Empire by AD 476 is no longer deemed to be synonymous with a long, preceding phase of decline. Historians can talk of the fall of the Western Roman Empire and debate its causes, or even the veracity of such a position, without invoking this Gibbonian narrative. The statement that the Roman Empire "fell," or the debates and arguments around this event or process, are not necessarily the myth *in and of itself*. To speak of "the fall of Rome" or "the end of Rome" does not *require* the invocation of decline, as the account of the academic historiography above makes clear.

If the "fall" is not purely in and of itself a form of this myth, can the same be true of "the decline of Rome?" Does the fall need to be invoked for the myth to work? The tradition of decline as a representational concept denoting moral, political, or theological decay is discussed at length in Chapter 3. It is one which profoundly informs this narrative, but also precedes it in its own mythic forms. It also precedes it in mythic forms of its own that influenced the Roman example. The Bible provides us with the expulsion from Eden and original "fall of man,"[63] Daniel's prophecy of four empires,[64] and the apocalyptic end times foretold in Revelations. Such ideas are present in the classical schema of Hesiod, in the now dead myths of Platonists, Manicheans and Persian Zoroastrians, and countless other religious traditions, the Hellenic timeline of four "ages," each worse than the last—Gold, Silver, Bronze, and then an Iron Age of universal wickedness.[65]

When dealing with the Roman story, however, this decline is focused around explaining a specific event, or set of events; whatever the nature, number, and length of its causes. The decline of the Roman Empire, and Roman civilization, is deemed to produce not simply decay to a lower state, but the very *destruction* of that civilization, to a greater or lesser degree, and the subsequent arrival of the "Dark Ages" in some form. The notion that Rome *fell* is integral to this myth: not simply that Rome was reduced in some measure from its earlier greatness. Such an idea is integral to Gibbon's *Decline and Fall*, which, as is argued further in Chapter 3, constitutes the real origin of the fully developed form of this myth. It is also a core tenet of the bleaker intellectual prophets of the twentieth century (as discussed in Chapters 4 and 5): self-appointed prophets like Spengler and Toynbee and Tainter, who all quote the Roman example when they envision, in the processes of the modern world, the coming collapse of civilization in its current form. Anthony Mann names his 1964 Gibbon-inspired epic *The Fall of the Roman Empire*, even though it never once discusses the actual history of the fourth and fifth centuries; instead, it purports to show the beginning of a long phase of corruption and decline, 200 years earlier, which thereby constituted the real and meaningful "fall."

When it comes to this myth, therefore, the decline and fall are mutually inclusive concepts. They are contained together in the presumption that a decline necessarily precedes a fall; and that the latter is the inevitable product of the former, unless the trend is halted or reversed. Such logic grafts the story with prophetic power; for, if Rome declined and fell, then evidence of a more modern decline may be the fingerprint of an oncoming collapse.

This method of comparative inquiry is central to the decline and fall. It is an approach which will be defined from here on as *negative classicism*; the inverse of traditional "classicism," or the reception of the classical world. The latter idea I must firstly explore here. It is bound up in the traditional conception of the *Classics*, namely, the study of the culture (literary and visual) and history of the Hellenic world—especially Ancient Greece and Rome during "Classical Antiquity" (600 BC—AD 200 traditionally).[66] Stemming from this is the concept of the "classical tradition," an idea popularized by works such as Gilbert Highet's *The Classical Tradition* (1949), one of the formative texts on the subject of this form of reception and representation. It signifies the ongoing transmission and influence of that ancient culture, *within* a context that is still tightly conditioned by its original, pure precedents. These literary, artistic, and intellectual prototypes are deemed to constitute a set of timeless and universal values, what Peter Rose calls "immutable reservoirs of fixed truth about a fixed human nature, a fixed human condition."[67]

An expression of this precept, "classicism," denotes the emulation of classical precedents which set the rules and standards for aesthetics, ideals and styles. It implies a strict canon of ideal forms. T.S. Eliot described how "The beginning of the twentieth-century has witnessed a return to the ideals of classicism," and stated these constitute "*form and restraint* in art, *discipline and authority* in religion, *centralization* in government ... the necessity for austere discipline."[68] Phases of "classicism" in Western culture invariably involve a reverence for the models and rules of Antiquity, even though their application has varied wildly. Amongst its myriad examples, classicism can be seen in the classical architecture that appeared during the Italian Renaissance, which emphasized a proportion and geometry that accorded to ancient styles, in the Palladian architecture in eighteenth-century England, in Molière's adherence to Aristotle's "unities," or the poetry of Dryder or Pope. Research into the classical tradition has also taught us about subjects varying from the ongoing transmission of ancient texts, to the afterlife of ancient rituals and conventions.[69]

Negative classicism represents a departure from this approach in several ways. While it involves the same comparative approach, whereby the culture of the present is seen or used to emulate the classical past, it is with an explicitly pejorative purpose. It is an ideologically charged approach to culture that adheres to certain implicit or overt maxims; namely, that

Rome was decadent; that it declined and was destroyed by this inner weakness; and that the society, nation, culture, or civilization of the author is falling in the same direction. It is one with little academic precedent. The only related usage of the term "negative classicism" can be found in Patrick Brantlinger's 1983 *Bread and Circuses: Theories of Mass Culture as Social Decay*, which uses it much more narrowly in terms of a perceived tension or debate between a high, pure, classicized culture, and modern mass culture, where proponents of the former see the former as being corrupted by the latter.[70] It is a usage reminiscent of the one here, though the remit is focused very selectively on the preservation of "higher" cultural ideals. Here, I am examining the appropriation of classical models of decline to attack or critique the contemporary world of the authors at large. Furthermore, negative classicism naturally lends itself in its themes to a consideration of Late Roman history; to find in the supposed decline and fall of Rome the lessons and warnings for a later age. By contrast, classicisms and classicists rarely touch on this later period of the empire's history.[71] The exact time frame, therefore, varies along with the nature of the approach.

It is here that I can define precise terms of which this myth consists. It is, in its simplest form, the idea that the Roman Empire was brought down in the fifth century AD due to a preceding internal decline that took a moral, cultural, and/or political form. For the empire to be conquered from without, Roman civilization had to first destroy itself from within. No other explanation is acceptable according to these parameters. Nor is any real attention paid to the Eastern Empire that survived another thousand years in some form. Rather it is dismissed, disparagingly, as a "Greek" empire, or by the anachronistic term "Byzantium": something somehow fundamentally different and inferior in character.[72] The fall of Rome in the fifth century is the end of the Roman Empire, and, consequently, suggests the termination of Roman civilization as a whole.

Such an analysis lends itself to being cast much more widely than a local historical concern. If the (Western) Roman Empire was not brought down due to the arrival of the Huns, or the loss of North Africa, or simple bad luck, but slowly rotted from the inside, then the lessons of its collapse may be transferrable to other empires, cultures and societies. The causes and mechanics of the decline and fall therefore mark the universal condition of nations, cultures or empires at their height. They are a prophecy, a prediction, and—frequently—a threat, which carry the stark moral force of the undoing of Rome.

For this myth to work, therefore, its representation must by absolute necessity remain constant and coherent. The "decline and fall of Rome" contains within this very statement an expression of its own internal logic. Historians who question the existence of this decline, or who suggest the "fall" in the West may be overstated, or who emphasize the continued existence of the Eastern Empire, are immediately banishing the myth from their own conceptual horizons. Without the conditions defined above, it carries no force, and the fall of Rome is simply a noted historical event; not a profound moral story, or a universal lesson of the relationship between greatness and hubris.

When considering this decline and fall in this way, it becomes apparent how the present is adapted to fit the enduring tropes of the Roman past. This makes this book an important variation on more established theories of representation, in which the past is a passive tool reanimated to fit the present; the *vehicle* rather than the *content* of its ideas. But the fall of Rome is not simply an arbitrary enabling device. I can illustrate this contrast by comparing it to the myth put forward in Richard Howells's *The Myth of the Titanic* (1999), a study of the Straussian myth-model in modern culture: as he says, "The story of the *Titanic* is a modern myth *par excellence*."[73] Howells argues that the original story of the *Titanic* sinking reflects the values of Edwardian society at the time—classist, nationalistic, patriarchal, and suffused with notions of honour, heroism and gentlemanly virtue.[74] Later versions of the *Titanic* story, however, radically alter this original Edwardian narrative, bar a few iconic details, such as the hubris around branding it unsinkable (actually a later legend).[75]

By contrast, the 1943 version of the *Titanic* commissioned by Nazi Propaganda Minister Joseph Goebbels, dispensed with any celebration of British values, and instead offered up a harsh anti-capitalist, anti-British and anti-American critique, with a fictitious German First Officer Peterson, describing the ship's reckless speed as evidence it was "run not by sailors, but by stock speculators."[76] During the Cold War, the film was banned by the British in Western Germany in the 1950s, but broadcast in the German Democratic Republic (GDP) due to its sentiments according with propaganda of the ruling regime.[77] As a contrast, James Cameron's 1997 recreation of the myth adopts the story as a personal romantic adventure; and, more implicitly, a class critique of Edwardian British society portraying a stifling and oppressive world from which the heroine is liberated by her American love interest. Some famous images, such as the performance of the band on deck as the ship sank, remain, but the story is fundamentally altered from the original Edwardian myth.[78]

Such a model of representations does not apply directly to the decline and fall. Instead, this is a myth which has remained atypically constant, through and before my period of study, and even through the emergence of new forms of mass media from the twentieth century. The views and judgements offered, both in terms of the moral perspective on Rome's fall, and its relevance to the contemporary world of its author(s), display a striking similarity in this regard. Its forms and associations have stayed broadly constant through the ages: a consistency we see to this very day. The myth shapes the forms of its recreation much more than the circumstances of production rework the original myth.

## Myth as Interdisciplinary Study

It is important for the purpose of this book that I explore those interconnected theoretical disciplines that play a central role in framing my research. I am concerned with the historical, social and cultural context of a "text," the role and reinterpretation of myth, the peculiarities of different media of transmission, and the sociology of representation. An interdisciplinary approach is therefore essential to this study. I am tackling questions about what constitutes myth, which is highlighted by social anthropology; examining symbolic representation, which is explored in semiotics; and discussing writings on popular culture, which receive treatment in media and film theory.

All these ideas are common to studies of "representation" and their forms. More specifically for the parameters of this book, the question of what constitutes "classical reception" and "the classical tradition," and their changing interpretation, needs to be given considerable scrutiny. The comparatively recent emergence of the study of representations of the ancient world throws up inevitable questions concerning their theoretical basis, intellectual value, and relationship to pre-existing fields of inquiry. A particular issue is how it co-exists with existing specialisms. As the field becomes more fashionable, it is increasingly an intellectual battleground of competing methodologies in history, cultural study, and social sciences.

It is important to note that the process of reviewing much of the relevant theoretical literature on myth and representation for this book is more about the active selection of the very parameters of study involved than a passive recital of an obvious and self-defined body of material. This book is concerned with the presentation and survival of ancient myths in a modern context. Consequently, a substantial body of theory must both be examined, and those ideas necessary to frame and elaborate my argument must be developed at length.

In any work that describes and explores a genre—especially when those boundaries have been little defined before—there is the risk of choosing a time frame that redefines the historical context of the subject matter through the nature of its selective dating. Academic works on the invention and reception of historical archetypes frequently postulate their own relevance to contemporary debates by proclaiming a "current" wave of film, media, or other such texts about their period, before proffering explanations for this. This provides us with a reason to keep the parameters of this book as inclusive as can be reasonably allowed. A consequence of this necessity is that the relatively *wide* chronological range of this book is balanced by a relatively *narrow* focus of appropriate subject matter; for instance, on narrative feature films intended for cinematic release. Admittedly, a strict demarcation of cinema from television, digital media, and film shorts can appear arbitrary, but such distinctions also prove important in the content and nature of the films themselves.

It is a long-established truism that popular representations of Rome, and of the pre-modern world in general, reflect and articulate political and cultural identities. In this tradition, the historical and iconographic themes of the "decline and fall" of Rome have often been appropriated by interest groups across the literate spectrum—writers, academics, filmmakers, historians, journalists—to tackle such ideas as the decline of empires and societies, perceived political and ideological "imperialism," whether in its virtues or flaws, and a range of related themes. The frequency and focus of this cultural output bears witness to the issues of the day.[79]

One would expect, therefore, that such representations would have attracted considerable academic attention, particularly in recent years. Yet little so far has been written specifically on this field.[80] This absence of directly comparable studies forces us to investigate a wide and varying field of literature for appropriate subject matter and/or methodological tools. It also, of course, presents a case for the justification of this book: both as a contribution to existing knowledge in the field of classical reception, and the broader arena of cultural representations of the past.

## Theories of Myth

In this section I will show how existing theory and methodology inform this study—while also demonstrating that there is little specifically written on this topic. The *re-presentation* of history, facts, people, ideas and situations in cultural forms is at the core of this book, making this an appropriate place to begin.[81] "Representation" as an academic notion defines the means by which members of a culture uses language—or any system involving signs—to generate meaning. Stuart Hall defines "culture" as a set of meanings constructed according to systems of representation. They are signs that are manipulated to create meaning in the world. This idea contains the premise, then, that "things"—entities such as objects, people or events—do not have in themselves any fixed, final, or true objective meaning: it is we who are within society and culture who create these.[82]

Representations not only articulate visual or verbal codes and conventions, but also the social practices and forces which underlie them. Producing meaning depends on the method and manner of interpretation: because meanings are always changing, codes operate more like social conventions than fixed, immutable laws. As meanings shift, the codes of a culture slowly, sometimes imperceptibly, change.[83] Furthermore, these meanings can vary or change from one culture to another. Therefore it is important for us to retain an appreciation of the inherent "relativism" of many cultural ideas, forms, and standards, and the need for some form of translation, even in the looser hermeneutic sense, as we move from the mindset of one conceptual universe to another. Elizabeth Chaplin argues that "Images and texts do not reflect their sources but refashion them according to pictorial and textual codes, in a way that makes them quite separate and distinct from the sources."[84] The challenge of studies such as my book, therefore, is in working out why exactly the past is represented in certain ways, and through certain dramatic forms—and how those portraits have changed over time, either in their form or final meaning.

As a concept, representation has antecedents in the classical period itself, the very period whose re-presentation is being discussed here. A key aesthetic and philosophical principle of Late Antiquity and the medieval era was *spolia* (or "spoils" in English), an artistic-historical term that refers to the reuse of art, architecture and texts. Spolia are ancient artefacts and materials which have been appropriated for a different context and purpose. In possibly one of the earliest examples of a theory of "representation," St Augustine allegorized the theft of Egyptian treasures by the Israelites in

Exodus to justify contemporary Christians taking the great cultural treasures of the classical world—art, literature, artefacts—and stripping them of their paganism to adapt them for their own motives. This was on the grounds that "all the branches of pagan learning contain not only false and superstitious fantasies ... but also studies for liberated minds which are more appropriate to the service of the truth, and some very useful moral instruction." Consequently, "these treasures ... which were used wickedly and harmfully in the service of demons must be removed by Christians ... and applied to their true function, that of preaching the gospel."[85]

*Spolia* is primarily used as an architectural term in modern scholarship, but in the realms of art, literature, philosophy and theology, examples abound. Augustine's very argument itself is a textual example of this practice, an allegorical appropriation of a historical/theological narrative. Such a recycling—in a literal and/or symbolic sense—produced very complex objects, which themselves facilitated a visual and conceptual dialogue between past and present. In this way the past and present become hybridized. The present is a multi-temporal representation, the ancient object layered with meanings foreign, sometimes alien, to its original context.[86] Such an idea not only informs such objects of the past, but continues to shape our constant *re-presentation* of them since.

For a modern approach to the field, the "social constructionist" approach to representation, as outlined by Stuart Hall, describes it as the construction of meaning through symbols and signs. As he says, "According to this approach, we must not confuse the material world, where things and people exist, and the symbolic practices and processes through which representation, meaning and language operate." This is not to deny the existence of the material world, but instead to say it is not *in itself* the source of meaning.[87]

It is important to point out that in the intellectual context of this study, the word *reception* is used primarily to denote the history of the meanings that have been imputed to historical events or artefacts; and the way that participants, observers, and historians have attempted to make past events meaningful for the present in which they live. This is different from the formal field of *reception theory*, which emphasizes the audience's interpretation of a text. I am emphasizing this distinction here because much of the pre-existing work on the "representation" of antiquity uses the word *reception* interchangeably with that, without connoting to the more formal discipline of reception theory.[88]

Focusing on the importance of our symbolic and cultural lives has important implications for our conception of what constitutes "truth." In this context, truth is primarily—though not exclusively—the product of human need.[89] Something can be true in the sense that it shapes and influences thinking—which can give a myth, story, or falsehood a similar importance, culturally and historically, to a quantifiable "fact." If you remove the layers of ritual and convention in human activity, little of it can be said to have a basis in an "objective" scientific reality. All human activity is an extension of the imagination—we inscribe our own realities onto the world, and representations act as mediators for these beliefs and ideas.

Emerging out of this is the modern scholarly notion of a myth, the importance of which cannot, in the context of this study, be underestimated, and which we will constantly refer to in this vein. Myth, in the sense that I am utilizing it, is a powerful conceptual model for understanding the role of belief in defining a particular conception of "reality," or the supposedly "true" meanings contained in the external world. It is a complex term that defies a simple or singular interpretation.[90] Myth has often carried a pejorative meaning, denoting a fiction, an error, a distortion or a lie—an idea which has frequently extended even to academic circles.[91] Its use in the study of classical representation is primarily as a technical literary and historic label for the stories and tales told in ancient societies—for instance, Greek and Roman myths about their gods or ancestors—not as a conceptual tool for those studies themselves. However, myth can be understood in a deeper sense neither as truth or falsehood, but as a sophisticated social representation.[92]

Theories of myth have varied considerably, running the whole gamut of functionalism, structuralism and semiotics. Percy Cohen outlined seven types of theory of myth, starting with "nineteenth century intellectualism," and finishing with their embrace by structuralism in the 1960s. The second category was a "mythopoeic" theory, which treated them wholly as an art form, lacking in any explanatory value; thirdly came the psychoanalytical ideas of Jung and Freud, which saw their plots and imagery as metaphors for unconscious desires; fourthly was the approach of theorists such as Emile Durkheim, who treated them as part of a religious system for maintaining social order and harmony; fifthly was the functionalism of Malinowski, in which myth legitimized social institutions; and the sixth category, as championed by Robert Graves, was concerned with the link between myth and ritual. The final category, pioneered in the structuralism of Strauss, saw individual myths as components of a larger narrative system, which played a somewhat abstract functional role in the "mediation of paradoxes"; and the analysis of which revealed a universality underlying human thought processes.[93]

Cohen's first category, nineteenth-century scholarship, comprehended myth as a way in which "primitive" man sought to understand and explain the world.[94] This set the academic precedent of examining primitive and distant cultures, and framing these observations in the context of universal human tendencies. Yet these theories reduce myth to a redundant and obsolete method of thought—a primitive counterpart to a post-Enlightenment age of reason and science. Andrew Lang's *Myth, Ritual and Religion* (1887) describes the "anomalous" and "irrational" elements in modern religious myths of otherwise "civilized" people as hangovers from humanity's original state of savagery.[95] The Orientalist Max Muller described myth as a "disease of language," a by-product of the limitations of primitive vocabulary in formulating abstract ideas. The anthropologist E.B. Taylor interpreted myth as a form of animism, a literal explanation for a natural phenomenon made by people too unsophisticated to conceive of impersonal laws of nature: with this outdated method of thinking surviving and persisting in religious faith.[96] Similarly, Émile Durkheim deemed religious mythic conceptions "erroneous applications of the law of causality."[97] A crucial shift in twentieth-century academic thinking was to reject this entirely "rationalist" dichotomy between myth and science, or reason and superstition.[98] This new trend primarily originated in the movement "functionalism", part of Cohen's fifth category of myth as social function, which argued that it played a vital social and cultural role: namely by sustaining and reinforcing the social order.[99]

In *Myth and Primitive Psychology* (1954), the anthropologist Bronisław Malinowski described how, "The function of myth, briefly, is to strengthen tradition, and endow it with a greater value and prestige by tracing it back to a higher, better, more superior natural reality of initial events."[100] It legitimizes organization within a society, and enshrines the sanctity of its sources of power and authority. This presents a powerful case for the importance of studying myth, by ascribing to it a social and political role: namely to validate and justify existing practices and conventions, by rooting them in a mythical past.[101] The rooting of ideas and ideologies—often at political instigation—in such a past has numerous historical precedents: Virgil's *Aeneid* glorified Roman virtues and supremacy, legitimizing the Julio-Claudian dynasty as descended from the heroes of Troy, while Foxe's *Book of Martyrs* enshrined the sanctity of the English Reformation by connecting the persecution of its advocates to the tradition of martyrdom in early Christianity.[102]

Notable in these ideas about myth, in contrast to the nineteenth-century approach, is a closer equation of the cultural and mental horizons of ancient and modern man. Malinowski compares the value of the "myth for the savage" with the way that "our sacred story lives in our ritual, in our morality ... controls our conduct."[103] Echoing Durkheim and Muller's focus on the connections between ritual, myth, and religion,[104] he defined a "special class of stories ... regarded as sacred, embodied in rituals, morals and social organizations ... which form an integral and active part of primitive culture."[105] This idea is of crucial value to this study, as the equation emphasizes conceptual and ideological continuities through human history, and the value the ancient world can have to "modern" (post-Enlightenment) culture and the more modern mind.

For Malinowski, however, these stories held their greatest value when viewed in their "original," pure state. He was critical of the academic study of ancient myths in their more contemporary literary forms, arguing that these were so distorted by subsequent generations of scribes, scholars and theologians that, "It is necessary to go back to primitive mythology ... (to study) a myth which is still alive."[106] While this may be true for discerning their original and ancient historical context, one cannot simply treat modern reinterpretations of older stories or idea simply as inferior distortions, of qualitatively less valuable than the "pure" form. Down the ages, myths have employed shifting forms and embodied mutable meanings. The story of Christ had a very different significance to the Emperor Constantine than it does to a modern-day Catholic—the *content* of the tale is broadly comparable, but the layering on of tradition and interpretation in subsequent centuries has greatly altered its context and significance.[107] But why should the ancient form have a qualitatively greater (or lesser) value than the modern? They are both of value to the cultures that originated or redefined them. We need to understand "modern" myths precisely because different societies express themselves in ways specific to them. Furthermore, those "ancient" stories usually have even earlier and more ancient forms—the Old Testament flood is predated by a Sumerian story, the virgin birth of Jesus has a long list of Hellenic precedents.[108] And these may themselves have grown out of oral traditions which are no longer extant. So the very idea of an "original" myth is a fraught and subjective concept in its own right.[109]

Malinowski's functionalism was largely eclipsed in the "structural anthropology" pioneered by Claude Lévi-Strauss (and occupying Cohen's final category of theory), who adapted the tools and methodology of Ferdinand de Saussure's linguistics in an effort to uncover the unconscious foundations of thinking in so-called "primitive" peoples. His anthropology was concerned with the abstract relationship between the elements of myths, as components of a "grammar": in his analysis, they comprise individual "mythemes" which take on meaning, like the units of language, only when combined in particular patterns. The anthropologist's task is, therefore, to uncover this underlying grammar—the rules and regulations which make it possible for myths to be "meaningful" to their audience and culture.[110]

Strauss claimed that beneath the vast heterogeneity of myth there can be discovered a homogenous structure, and only by understanding this structure can we truly grasp the meaning of any individual myth. His methodology was to attempt to reintegrate all the component myths into a single semiotic structure, for, "If there is meaning to be found in mythology, it cannot reside in the isolated elements which enter into the composition of a myth, but only in the way those elements have combined."[111] Strauss rejected Malinowski's focus on what he called "obvious narrative," which communicated only the "apparent content" of a myth. Instead, Strauss proposed looking deeper, into the *latent* content of myth.[112] He outlined the relationship between the two using the structural analogy of an orchestral score. The "narrative" sequences were comparable to the melody, and were to be read chronologically from left to right. Conversely, the "schemata" were comparable to the counterpoint and harmonies: they were to be read from top to bottom, making sense not in isolation but in relation to each other.[113]

This relationship between the individual elements and broader themes defined the nature of a "story." It means that cultural text can have a very specific content and purpose, whilst also reflecting much deeper themes. The approach of Strauss, therefore, allows us to make some universal and non-hierarchical claims for cultures, whether modern or ancient, distant or near. Myths, Strauss argued, were assembled from deep-rooted unconscious archetypes common to all humankind, using a process he called "*bricolage*" (an analogy with a French handyman), or the assemblage of the available cultural materials of our conceptual landscape.[114] The term denotes the purpose and order we project onto an otherwise meaningless material canvas, even as we imagine those qualities to be inherent to it. To Strauss, all myths have a similar socio-cultural function in society: to make the world explicable, to magically resolve its problems and paradoxes, thereby providing order and stability to our social arrangements.[115] They consist of "binary oppositions"—good and bad, order and chaos—their interplay and mediation giving meaning and context to both. The tension between them is overcome by the mediation of other forces in the myth that resolve the story into harmony. It is a logical model for reconciling the conflicts and contradictions of their lived experiences.[116] It is also reminiscent of Hegel's dialectic—a philosophical model which treated the advance of society as a counterpoint of tensions and resolutions between competing ideas—theses and anti-theses which produced "synthesis."[117] As Strauss says, "Mythical thought always progresses from the awareness of its oppositions toward their resolution ... the purpose of myth is to provide a logical model capable of overcoming a contradiction."[118]

Taking these ideas to their furthest conclusion, the structuralism of Strauss sees myth as an expression of fixed and universal social and mental structures. Consequently, this means that *universal laws govern mythic thought*. The logic of this could be, and was, taken even further. For Strauss, myth was the testing ground for a broad and sweepingly reductionist outlook on the human condition. If something so seemingly wild and random could actually be conditioned by universal laws, then *all* human thinking must be the product of similar coherent structures—meaning that discernible rules governed the entirety of human thinking, individually and collectively. "If the human mind appears determined even in the realm of mythology, *a fortiori* it must also be determined in all its spheres of activity."[119] In essence he argued for the equality of the savage and civilized minds. Whatever their surface distinctions, the two were composed of the same structures, and possessed the same internal logic of thought.

This principle has important connotations for judging the very concept of "myth"—in regard to both its academic consideration, and the conventional, everyday use of the word. Strauss's anthropology considers mythic reasoning and narrative to be neither a falsehood nor a sign of cultural or cognitive inferiority, but instead views them as a *social tool*: as rigorous, logical and coherent as modern science. The difference between the two therefore lies not in the quality of the intellectual process involved, but in the nature of the material to which it was applied.[120] Myth, to Strauss, could no longer be described as the intellectual predecessor of logic and reason, for man "has always been thinking equally well." This idea underpins the approach taken here. Myth and history combine today just as they always have: and, as will be argued, a collective mythic consciousness exists co-terminally with a historical one.

It is important to point out here that his anthropology, while very useful to this study, is liable to a number of profound criticisms that limit its final significance. The system is highly reductionist: it contracts history and humanity to a single idea, or supreme motive force. In doing so it transforms individuals into algorithms, the preconditioned output of vast mathematical systems.[121] The problem here is symptomatic of a hazard faced by the social sciences in general, namely that they are grounded in the vagaries and ambiguities of human behaviour, yet attempt to imprint onto it a precise, mathematical elegance. Siegfried Kracauer expressed a fear about the impact of social theorizing, declaring that:

the social sciences today avail themselves increasingly of computers to establish formal theories covering various social processes ... it appears that, for its perpetuation, modern mass society depends on the predictability—i.e., the manipulation—of all individual responses and behaviour patterns that are socially significant. We have already gone far in preconditioning people's attitudes: should society carry on this way, the so-called "personality" would dwindle to a mathematical point—man, that is, would become a statistician's dream.[122]

The Straussian equation of the logic of ancient and modern man has significant limitations. Cognitive relativism of this kind can imply that modern science is nothing more than a myth in itself—another narrative or social construct by today's generation of "story-telling natives." Strauss even called into question the claim that Western scientific rationalism held any intrinsic superiority over mythical forms of thinking.[123] Yet, though the unconscious process of myth-making and the deliberate rationality of the scientific method may be born of the same psychological imperatives—to comprehend a meaning and order in our environment—they do not possess the same logic of inquiry, or empirically mediated relationship with the outside world.[124] Scientific theories are conditioned by very different forces than those which shape myth. New scientific data and theories often arise *in opposition* to existing social and cultural narratives, however powerful those may be. The impact of Darwinism on Victorian society is an example of a religious mythic system of ancient origins violently and irreparably shaken by evidence from the objective world.[125] Furthermore, this idea assumes there has been little essential change in what constitutes "humanity," that the individual and social experience has stayed fundamentally constant, and therefore that the vastly altered conditions of human existence—social, technological, scientific, conceptual—have not in any way qualitatively altered the thinking patterns or cultural programming of society. Placing a primacy on fixed cultural relations in defining human existence is itself a reaction to earlier, more material models of behaviour. Yet omitting the primacy of such factors comprises an overreaction of extreme proportions—Terry Eagleton describes how rampant "culturalism" ignores such forces as "labour markets, commodity prices, raw materials, political forces" in shaping human affairs.[126]

There are no simple methodological tools or shortcuts to comprehending a text, culture, or society. This idea is readily accepted across the breadth of contemporary historiography, which incorporates many of the practices of the social sciences, in a hermeneutic context, *without* being beholden to its pseudoscientific excesses.[127]

Despite these reservations about the more reductionist elements of structural anthropology, a number of ideas within it are still highly germane to this study. Firstly, there is the premise that specific myths and stories cannot be fully comprehended in isolation, but must be examined as part of a broader system. This supports an idea central to this study, that we must embrace culture in its entirety—whether in "high" or "low" forms, or old or new media—in our attempt (as is the final aim of all history) to meaningfully comprehend society as a whole. This is particularly true in more modern times, when these myths have proliferated across a range of new media, whether in literary, dramatic, or visual forms. Furthermore, this anthropology demonstrates how culture can be understood not as the product of individual authorship, but as a collective tradition. Elements or details of a narrative may originate with a specific author, but the components and themes of any tale are far more deep-rooted than that. It is therefore better to attribute their authorship to societies rather than individuals. This accords in particular with the emphasis on the value of mass and popular culture in studies such as this, and the web of tradition that I will demonstrate can be seen in the concept of the decline and fall.

Secondly, the equation made by Strauss between ancient and modern man lends itself powerfully to the idea that myths continue to carry enormous relevance in the post-industrial age. Consequently, one must consider in what cultural forms these modern myths reside. It can be convincingly argued that popular culture is now the "repository and purveyor of myth."[128] Such an idea receives detailed treatment in Richard Howells's *The Myth of the* Titanic (1999), which begins with a set of theoretical observations about the parallels between ancestral myths and mainstream contemporary culture, and explores this connection by applying it to the case study of popular depictions of the sinking of the Titanic.[129] But this theory is not locked specifically to the Titanic, or Edwardian society, or even modern Europe—the connections that can potentially be made are deemed more universal.[130] Howells takes the universalism of Strauss and inverts its central theme, arguing that if primitive man was as intellectually sophisticated as modern man, so the latter might be considered to still think like the primitive.[131] Out of this perspective comes a universal definition of myth as "narrative tools" that "codify abstract ideas into concrete form."[132] Their truth lies not in any objective historical realities they describe, but in their value to those who absorb and mediate the narrative.

This treatment of the past emphasizes a cultural outlook on history in which primacy is accorded to uncovering people's beliefs, and their impact on the historical record, over the importance of the strictly "real."[133] Furthermore, it allows for the consideration that myths possess both "temporal" and "universal" dimensions. At a temporal level they demonstrate the concerns and values of specific societies. At a universal level, they are a window into a much deeper cultural consensus that crosses the chasm of time and space. This also follows in the methodological tradition of John Grierson, who draws on Hegelian and Kantian philosophy to distinguish between the "noumenal" and "phenomenal." The former is meant as a more abstract truth underlying all human experience; the latter simply the local, empirical and particular. Grierson advocated the use of the phenomenal in pursuit of the noumenal or real truth in a story.[134] In the context of this study, one can say that ancient stories will only continue to function through their continuing recalibrations for new generations of audience—yet at the same time, archetypal themes exist at their core, largely preserved in original form, and ubiquitous in their meaning and value.

Finally, of great value to this study is the contrast Strauss makes between the *overt* and *latent* content of a myth—or between their *apparent* subject matter and a deeper, underlying meaning. This is an approach to representation that can be extended to any "text," whether cultural, literary or historic; or high culture versus the vernacular.

## Historiography, Myth and Literature

History does not at first appear to have much in common with myth—in fact it seems diametrically opposed to its very principle. As Malinowski, otherwise a strong proponent of their study, says, "Myth, taken as a whole, cannot be sober, dispassionate history, since it is always made ad hoc to fulfil a certain sociological function, to glorify a certain group, or to justify anomalous status."[135] Attempts to distinguish myth from history are seen as early as Thucydides, who criticized those writers "less interested in telling the truth than in catching the attention of their public, whose authorities cannot be checked and whose subject-matter, owing to the passage of time, is mostly lost in the unreliable streams of mythology."[136] The drive to arrive at truthful depictions, free from such tall tales, culminated in the transformation of history into a professional discipline in the nineteenth century. This is best expressed in the empiricism of Leopold von Ranke, which strove towards an objective comprehension of the "truth" in human history, through the use of primary sources with a "proven" authenticity.[137]

However, this clear distinction breaks down on a number of grounds. The first and most obvious one can be summarized quite simply: myth is just a specific *form* of history; not the history of "what happened," but what people thought and believed. As people accept and absorb myths, they become the basis for ideas and actions that shape history. On these grounds, it is a mere technicality (or incidental fact), for instance, whether Robert Darnton's "Great Cat Massacre" ever actually took place: the point is that people chose or came to believe that it happened, and invested the event with cultural value.[138] Similarly, the factually plausible events of Christ's life are not nearly as important to the subsequent history of the Christian faith as the mythic version of the story that came to be mediated through the Gospels, and came to define the institutional (Catholic) Christian Church and its theology.

From all this, one can argue that the content of myth falls comfortably and squarely within a subset of the "history of ideas." Their use as a historical tool is no less than any other for exploring the past. The issues of truth and falsehood in past events, and their interpretations, then become somewhat moot to the purpose of this and related studies. Myth has always been the negotiation of fact and fiction, event and concept, a weaving of the real and imaginary. It represents the construction of a meaning and order that generates a new value truth of its own: "The value of myth lies in its values."[139] Studying belief is not qualitatively different to studying reality, because those beliefs are a human reality *in themselves*, and provide a foundation for historical awareness and action, whether embodied in social, political, or cultural forms.

## HISTORICAL "CONSCIOUSNESS" AND NARRATIVE

Leading on from this discussion, a broader challenge that to traditional conceptions of history, or our collective "consciousness of history," should be considered. In recent decades, there have been widespread, sometimes radical, critiques of historical methodology that challenge the formally clear boundaries between this and fictional forms of representation, and question much about the nature of knowable historical truth, particularly as mediated through historical texts. Much of this falls loosely within the umbrella of academic "Postmodernism," a wide-ranging concept which, when deployed as a critical technique, involves scepticism towards the hard certainties in *any* field of inquiry. Jean-François Lyotard in *The Postmodern Condition* (1979) describes postmodernism as marking a "crisis of knowledge" in Western societies, and defines the movement at its essence as "incredulity toward metanarratives" and their "reliance on some form of "transcendent and universal truth.'"[140] These metanarratives include such unifying conceptual schemes of human history as Marxism and the Enlightenment, and he further refers to those "metadiscourses" that make appeal to such grand narratives and ideologies, for instance "the dialectics of Spirit, the hermeneutics of meaning, the emancipation of the rational or working subject, or the creation of wealth."[141] Lyotard deems these approaches a teleological, totalitarian imposition of narrative on human nature. They "operate through inclusion and exclusion, as homogenizing forces, marshalling heterogeneity into ordered realms; silencing and excluding other discourses, other voices in the name of universal principles and general goals."[142] Consequently he sees the need for their replacement with a more relativist notion that there is no certainty of ideas, only contending "local" narratives of interpretation.

These ideas have been brought to bear, sometimes quite radically, on traditional notions of historical truth. Mieke Bal and Norman Bryson describe historical context as more a conceptual construct than an objective reality, which can be used by historians in their interpretation of an idea or source.[143] Michael Foucault criticized using historiographical assumptions—and narratives of "progress" and "meaning"- in descriptions of the past.[144] Karl Popper in *The Poverty of Historicism* went further, expressing a fundamental outlook that "belief in historical destiny is sheer superstition ... there can be no prediction of the course of human history by scientific or any other rational methods," due to both the innumerable components and characteristics of a society, and the impossibility of modelling future growth in scientific or technical knowledge.[145] These critiques become especially relevant when examining the more "literary" and subjective qualities of historical authorship. The key useful point that they make here is that the historical context in which a literary work is written is not (simply) a factual, independent series of events that exists in a realm separate and distinct from the observer. Hans-Robert Jauss describes literary work as "the product of reciprocal interaction of work and readers, from whose experience it is inseparable."[146] Terry Eagleton observes that the meaning of a text exceeds the intentions of its author—as it is passed from one cultural and historical context to another, new and unforeseen potentials in a work can be realized.[147] The reader, therefore, "Makes implicit connections, fills in gaps, draws inferences and tests out hunches ... drawing on a tacit knowledge of the world in general and of literary conventions in particular. The text itself is really no more than a series of 'cues' to the reader, 'invitations to construct a piece of language into meaning.'"[148] From his semiotic deconstructions, Barthes came to deny a distinction between history and literature, seeing the former as nothing but another deceptive discourse; a surreptitious, imaginary elaboration of cultural values.[149] In *The Past Is a Foreign Country* (1995), critic and cultural theorist David Lowenthal observes that,

> The most pellucid pearls of historical narrative are often found in fiction, long a major component of historical understanding ... The segregation of historical from fictional narrative was a by-product of late-Renaissance concern about the validity and accuracy of historical sources ... as history retreated to the arid confines of empirical rigour, novelists took over the richer if more fanciful aspects of the past that historians relinquished ... historical fiction shares with history the burdens of hindsight, not just to make the past intelligible but to account for processes of change not originally apparent. All accounts of the past tell stories about it, and hence are partly invented ... The history-fiction difference is more one of purpose than of content.[150]

Here, the argument is not to emphasize that history writing is inherently pregnant with fictional narrative (though the last quoted line reiterates that idea), but that academic developments in the discipline required a different form of literature to satisfying the purpose of making the past meaningful and intelligible for a broader audience.

Most in line with the approach of this book are the works of Stephen Bann and Hayden White, which provide a detailed critique of the distinct categorization of historiographical and fictional literature. Their arguments play a crucial role in the outlook of this study; both in the interconnections they highlight between history and other forms of representation, and for the attention they draw to the evolution of historiography in the nineteenth century. Bann is concerned with how the emerging discipline of history had to negotiate its own conceptual corner within the emergence of other professional and "scientific" fields. He contends that the nineteenth century witnessed the emergence of "historical poetics"—a system of rhetorical techniques that appeared in tandem with a deepening conception of historical consciousness.[151] Hayden White applies this idea to a broader critique of historical literature as a genre by comparing four major historians (Michelet, Ranke, Tocqueville, and Burckhardt) and four principal *philosophers* of history (Hegel, Marx, Nietzsche, and Croce) from the nineteenth century, contending that the "works of the principal philosophers of the nineteenth century differ from those of their counterparts in what is sometimes called "proper" history (Michelet, Ranke, Tocqueville, and Burckhardt) only in emphasis, not in content."[152] White describes historical narratives as "verbal fictions, the contents of which are more invented than found," and argued that they were narratives with more in common with literature than science.[153] His concern is instead with critically establishing the "poetic" elements in historiography and philosophy of history "in whatever age they were practiced."[154] Crucially, for my purpose, White argues that while these descriptions proceed from empirically validated facts or events, they necessarily require imaginative steps to place them in a coherent story. He therefore states that "the techniques or strategies that (historians and imaginative writers) use in the composition of their discourses can be shown to be substantially the same, however different they may appear on a purely surface, or dictional, level."[155]

The consequence of all this is that, in White's view, what we may consider "facts" are instead deemed "constructed: in the documents attesting to the occurrence of events, by interested parties commenting on the events or the documents, and by historians interested in giving a true account ... and distinguishing it from what may appear to have happened. It is the "facts" that are unstable, subject to revision and further interpretation, and even dismissible as illusions on sufficient grounds."[156] The assertion he derives from an examination of nineteenth-century historical consciousness is that all "proper" history or historiography is a form of philosophy. Its authors possess no absolute theoretical grounds to legitimately claim their authority, and so are forced to choose between "contending interpretative strategies." Consequently "the grounds for choosing one perspective on history rather than another are ultimately aesthetic or moral rather than epistemological."[157] Historiography to White is essentially a *literary* genre, following literary tropes and conventions, and conforming to genres and poetic archetypes that are driven first and foremost by "ideology." All historical discourses, according to this mode of analysis, are forms of "fiction." All history involves storytelling and a plot.[158] This means that its claim to possessing real truth or objectivity can be seriously challenged.

This leads on to White's most important concept for this study, that of the "metahistorical understructure." He postulates a "deep level of consciousness on which a historical thinker chooses conceptual strategies," and describes how the "historian performs an essentially poetic act." This act produces the accessible vision of literature, for the "coherence of literature as an event is primarily mediated in the horizon of expectations of the literary experience of contemporary and later readers, critics, and authors." Such metahistory, as defined by White, draws to the overlapping forms of nineteenth-century historical representation—its "professional" history, museum displays, paintings, plays, and eventually films.[159] It is an *integrated regime of historical representation* at work that incorporates both high and low cultural forms.

While there is a great deal of value in the above approaches, some important criticism of it can be noted. It should be pointed out that one very easy consequence and extrapolation of these postmodern critiques of history is an unbridled, extreme relativism; one that can only end in the deconstruction of *all* accessible meaning. Karl Popper describes historical events as "unique" and "non-repeatable" processes, without comparable cases—thereby depriving us of much of the value of comparisons of past events, or even the study of history itself.[160] Similarly, Lévi-Strauss "called into question claims that Western scientific rationality possessed any intrinsic superiority over mythical forms of thinking." Saussure, arguing for the subjectivity of semiotic experience, held that "language shapes images of reality but does not refer to it."[161]

The problems with this outlook are manifold. In terms of our ability to positively construct a comprehension of the past, they offer very little of use to historians, anthropologists, or social scientists—being more concerned with emphasizing just how much we *can't* say than with suggesting anything useful that we can. Such reductionism leads to absurd and self-contradictory extremes. If we take White and other deconstructionists too literally, and conclude that historical events exist only in the mind of the historian, then we would also have to conclude that there are no connections between different things that happened in the past. By a logical irony, this would also render White's own thematic assemblage of nineteenth-century writers invalid, as it reduces such analysis to a reflection of the interior of his own mind, rather than of the outside world.

Much of the postmodern critique of Western scientific, rationalist, and empiricist historical worldviews is an outgrowth of a progressive ideology that holds that their perceived status as "universal truths" has proved a justification for abuses of power and authority, is a legacy of colonialism, and a form of cultural imperialism.[162] This attack on hegemonic Western value systems is a key component of a revisionist and rebellious movement in society, the arts, and politics.[163] It may (or may not) be a valid one in these respects, and is a core component of the approaches in postcolonial literature.[164] However, not all historical writing succumbs completely to such distorting ideals of purpose, or an overt teleological frame. White's model works very well for the post-Enlightenment writers that reflected and glorified its more Whiggish ideals. It applies very effectively to the eloquent, propagandist rhetoric of Gibbon's *Decline and Fall of the Roman Empire*, and much of the subsequent literature, media and material inspired by this—which is precisely why it is a very appropriate model for this book. It also describes well the histories of the nineteenth century that focused on the medieval world, and which informed the cultural output explored here. The extent of their influence was such that the medievalist Norman Cantor argued that "any bright American college sophomore who today takes a good survey course on medieval history has a better understanding of the components of the medieval world than anyone who wrote before 1895."[165]

This approach is *not*, however, as strong a fit with modern historical scholarship as an *academic* discipline, which places a more conscious distance between itself and the ideals and techniques White placed under the microscope. Arthur Marwick puts this point forward by praising White's "brilliant analysis of the rhetorical techniques of some famous early nineteenth-century historians ... *before* the emergence of professional history (emphasis added)." Consequently, he criticized him for showing "very little acquaintanceship with what historians write today."[166]

There are a number of important conclusions to be drawn from this discussion of history, myth, and literature. Historical writing does not exist independently of cultural or social activity, or present us with an unchanging objective truth. Much of it consists of a series of debates between historians, an ongoing dialogue on the past. Furthermore, *all* forms of representation, including the historical, are potentially loaded with cultural and ideological values, whether latent or more overt. Consequently, a work of history can be treated as a cultural or "mythic" text as much as any other. Just as myth involves a negotiation of fact and fiction, so history occupies an ambiguous position between art and science, and the gap between reality and representation is not always clear. A critical examination of these traditions of historical scholarship is vital to understanding the very material forms that such representations acquire when translated into other cultural media. Without being beholden to its more extreme postulations, much of the postmodern critique of history can be integrated into the conception of myth in this study. This is not to deny any and all historical objectivity, or to reduce it to White's depiction of a rudderless "conceptual anarchy,"[167] but simply to argue for its lack of primacy, compared to such forms of myth, in defining the cultural historiographical record. The value of the above critiques of rigid historical paradigms is not that they abolish any meaningful concept of truth or fact, but that they help soften the boundaries between historical discourse and fiction, truth and falsehood, and scholarship and propaganda. This allows one to focus on beliefs over realities, and the complex and recursive relationship between historical and artistic representations. There is no reason for this approach—and studies of representation in general—not to constitute an entirely and perfectly valid field of historical study, within the ever widening remit of the discipline today.

## Classics and the Vernacular

One of the key themes at play in studies of representation is the longstanding debate about the meaning, interpretation, and ultimate value of popular culture. The very term "value" is of course itself a contested category, beholden to a plurality of meanings. It includes the culture of—or sometimes deemed imposed on—the "working class"; those mass cultural forms unique to post-industrial society; or rural and folk practices, and/or their appropriation and re-articulation in the contemporary world.[168]

Within this variety of approaches is a debate of particular pertinence, namely the perceived disjunction between "high" and "popular" cultural forms. The latter have been frequently portrayed as conflicting with traditional ideals of high culture, which was famously described by Matthew Arnold as representing, "The best that has been thought and said."[169] T.S. Eliot declared that culture is inclusive of everything from dog races and Wensleydale cheese, to Gothic churches and the music of Elgar: yet he also advocated a system of cultural segregation to maintain the division between high and low cultural forms.[170] Astonishingly, Eliot also argued against encouraging the majority to partake in high culture, as this would "adulterate and cheapen" it—consequently its minority status was necessary for its very survival and preservation.[171] These ideas echo deep-rooted and long-lasting fears about allowing the masses to become a dominant force in culture, thereby realizing the tyranny of the ignorant majority over cultivated minority taste.[172] More recently, John Storey speaks of seeing "a neo-conservative revival of the distinction between high and popular culture.".[173]

The long tradition of popular culture being reviled by academics also comes from the political left, as embodied in particular by the Frankfurt School, which perceived mass culture to be an expression of the dominant ideology of elites: a "False Consciousness" generated to secure the stability of exploitative capitalism. Popular cultural forms are seen in this school of thought as ideological weapons, fashioned by the owners of the means of cultural production to make capitalism appear natural and inevitable. They reflected not the people's authentic values and interests, but the indoctrinating propaganda of their "master's voice."[174] Kracauer in particular took this approach to connect cinema and representations of the pre-industrial world, arguing that films set far in the past were deceptions disguising realities about the present day. He believed that the presentation of current events in cinema posed a threat to the institutions of power or the "excitable masses," who could potentially turn against those institutions. Consequently, he suggests that it is in the interests of those institutions to project their attention into the remote past of the ancient or medieval worlds to rob them of this subversive potential.[175]

Debates about culture and value tie intimately into the consideration of how, why, and even whether antiquity and the classics maintain a significant and meaningful presence in the modern world.[176] The significance of this tradition of learning, derived from the culture of the ancient world, has long been deemed to be immense, bordering on the sacred. Christopher Higbert describes in *The Classical Tradition* how without its Hellenic heritage "...our civilization would not merely be different. It would be thinner, more fragmentary, less thoughtful, more materialistic ... it would be less worth to be called a civilization, because its spiritual achievements would be less great."[177] This sacrosanct reverence lends itself to a view in which classical archetypes are deemed to be a special form of high culture, antithetical to the popular. The timeless, universal values of the "classic" are therefore weighted against the seemingly mundane and localized interests of popular culture. Consequently, the appropriation and reinvention of these formal, sacrosanct texts into new, popular, and interpretative dramatic forms has been frequently deemed anathema to the classical tradition—an intellectual perversion, portrayed by its detractors as "cultural vandalism" and "vulgar attempts to attract students to a discipline in crisis,"[178] or to the trivial interests of popular culture.[179] In *Backing into the Future: The Classical Tradition and Its Renewal* (1994), Bernard Knox describes a fear that progressive cultural attitudes threaten to "abolish the cultural traditions on which the West's sense of unity and identity is founded ...", and that "it is only to be expected that in this age of cultural dilution, of plastic substitutes, of mindless television shows ... the genuine article is no longer valued."[180]

Popular culture can easily be perceived as a threat to the "classic," and a modern form of barbarism.[181] As the archetypal "mass medium" of the twentieth century, cinema in particular has been a challenge to the more "elite" elements of both high culture and "classicism," and a focal point for much of this disaffection. Many writers and intellectuals have expressed disquiet at the public's taste for the representation of historical and classical romance on-screen.[182] Walter Benjamin and D.W. Griffith's hopes for the potential of cinema as a principal cultural device have constituted some of the worst fears of many traditional classicists.[183] Quentin Leavis, writing in 1932, outlined the detrimental impact of cinema as alienating modern man from the great literature of the past, seducing him with the "frivolous stimuli" of "cheap and easy pleasures offered by the cinema."[184] This trend is not just confined to representations of the ancient world—Arthur

Lindley describes how "One could note the absence of books by medievalists as well as books of any kind devoted to medieval film.".[185]

Popular cultural forms have often then been disregarded by many writers, historians and intellectuals as a means for constructing the past—or *a* past—that might have a legitimacy and value of its own. The superficially exciting allure of popular media leave them open to qualitative judgments of their worth. Yet it has become increasingly recognized that one cannot ignore popular culture in favour of "high" or "elite" materials, because, subjective aesthetic considerations aside, the former far better illuminates broader social and historical phenomena. The centrality of popular culture to contemporary society and the modern state is increasingly being emphasized by many theorists. This more contemporary approach to culture eschews value judgements about its intellectual worth, and instead focuses on its *anthropological* treatment, as the lived experience and activities of a society, and the meaning and values implicit in them.[186] It should be noted, in fact, that "Classics" as a field itself involves the study of ancient forms of popular culture; arena tournaments, "street Latin," and graffiti from the walls of Pompeii have all been the subject of extensive study. As T.S. Eliot put it, "Even the humblest material artefact ... is an emissary of the culture out of which it comes."[187]

If we assume that mass cultural artefacts have to satisfy commercial imperatives and compete in a market for public attention—in contradiction to the extreme dismissals of the Frankfurt school—then they can prove to be powerful indices for public concern. Popular culture occupies an increasingly central position in society. Being vernacular does not make it peripheral. It is crucial to note that in modern (post-industrial) times, mass production and mass popular culture have subsumed society and become the salient feature of social life. Symbolic production is a central component of this post-industrial economy. We live in a world deluged with images, where the bulk of people's ideas about the past come from cinema and television—feature films, documentaries, news programmes, and the like. Consequently, the centrality of popular culture and visual culture to modern society is being increasingly emphasized by historians and intellectuals. Vachel Lindsay was already describing America, in 1919, as utterly transformed by photography, cinema and advertisements into a "hieroglyphical" civilization resembling Egypt.[188] Umberto Eco describes us as a civilization "now accustomed to thinking in images ... It is the visual work (cinema, videotape, mural, comic strip, photograph) that is now part of our memory.".[189]

Within this new paradigm, popular culture becomes an ideal barometer for shared social experience. Seen in this light, one does not need to focus on how film—and other, related forms of representation—gets the past wrong, or theorize on the purpose of film as a presentation of the past, or what it should do for the past, or how it "should" construct history. Rather, it is better to be concerned with *how* historical filmmakers have been working, and grasp the rules of engagement by which history is rendered on screen, and elsewhere outside of academic treatises. As a symbolic source for modern times, it can be considered to denote deep, commonly held myths and mores. Just as drama and theatre did in an earlier age, in the face of much traditional opposition, so cinema has proven itself as a vehicle for creative and artistic talents.[190] Furthermore, the popular appropriation of antiquity challenges any sense of "ownership" that scholars, traditionalists, and cultural "elitists" may feel about the ancient world, literature and classical learning. Rosenstone suggests that historical film is troubling and disturbing most professional historians, for the simple reason that, "Film is out of the control of historians. Film shows that academics do not own the past. Film creates a historical world with which the written word cannot compete, at least for popularity."[191]

In recent centuries, classically influenced texts and commentaries have changed enormously, as the very conception of "classics" and the classical world has been varyingly understood. Furthermore, the range of what has been deemed to count as classics has been constantly defined and redefined. Mary Beard and John Henderson define the field as "a subject that exists in that gap between us and the world of the Greeks and Romans."[192] Consequently, its aim can be seen as not just the uncovering of the ancient world, but *defining and debating our own relationship to that world*. This leaves it more open to discussing novel cultural forms, such as cinema, than the historically rigorous parameters of "classicism" would naturally appear to allow. In this vein, Martin Winkler describes classics as "a versatile and exciting discipline, capable of combining methods of traditional scholarship with an openness to modern critical thought in its approaches to the ancient cultures and to the classical tradition."[193] Because Greco-Roman culture has lost much of its privileged status, the post-Roman centuries are no longer automatically viewed as the "Dark Age" that followed the demise of a great civilization. Nowadays, instead of "civilizations", we apply the word "cultures". Civilizations as a concept can be unfashionable or uncomfortable as an exclusionary label.

Decoupling the distinctions between high and popular culture in this way allows for a richer academic engagement with the wide array of cultural discourses between the ancient and modern worlds. It enables a productive exchange between scholarship on ancient culture and cultural theories of the popular. These are different, though interrelated, fields of inquiry; drawing on similar material, but which is filtered through the lenses of different societies, and calibrated to a changing set of social and cultural criteria.

The history of the reception of antiquity cannot ignore its modern cultural formations, extensive and all-pervading as they are. Both high and low culture meld fact and fiction. Classical representations pervade not just high culture but *all* culture: this process is not composed solely or primarily of elite responses, but ranges across the cultural spectrum. Such an approach has far more value to the study of contemporary culture and society, and the varied interrelations of past and present, than a narrow focus on high culture, or its expression via the concept of an innately purer and superior "Classical Tradition."

There are a number of valuable approaches to the post-industrial representation of antiquity, and these include such interdisciplinary approaches as the psychoanalytic, structuralist, political, and historical.[194] However, the nexus of this project is "historical" forms of representations of decline, and their mutual relationship. Those artistic/imitative and psychological fields of inquiry commonly explored in such studies are of limited importance. Film, however, is central, as it is the primary means by which the ancient (and medieval) past is featured in popular culture. The reception of antiquity in relation to film has become an increasingly vigorous field of study in the past few decades. It was largely initiated by Jon Solomon's *The Ancient World in the Cinema* (1978), an encyclopaedic study of various classical topics in film.[195] Research in this field has typically taken two directions. There are those works focused on *direct* representations of the past in present cultural texts. For instance Maria Wyke's *Projecting the Past* (1997) highlights this through a number of case studies: Spartacus, Nero, Cleopatra and the city of Pompeii. For example, the book provides a history of how men's attitude to women is displayed in evolving representations of the sexuality of Cleopatra.[196] Most recently there is *The Fall of the Roman Empire: Film and History* (2009), a collection of essays, edited by Martin Winkler, providing a critical re-evaluation of a highly controversial epic film, featuring topics from the representation of

Roman history onscreen to the wider discourses surrounding the place of Anthony Mann's film in our culture.[197]

While all these discussed approaches to classical scholarship are far from universally appreciated, they now mark one of the dominant attitudes in the study of ancient texts in relation to the contemporary world. Considerable in scope though they are, however, there are several grounds in which they can be deemed to fall short. This approach is typically driven by a very specific motivation; namely, the retooling of the discipline of classics for the modern world, and a modern audience, and thereby ensuring its ongoing survival. An evident purpose of these comparative studies is to subvert conventional attitudes to classicism. It attempts to redeem the "worth" of classical representation,[198] and can also be related to a broader movement to rehabilitate popular culture by finding "high" art values residing in low art forms.[199] This agenda has been the most common criticism of this new form of reception from traditional classical scholars, who have believed such compromises to be unnecessary at best, and "dangerous" or demeaning to the form at worst.[200] Thus, it is always necessary to keep the contemporary horizon of interest of the comparative interpreter in view. This book makes a conscious effort to avoid these kinds of subjective assessments of quality or worth, taking as its premise that the most valuable evaluations of cultural forms are made by those who seek not to praise or condemn, but rather to understand.[201]

With regard to these trends in classical reception, it needs to be reiterated that the theme of the decline and fall has received comparatively little attention in these approaches. Most scholarship on antiquity in more modern media has been taken up by traditional classicists, whose academic background and consequent area of focus are on the depiction of a much earlier "high" period of Greco-Roman culture and history. Consequently, while there are works on specific relevant topics, for instance a recent study of Anthony Mann's *The Fall of the Roman Empire* (Paramount Pictures, 1964),[202] there is not yet any coherent synthesis or study of this theme.

## FILM AND A CONSCIOUSNESS OF ANTIQUITY

In regard to the popular cultural presence of antiquity, film has been crucial to the formation and wide dissemination of a historical consciousness of Ancient Rome. Cinematic resurrections of it are one of the chief transmitters of twentieth-century knowledge of the Roman world. This does not resemble a "break" from past cultural traditions, so much as its re-mediation in new forms. Historical film has its roots in the "histories," literature and novelizations of the nineteenth century. Cinema's representation of Rome in the twentieth-century was forged in the discourses of the nineteenth, while film as a medium has its roots in the representational forms of that century; it fitted a principle of that period to make the past reawaken in the present, and grew out of technologies such as engraving, lithography and photography.[203]

The significance for us here lies in the fact that films are stories that situate us in a value-laden world. Cinematic representations are fictions, but fictions that bring up a constellation of meanings for their audiences. As every film is a product of its own culture, it reflects in some way the mores and concerns of the ordinary people. For the past century, cinema has been a revealing index of social and cultural concerns. Siegfried Kracauer contended that, "The films of a nation reflect their mentality." German expressionist films suggested a dark and moody angst lurking within the cultural flamboyance of Weimer Germany.[204] Italian Neo-realism depicts the harshness of life in that country after the Second World War.[205] Early Soviet cinema revelled in the modernist machine age.[206] Different genres have proved radically mutable in meaning even where they retained technical and stylistic consistency of form. Science fiction evoked communist paranoia in the 1950s and utopian and philosophical idealism in the 1960s. Film takes a very prominent position in the wider study of classical reception, precisely because the themes of the classical past—and the decline from those glories, the fall and loss of that world—are, to the modern mind, still laden with myth and meaning.

These discourses were therefore part of a wide, integrated and evolving regime for representing the past. Classical Antiquity endowed the USA with the legitimacy of a cultural, moral and intellectual tradition linking its "New World" to Athenian Democracy. As Maria Wyke points out, "The two nations most prolific in the manufacture of cinematic histories of Rome—Italy and the United States—were also those that assiduously created a whole array of "invented traditions" to connect themselves to a Roman past now appropriated as their own."[207] Cinematic reconstructions of Roman history have mirrored both the evolution of their genre and industry, and wider cultural and historical developments. In the 1910s they sought to legitimize cinema as a new art form, in the 1930s they served as a showpiece for commodities and the bourgeoning consumer culture, and in the 1950s they came to challenge the assault of television on film industry profits.[208]

In emphasizing the mass cultural significance of cinema, it should be pointed out that I am drawing a contrast to the aforementioned "auteur" theory in regarding films—or at least relatively mainstream ones—as the outcome of a team or social group, rather than an individual's creativity. Films need a public, have financial backers and often appeal to a heterogeneous mass audience, therefore they can often be easily seen as reflections of the collective mentality of a nation—a historical text that society writes about itself. This makes it an inherently collaborative medium. Samuel Bronston, the producer of Anthony Mann's *The Fall of the Roman Empire*, described his role in this manner: "I consider myself a twentieth-century artist whose medium consists of the most complicated elements: armies of talented people, huge financial capital, awesome communication technologies, and a collection of creative peers whose brilliance and discipline set a standard of quality that is still a global source of inspiration."[209]

Films are stories that situate us in a value-laden world. Cinematic representations are fictions, but fictions that bring up a constellation of meanings for their audiences. As every film is a product of its own culture, it reflects in some way the mores and concerns of the ordinary people. Because mainstream movies were turned out on an assembly-line basis in such massive numbers, tuned to appeal to a vast audience base, they were often better indices of public concerns, and shared myths and mores, than individually conceived artistic projects of the so-called auteur.[210] On this note, Geoffrey Richards points out that many of the early critics of cinema missed out just how well these hugely commercially successful films reflect the tastes and attitudes of their audiences.[211] Consequently, I am not treating the medium as being defined by the interplay of free signifiers, divorced from historical realities. Rather, cinema's very complex relationship to history necessitates an interdisciplinary approach. Both films and history are entry points to a unified system of culture.

## Truth and Accuracy in Historical Cinema

The visual and literary arts, in both high and low culture, have always combined fact with fiction when dealing with history: even when purporting to be offering an accurate and meaningful account of a historical event or process. This is especially true when examining a distant past which is not easily recovered; where the setting is idealized, the proper context, beliefs, and motives can be exotic to modern audiences, and the sources are fragmentary and obtuse.

The impulses behind historical cinematic presentation of this sort could be varied and competing. There was the pursuit of strict historical authenticity, or the communication of some essential, selected historical truth. The importance of the authentic haunts discussions of films about the past.[212] There is a broad range of academic studies on historical film which seeking to defend it against charges of inaccuracy, and to establish criteria for its quality and claims to authenticity different from those of academic historiography.[213]

This authenticity therefore takes a number of forms. Directors who make the strongest claims for a return to a medieval or otherwise historic reality often draw on specific details—such as the armour, heraldry, architecture or other such details, to craft a supposedly authentic *mise-en-scene* of authorization.[214] Whether the deeper content is indeed "truthful," or even intended to be, such a strategy can be highly successful in engendering that response. The reception of Jean-Jacques Annaud's 1986 film *The Name of the Rose*, set in a fourteenth-century Benedictine Abbey, indicates it largely succeeded in producing the "effect" of authenticity, and projected an image of its devotion to historical accuracy. Author Umberto Eco, who wrote the book on which the film was based, did his best to foster the perception of the accuracy of *The Name of the Rose*, describing the desire of the director "to reproduce the period in all its details."[215] *The Guardian* expressed admiration for Annaud's "obsessive attention to historical authenticity, from specially-woven monks habits to having all the fillings and crowns removed from the actors' mouths."[216] This desire for authenticity, or "truth" of a sort, is not unique to factual and historical film—it was a much-touted selling point of the *Lord of the Rings* trilogy, and in other examples of "medieval fantasy."[217] D.W. Griffith, the filmmaker of ancient-themed epics such as *Intolerance* (Triangle Film Corporation, 1916) and *The Ten Commandments* (Paramount Pictures, 1923),[218] believed cinema had a unique role in transmitting a historical consciousness to the public, and would one day usurp history books in that role; its intimacy and immediacy made it a powerful and provocative way of capturing the public imagination.[219] Indeed, as David Williams argues, the demand for such authenticity—for "the real thing"—works subtly and unconsciously in the minds of all watchers of film.[220] Alternatively, this authenticity can be less a purposeful pursuit than it can be a veneer or smokescreen, one contrived both for entertainment purposes and/or to convey an ideology of some sort.[221] Historical film suits this purpose particularly well, as it allows for a pointed comparison, whether direct or implicit, to be made with the modern world. It can enshrine such comparisons, however trite, with the shroud of authority.

Exotic and distant, the ancient and medieval worlds catered for this purpose in varying ways. Cecil B. DeMille cared greatly about maintaining the visual accuracy of his material, but not the content—his characters may wear historically accurate garb and drink out of the right goblets, but their dialogue is replete with modern slang, and anachronistic assumptions about the lives of the ancients.[222] Roland Barthes noted the stereotype of the "Roman fringe"—an arbitrary sign, unrelated to actual historical practice, which nevertheless serves as a period marker, and signifier of *Romanitas*, or Roman-ness, in certain films set in ancient Rome, such as Joseph L. Mankiewicz's *Julius Caesar* (1954).[223] Medieval artists and audiences would have found the Roman fringe an entirely comprehensible signifying system.

This kind of "historical myopia" is partly a function of the desire to produce films which entertain enough to be commercially viable. It is a common treatment of the subject in cultural and media theory.[224] However, it is far from the exclusive purpose of history in cinema—even of commercial, epic filmmaking. In particular, the concept of authenticity can be central to the ideology of historical cinema—and therefore those ancient and medieval films that incorporate the decline and fall myth— even and indeed especially where that ideology contrasts to the reality of the production, its use of facts and sources, and the intentions of the author.

It should be noted here that central to many medieval or early-medieval films through the twentieth and twenty-first centuries is the idea that the Middle Ages are represented as a form of *prehistory*, rather than as part of a secular historical narrative. The distinguishing difference in this approach is that it projects a world in which the supernatural conjoins with the real. Such cinema is much more likely to include miraculous or supernatural events than representations of later historical periods. These can be overt, or embody more implicit examples woven into the historical record. Literary inventions such as Arthurian Knights or Siegfried can be portrayed as often as historical figures like Charlemagne and Saladin.[225] This tendency proves almost as common in historical representations as it is in purely fictional or stories. These frequently belong to the "mode of the marvellous," where the supernatural is accepted as existing within the world by its characters. This lack of strict realism explains much of the perceived inferiority of these genres of cinema. The cut-off point from this pre-historical time appears to be the transition from the Middle Ages to modernity—or what Arthur Lindley describes as "dreamland" and real "history."[226] The genre—if it can be called that—is easily open to an injection of fantasy and the supernatural. It fits best in the dream-like qualities imposed on the "Dark Ages"; a construct that can stretch in the historical imagination over the early medieval world, the "other" fringes of society, and the end of Late Roman history, and which also allows one to explore themes of the contrast between "barbarity" and civilized values.

In both their sources and common purpose, historical cinema and historiography have many affinities. These, however, are not necessarily the ones argued by the advocates of the former, arguments which can resemble an apologetic for the perceived intellectual inferiority of the art form.[227] As with the attempts by some classicists to rehabilitate the aesthetic value of popular culture, these arguments for the inherent worth—either in artistic merit or historical truthfulness—of a cinematic representation, are not the purpose or primary concern of this book. Instead, we can demonstrate the value of these representations as indicators of cultural myths and mores; insights into the reception and reworking of the past. This value is not in any way determined by their ability to capture factual "truth."

The mediating dynamic of the motion picture has become a vehicle for historians (and classicists) to reinterpret, sometimes radically, the role of their discipline. Historical film must be taken seriously on its own terms; as an interpretation and poetic speculation on the past, and a key component of a wider cultural *discourse* with that past that frames our relationship to it. The analysis of historical film, and all forms of historical representation, opens up not one but two avenues of inquiry—the study of contemporary society through the representation of the past, and, less overtly, the study of *the modern transmission of historical consciousness*. These representations make up a "cultural historiography" of their own: a tradition in which culture acts as the primary agent in the ongoing reception by the present of the past. They shadow and shape the collective historical imagination. In this study, the force of this tradition is witnessed in the evolving conception of the decline and fall.

## Notes

1. Arnold H.M. Jones, *The Later Roman Empire 284–602: A Social, Economic and Administrative Survey*, 2 vols (Baltimore: John Hopkins (ori. Pub. 1964), 1986).

2. Bryan Ward-Perkins, "Jones and the Late Roman Economy," in David M. Gwynn (ed.), *A.H.M Jones and the Later Roman Empire: Brill's Series on the Early Middle Ages*, vol. 15 (Leiden: Brill, 2008), p. 193. The book derives from a seminar series in Oxford to commemorate the 40th anniversary of the publication of *The Later Roman Empire*.
3. Peter Brown, "The Later Roman Empire," *The Economic History Review*, XX (1967), p. 327.
4. Op. cit., pp. 328–9.
5. Jones, p. 1027.
6. Ward-Perkins (2008), p. 195 gives an excellent example in the form of Friedrich Oertel, "The Economic Life of the Empire," in *The Cambridge Ancient History*, XII (Cambridge: Cambridge University Press, 1939), pp. 269–70, which describes how "a complete State-socialism was in force ... with its terrorism by officials," and which "stamped subjection ... to the will of God." See also Michael I. Rostovzeff, *The Social and Economic History of the Roman Empire* (Oxford: Oxford University Press (ori. Pub. 1926), 1957), who had pushed the argument for this socio-economic erosion and class tension in more Marxist terms. Roger Collins, analyzing Rostovtzeff's Marxian account of the collapse of the Western Empire, made the observation that "this is one of those topics than can tell the reader more about a historian's personal prejudices than about the historical reality that he seeks to describe." See Roger Collins, *Early Medieval Europe, 300–1000 AD* (London: Macmillan, 1991), p. 99. An escapee from the Russian Revolution, he attributed the collapse of the Roman Empire to an alliance between the rural proletariat and the military in the third century AD. Despite a personal opposition to communism, Rostovtzeff applied Marxian language to his analysis of the collapse of Rome, utilizing notions of class conflict between the proletariat and bourgeoisie, and a "capitalist rural economy," in his picture of the ancient world. For a critique of this, see Meyer Reinhold, "Historian of the Classic World: A Critique of Rostovtzeff," in Meyer Reinhold (ed.), *Studies in Classical History and Society* (New York: Oxford University Press, 2002), pp. 83–91. For "rural capitalism" see Rostovzeff (1957), p. 187.
7. Jones, p. 1045.
8. Ward-Perkins (2008), p. 197.
9. Jones, p. 1045.
10. He describes, for example, a tax on manufacturers and traders as "this terrible tax, which drove the merchants and craftsmen of the empire to desperation." Op. cit., pp. 871–2.
11. The core of this argument is found on the following pages: Op. cit., pp. 563–606 for the bureaucracy and its failings, pp. 772–780 and

pp. 808–12 for the condition of the peasant, pp. 794–802 for that of the *coloni*, pp. 812–23 for the *agri deserti*, pp. 933–4 for burden of the church, pp. 1035–8 for military deficiencies, pp. 1038 for economic decline, pp. 1040–44 for poverty and depopulation, pp. 1045–8 for idle mouths, pp. 1053–8 for administrative abuse, pp. 1048–52 for repressive legislation, and pp. 1058–64 for the loss of public spirit.
12. Op. cit., p. 1067.
13. Brown (1967), pp. 329–30.
14. Ward-Perkins (2008), p. 193.
15. Jones, p. 1068.
16. Ward-Perkins (2008), p. 193.
17. Jones, p. 1058.
18. Ward-Perkins (2008), p. 205. See also Peter Garnsey, "Writing the Late Roman Empire: Method and Sources," in Gwynn, p. 34.
19. Averil Cameron, "A.H.M Jones and the End of the Ancient World," in Gwynn, p. 243.
20. For an overall account of this see Luke Lavan, "A.H.M Jones and 'The Cities' 1964–2004," in Gwynn, pp. 167–192, for the cities; and Ward-Perkins (2008), pp. 193–212 for the economy.
21. For modern appraisals of the archaeological evidence see Bryan Ward-Perkins, "Specialized Production and Exchange," *Cambridge Ancient History*, XIV (2000), pp. 350–61, Ward-Perkins (2008), pp. 208–209, and Simon Swain and Mark Edwards (eds), *Approaching Late Antiquity: The Transformation from Early to Late Empire* (Oxford: Oxford University Press, 2006).
22. Jones, pp. 812–23 and pp. 1039–45.
23. For the revised view on the *agri deserti* see Chris R. Whittaker, "Agri Deserti," in Moses I. Finley (ed.), *Studies in Roman Property* (Cambridge: Cambridge University Press, 1976), pp. 137–65.
24. Jones, pp. 812–23, quote at p. 821.
25. Op. cit., p. 1040.
26. Op. cit., p. 808, as quoted in Ward-Perkins (2008), p. 200.
27. Jones, pp. 757–63.
28. John H.W.G Liebeschuetz, *The Decline and Fall of the Roman City* (Oxford: Oxford University Press (ori. Pub. 1972), 2001), pp. 104–5.
29. Peter Heather, "Running the Empire: Bureaucrats, Curials, and Senators," in Gwynn, pp. 112–14. See also T. A. Kopecek, "Curial Displacements and Flight in Later Fourth-Century Cappadocia," *Historia*, XXIII (1974), pp. 319–42.
30. *Codex Theodosius*, 12.1 on curial restrictions.
31. Jones, p. 1051.
32. Op. cit., pp. 1051–2.

33. Op. cit., p. 1046, see also Ward-Perkins (2008), pp. 197–8.
34. Jones, p. 980.
35. Peter Brown, *The Rise of Western Christendom* (Oxford: Blackwell, 1996).
36. Cameron (1993), pp. 126–7.
37. For an overview of these processes see Peter Brown, *The Rise of Christendom: Triumph and Diversity 200–1000 AD* (Oxford: Blackwell (ori. Pub. 1996), 2002), Ramsey Macmullen, *Christianizing the Roman Empire: AD 100–400* (New York: Yale University Press, 1984), and Gwynn, "Idle Mouths and Solar Haloes: A.H.M Jones and the Conversion of Europe," in Gwynn, pp. 213–230.
38. Symmachus, *Relatio*, III, 11–16 on the confiscation of state subsidies for pagan ceremony by Gratian, and the retention of lands by the treasury dedicated to Vestal Virgins or pagan ministers. Libanius, *Pro Templis*, XXX on the ruin and despoliation of the temples.
39. Cameron (1993), pp. 81–3.
40. Liebesheutz, pp. 137–167, Cameron (1993), pp. 71–73.
41. David M. Gwynn, "Idle Mouths and Solar Haloes: A.H.M Jones and the Conversion of Europe," in Gwynn, p. 225, see also p. 228. Gwynn also points out that Jones does not entirely abandon the idea of Christianity "sapping" Roman society, pp. 225–6. The quotes are from Jones, pp. 1026–7.
42. Jones, p. 1027.
43. Ward-Perkins (2008), p. 196.
44. Jones, p. 1067.
45. Pat Southern and Karen R. Dixon, *The Late Roman Army* (London: Routledge, 2000), pp. 13–14 on Gallienus' mobile cavalry army, which took 12 days to march from Milan to the Rhine.
46. Ammianus, *Res Gestae*, XXVIII. 6.26.
47. For more on this see Simon Corcoran, *The Empire of the Tetrarchs: Imperial Pronouncements and Governments AD 284–324* (Oxford: Oxford University Press (ori. Pub. 1996), 2000), especially p. 440.
48. Peter Heather, *The Fall of the Roman Empire: A New History of Rome and the Barbarians* (Oxford: Oxford University Press, 2005), p. 448. See also Peter Heather, *Goths and Romans 332–489* (Oxford: Clarendon Press, 1991).
49. Heather (2005), pp. 386–397, p. 447.
50. Bryan Ward-Perkins, *The Fall of Rome and the End of Civilization* (Oxford: Oxford University Press, 2005), p. 57 emphasizes the role of bad luck and bad judgement in the erosion of imperial resources and territory. Heather (2005), pp. 272–80 deals with the particular significance of the loss of North Africa.

51. Ralph W. Mathisen, *Roman Aristocrats in Barbarian Gaul: Strategies for Survival in an Age of Transition* (Austin: University of Texas Press, 1993), and Ward-Perkins (2005), pp. 56–7.
52. Christopher Wickham, *The Inheritance of Rome: A History of Europe from 400 to 1000 AD* (London: Penguin, 2009), p. 3. See also Henri Pirenne, *Mohammed and Charlemagne* (Massachusetts: Courier Dover Publications (ori. Pub. 1937), 2001).
53. Ward-Perkins (2005), p. 62, and Collins, pp. 94–95, quote on p. 95. As he further elaborates, "This, at the time, was seen by the emperors as a temporary expedient, and in no sense did they feel that they were alienating their intrinsic authority over the empire."
54. Walter Goffart, *Barbarians and Romans AD 418–54: The Techniques of Accommodation* (New Jersey: Princeton University Press (ori. Pub. 1980), 2001), p. 35, as referenced in Ward-Perkins (2005), p. 10.
55. Ward-Perkins (2005), pp. 14–31 on the destruction from wrought by the invaders, and pp. 123–168 on its economic and cultural consequences.
56. Eileen Power, *Medieval People* (Gutenberg Project: Public Domain (ori. Pub. 1924), 2004), pp. 1–17.
57. André Piganiol, L'Empire Chrétien (Paris: Presses Universitaires de France, 1947), p. 422. See also "Review: L'Empire Chrétien," Kenneth M. Setton, The American Journal of Philology, vol. LXXIX, pp. 329–333.
58. Walter Goffart, "Rome, Constantinople, and the Barbarians," *American Historical Review*, LXXXVI (1981), p. 21. Says Ward-Perkins, "There is certainly a link between interpretations of the Germanic invaders as primarily peaceful, and the remarkable (and deserved) success that modern Germany has had at constructing a new and positive identity within Europe, after the disastrous Nazi years." Bryan Ward-Perkins, *The Fall of Rome and the End of Civilization* (Oxford: Oxford University Press, 2005), p. 173.
59. Collins, p. 98.
60. Jones, p. 1067.
61. Cameron (2008), p. 243.
62. Heather (2005), pp. 120–21.
63. Genesis 3:14–24. This idea does not originate with Judaeo-Christian legend. It has been strongly linked by modern scholarship to the Babylonian story, through the "Temptation Seal," which presents two figures (male and female) on each side of a tree, holding out their hands to the fruit, while at the back of one is a serpent, suggesting a very similar legend, for which see Thomas C. Mitchell, *The Bible in the British Museum: interpreting the evidence* (London: British Museum Press (ori. Pub. 1988), 2004), p. 24.

64. Daniel 2:31–40 and 2:38–44. The prophecy Jerome perceived as completed in his own time: see Jerome, trans. Gleason Leonard Archer, *St. Jerome, Commentary on Daniel* (Oregon: Wipf & Stock Publishers, 2009). pp. 15–157.
65. See Glenn W. Most, *Hesiod: Theogony, Works and Days, Testimonia*, Loeb Classical Library, LVII (Harvard: Harvard University Press, 2006), and Robert Bartlett, "An Introduction to Hesiod's Works and Days," *The Review of Politics* CXVIII (2006), pp. 177–205. See also Barry J. Gordon, *Economic analysis before Adam Smith: Hesiod to Lessius* (New York: Barnes and Noble, 1975), and Jacqueline de Romilly, *The Rise and Fall of States According to Greek Authors* (Ann Arbor: University of Michigan Press, 1991), p. 199, for the links between this and early political and economic thought.
66. Mary Beard and John Henderson, *Classics: A very short introduction* (Oxford: Oxford University Press, 1995). This definition now sometimes encompasses "Late Antiquity," up to circa AD 600. See Brown (1989) for this more inclusive revision.
67. Peter W. Rose, "Teaching Greek Myth and Confronting Contemporary Myths," in Martin M. Winkler (ed.), *Classics and Cinema* (Lewisburg: Bucknell University Press, 1991), p. 18.
68. Cited in Roland Bush, *T.S. Eliot: The Modernist in History* (Cambridge: Cambridge University Press, 1991), p. 172. See also T.S. Eliot, *What is a Classic?* (London: Faber and Faber, 1945).
69. For details on these many adaptations, see Craig W. Kallendorf (ed.), *A Companion to the Classical Tradition* (Oxford: Blackwell Publishing, 2007), Kenneth Clark, *The Nude: A Study in Ideal Form* (New Jersey: Princeton University Press, (ori. Pub. 1956), 1972), and Gilbert Highet, *The Classical Tradition: Greek and Roman Influences on Western Literature* (Oxford: Oxford University Press, 1949).
70. Patrick Brantlinger, *Bread and Circuses: Theories of Mass Culture as Social Decay* (London: Cornell University Press, 1986), pp. 42–44.
71. See the section of the Introduction of this book entitled "Representation and Myth," pp. 5–10.
72. The first reference to a "Byzantine empire" occurs in George Finlay's *History of the Byzantine Empire from 716 to 1059* (New York: Dutton and Co., 1906), although there are some earlier comparable uses by German authors from the sixteenth century: see John H. Rosser, *Historical Dictionary of Byzantium* (Massachusetts: Scarecrow Press, 2011), p. 2.
73. Howells (1999), p. 37.
74. For example, the men escort the women and children to the lifeboats, and then "die like gentlemen." Op. cit., p. 80.
75. Op. cit., pp. 229–232.

76. Werner Klingler, *Titanic* (Universum Film AG, 1943).
77. Paul Heyer, *Titanic Century: Media, Myth, and the Making of a Cultural Icon* (Santa Barbara: California, 2012), p. 143.
78. James Cameron, *Titanic* (Twentieth Century Fox, 1997). For an analysis in this regard see Richard Howells, "Review of Titanic (1997)," *Film and History*, XVIII (1998), pp. 70–71. See also Howells (1999), pp. 3–5.
79. It has seen a prodigious increase in the geopolitical climate since 2001: for instance see Murphy (2007), and Allen Massie "Return of the Roman," *Prospect* (November 2006), available online at http://www.prospectmagazine.co.uk/features/returnoftheroman
80. See "Representation and Myth," p. 8, in the Introduction to this book.
81. For more on this concept see Lisa D. Matson, *Re-Presentations of Dante Gabriel Rossetti: Portrayals in Fiction, Drama, Music, and Film* (New York: Cambria Press, 2010).
82. Stuart Hall, *Representation: Cultural Representations and Signifying Practices* (London: Sage, 1997), p. 25.
83. Elizabeth Chaplin, *Sociology and Visual Representation* (London: Routledge, 1994), p. 1.
84. Op. cit., p. 3.
85. Augustine, *On Christian Teaching*, trans. R.P.H. Green (Oxford: Oxford University Press, 1997), II, pp. 64–5.
86. For more practical examples of this tradition see Lex Bosman, *The power of tradition: Spolia in the architecture of St. Peter's in the Vatican* (Wilco: Hilversum, 2004), and Dale Kinney, "Rape or Restitution of the Past? Interpreting Spolia," in Susan C. Scott (ed.), *The Art of Interpreting* (Pennsylvania: University Park, 1995), pp. 53–67.
87. Hall, p. 25.
88. Reception theory focuses on the relationship between author and audience in the construction of meaning from a text: a negotiation between the former's intentions, and the complementary or contradictory reception of the latter, based on their own cultural background. On this see Terry Eagleton, "Phenomenology, Hermeneutics, and Reception Theory," in *Literary Theory* (Oxford: Blackwell Publishing (ori. Pub. 1983), 1996), pp. 47–78, and Robert C. Holub, *Crossing Borders: Reception Theory, Poststructuralism, Deconstruction* (Madison: University of Wisconsin Press, 1992). A good example of this interchangeable use is in *The Classical Receptions Journal* (Oxford: Oxford University Press, 2009–11).
89. Howells (1999), p. 50.
90. Peter Burke, "History as Social Memory," in Thomas Butler (ed.), *Memory: history, culture and the mind* (Oxford: Blackwell, 1989), pp. 97–113.

91. Roland Barthes describes myth as "its function is to distort," in *Mythologies*, trans. Annette Lavers (London: Vintage Classics (or. pub. 1972), 2009), p. 121.
92. The critical treatment of "myth" dates as far back as the Pre-Socratics. Euhemerus, an early mythographer, rationalized them as historical events which had been distorted and amplified to reflect the *mores* or values of their society. The Renaissance-era *Theologia Mythologica* (1532), a treatise of Classical mythology, treated the Hellenic pantheon as an allegory for the natural order. On these see Jean Seznec, *The Survival of the Pagan Gods: The mythological tradition and its place in Renaissance humanism and art*, trans. Barbara F. Sessions (New Jersey: Princeton University Press (ori. Pub. 1953), 1992), p. 11.
93. For all these see Percy S. Cohen, "Theories of Myth," in *Man*, IV (1969), pp. 337–353: a paper delivered at the Malinowski Memorial Lecture at the London School of Economics and Political Science, on the 8th May, 1969.
94. A good example is Max Muller's emphasis on solar myths (within which he controversially incorporated Christian doctrine). See Jon R. Stone (ed.), *The Essential Max Müller: On Language, Mythology, and Religion* (New York: St Martin's Press, 2002).
95. Andrew Lang, *Myth, Ritual and Religion* (New York: Cosimo Classics (ori. Pub. 1887), 2005), pp. 40–41, "so the anomalous and irrational myths of civilized races may be explained as survivals of stories which, in an earlier state of thought and knowledge, seemed natural enough .... We seek for the origin of the savage factor of myth in one aspect of the intellectual condition of savages."
96. Max F. Muller, *Three Lectures on the Science of Language* (Chicago: Open Court Publishing, 1899), p. 11, Edward B. Taylor, *Primitive Culture* (London: John Murray, 1871), p. 21.
97. Eric Csapo, *Theories of mythology* (London: Blackwell, 2004), p. 140.
98. Robert Segal, *Myth: A Very Short Introduction* (Oxford: Oxford University Press, 2004), p. 3.
99. Csapo, p. 140.
100. Bronisław Malinowski, *Magic, Science and Religion and Other Essays* (Illinois: Waveland Press (ori. Pub. 1954), 1992), p. 146.
101. Op. cit., p. 117, p. 144. The idea is not wholly original, and it echoes Plato, who in *The Republic*—a model for an idealized autocracy—outlined sample myths that could serve the benevolent ruling class as useful fictions in ensuring obedience from the various classes of citizen. See Plato, *The Republic*, trans. Desmond Lee (London: Penguin, 2007), p. 3. It is also demonstrated in the Marxist aesthetic philosophy of "Socialist Realism," which states that the ideal role of art is in communicating and

reinforcing Communist values. See James C. Vaughan, *Soviet Socialist Realism: Origins and Theory* (London: Macmillan, 1973).
102. See for example Philip R. Hardie, *Virgil's "Aeneid": Cosmos and Imperium* (London: Clarendon Press, 1988).
103. Malinowski, p. 177.
104. Csapo, p. 140 explores this connection in detail.
105. Malinowski, p. 178.
106. Op. cit., p. 177.
107. For the evolution of these ideas after Constantine see Ramsay Macmullen, *Christianizing The Roman Empire AD 100–400* (London: Yale University Press, 1984) and Peter Brown, *The Rise of Western Christendom Triumph and Diversity 200–1000 AD* (Oxford: Wiley-Blackwell (ori. Pub. 1973), 2002) for the development of early Christian ideology.
108. For examples of these myths see Alan Dundes (ed.), *The Flood Myth* (Berkeley: University of California Press, 1988). The interrelation of history and myth in theology is also discussed in Richard Howells, *The Interpretation of Popular Culture as Modern Myth* (PhD diss., Cambridge University, 1994), pp. 32–33.
109. For more on the potential contrast between myth and stories, see Umberto Eco, "The Myth of Superman," *Diacritics*, trans. Natalie Chilton, II (1962), p. 107. Eco contrasts the concept of the "myth" and "novel" as embodying opposed and mutually exclusive narratives; myth follows an established, known, and pre-determined pattern, while in a story the primary concern is finding out what happens next.
110. Lévi-Strauss (1968), pp. 203–6.
111. Claude Lévi-Strauss, *Structural anthropology II*, trans. Monique Layton (London: Penguin, 1978), pp. 60–67, p. 65. Similarly he says that, "A myth must never be interpreted individually, but in relation to other myths which form a transformational group," Strauss (1968), p. 217.
112. Edmund Leach (ed.), *The Structural Study of Myth and Totemism* (Tavistock: London (ori. Pub. 1967), 2004), p. 21.
113. Op. cit., p. 17.
114. Claude Lévi-Strauss, *The Savage Mind*, trans. George Weidenfield (University of Chicago Press: Chicago, 1966), p. 11. The application of bricolage to social structures is notable also in Jacques Derrida's essay "Structure, Sign, and Play in the Discourse of the Human Sciences," in Jacques Derrida, *Writing and Difference*, trans. Alan Bass. (London: Routledge (ori. Pub. 1967), 2001), p. 284
115. Strauss (1968), p. 224.
116. Op. cit., p. 229.
117. Beiser C. Frederick, *Hegel* (London: Routledge, 2005) for a good summary of the details of his philosophy and its wider influence, particularly on Marx.

118. Strauss (1968), p. 224, p. 22.
119. Claude Lévi-Strauss, *Mythologiques*, 4 vols (Chicago: University of Chicago Press (ori. Pub. 1969), 1983), I, p. 10.
120. Howells (1999), p. 43.
121. Clifford Geertz, *The Interpretation of Cultures* (Basic Books: New York (ori. Pub. 1973), 1993), p. 18, —"Nothing has done more, I think, to discredit cultural analysis than the construction of impeccable depictions of formal order in whose existence no-one can quite believe."
122. Siegfried Kracauer, *History: The Last Things Before the Last* (New York: Marcus Weiner (ori. Pub. 1969), 1995), pp. 24–5.
123. Strauss (1978), p. 65.
124. See Alan Sorkal and Jean Bircmont, *Fashionable Nonsense: Postmodern Intellectuals' Abuse of Science* (London: Picador, 1999), and Alan Sorkal, *Beyond the Hoax: Science, Philosophy and Culture* (Oxford: Oxford University Press, 2008) for criticisms of the application of concepts of relativism and postmodernism to science.
125. On its historical significance in this regard see Peter J. Bowler, *Evolution: The History of an Idea* (California: University of California Press, 2003).
126. Eagleton, p. 205.
127. Marwick, p. 14.
128. Howells (1999), p. 37.
129. Op. cit., p. 37, "The story of the *Titanic* is a modern myth *par excellence*," and p. 144, which describes the *Titanic* myth as a modern reworking of the Hellenic themes of hubris and nemesis.
130. Op. cit., p. 158.
131. Op. cit., p. 43.
132. Op. cit., p. 4. Umberto Eco asserts that "it is possible to find elements of revolution and contestation in works that apparently lend themselves to facile consumption"—i.e. works of popular culture; as quoted in Peter Bondanella, *Umberto Eco and the open text: semiotics, fiction, and popular culture* (Cambridge: Cambridge University Press, 1997), p. 99.
133. Howells (1999), p. 2, p. 11.
134. Howells (1999), pp. 158–9. Campbell similarly described two different orders of mythology: those myths that "are metaphorical of spiritual potentiality in the human being," and those "that have to do with specific societies," in Joseph Campbell, *The Power of Myth* (New York: Doubleday, 1988), p. 22.
135. Malinowski, p. 125.
136. Thucydides, *The History of the Peloponnesian War*, trans. Rex Warner (London: Penguin, 1973), 1.21.2. For more on the ancient treatment of history and historians see Moses I. Finley, "Myth, Memory and History," *History and Theory*, IV (1965), pp. 281–302.

137. Peter Novick, *That Noble Dream: The Objectivity Question and the American Historical Profession* (Cambridge: Cambridge University Press, 1988), pp. 21–31.
138. Howells (1999), p. 2.
139. Op. cit., p. 48.
140. Jean-François Leotard, *The Postmodern Condition: A report on knowledge* (Manchester: Manchester University Press (ori. Pub. 1979), 1984), pp. xxiv-xxv. See also Perry Anderson, *The Origins of Postmodernity* (London: Verso, 1998), pp. 24–27.
141. Leotard, p. xxiii.
142. Storey, p. 150.
143. Mieke Bal and Norman Bryson, "Semiotics and Art History," *The Art Bulletin*, LXXIII (1991), pp. 174–298, see also Mieke Bal and Norman Bryson (eds), *Looking in: The Art of Viewing* (Amsterdam: Routledge, 2001).
144. Richard Evans, *In Defence of History* (London: Granta Books (ori. Pub. 1997), 2001), pp. 195–6, and Ronald J. Johnston, *The Dictionary of Human Geography* (London: Wiley-Blackwell, 2000), p. 292.
145. Karl Popper, *The Poverty of Historicism* (London: Routledge (ori. Pub. 1957), 2002), p. ix.
146. Hans-Robert Jauss, "Literary History as a Challenge to Literary Theory," *New Literary History*, II (1970), pp. 7–37.
147. Eagleton, pp. 61–63.
148. Op. cit., p. 66.
149. Roland Barthes, "The Discourse of History," *Comparative Criticism*, III (1981), pp. 7–20.
150. David Lowenthal, *The Past Is a Foreign Country* (Cambridge: Cambridge University Press (ori. Pub. 1985), 1995), pp. 224–226 and p. 229.
151. Bann (1990), pp. 4–5. Also Stephen Bann, *The clothing of Clio: a study of the representation of history in nineteenth-century Britain and France* (Cambridge: Cambridge University Press, 1984).
152. Hayden White, *Metahistory: The Historical Imagination in Nineteenth-Century Europe*, (Baltimore: John Hopkins, 1973), p. xi.
153. Hayden White, "The Historical Text as Literary Artifact," in Hayden White (ed.), *Tropics of Discourse: Essays in Cultural Criticism* (John Hopkins: Baltimore, 1978), p. 82.
154. White (1973), p. xii.
155. White (1978), p. 121.
156. Hayden White, "Response to Arthur Marwick," *Journal of Contemporary History*, XXX (London: Sage, 1995), pp. 233–246.
157. White, *Metahistory*, p. xii. See also on White's ideas, Robert Doran (ed.), *The Fiction of Narrative: Essays on History, Literature, and Theory, 1957–2007* (Baltimore: The Johns Hopkins University Press, 2010).

158. White (1973), p. ix, describes history as "verbal structure in the form of narrative prose discourse."
159. Op. cit., p. x.
160. Popper, p. 47. See also John Dunn, *Rethinking Modern Political Theory: Essays 1979–83* (Cambridge: Cambridge University Press, 1985), which criticizes the perceived limitations of modern political thinking by delving into its ideological origins. Also John Dunn, *The History of Political Theory and Other Essays* (Cambridge: Cambridge University Press, 1996).
161. Mark Gilderhus, *History and historians: a historiographical introduction* (Prentice-Hall: Upper Saddle River, 2000), pp. 134–6.
162. See Edward W. Said, *Orientalism* (London: Penguin (ori. Pub. 1979), 2003), on pejorative Western representations of the "Orient," and Michael Foucault, *The Archaeology of Knowledge*, trans. Sheridan Smith (New York: Routledge, 2002), for his critique of value systems such as the "Enlightenment.".
163. John Storey, *Cultural Theory and Popular Culture: an Introduction*, (New Jersey: Prentice Hall, 2000), pp. 147–8, on the cultural reaction against "Modernism" from the 1960s.
164. See for instance, Gaurav G. Desai and Supriya Nair (eds), *Postcolonialisms: An Anthropology of Cultural Theory and Criticism* (Oxford: Rutgers University Press, 2005).
165. Cantor (1991), p. 37.
166. Marwick, p. 14.
167. White (1973), p. 13.
168. Storey, pp. 44–47.
169. Matthew Arnold, *Culture and Anarchy* (New York: Macmillan, 1882), p. 31.
170. T.S Eliot, *Notes Towards the Definition of Culture* (London: Faber and Faber, 1973), p. 31.
171. Op. cit., pp. 106–7.
172. Dominic Strinati, *An introduction to theories of popular culture* (London: Routledge, 2004), p. 7.
173. Storey, p. 15, p. 155, p. 160.
174. Adorno (1991), pp. 85–6. For a modern formulation of the concept of "false consciousness" according to a corporate-media model, see Edward Herman and Noam Chomsky, *Manufacturing Consent: The Political Economy of Mass Media* (New York: Pantheon, 1988).
175. Siegfried Kracauer, *The Mass Ornament*, trans. Thomas Y. Levin (Massachusetts: Harvard University Press (ori. Pub. 1927), 1995), p. 65. Kracauer's sense of the purpose of film, and his criticisms of the use of the medium in ways which detract from this, are closely related to his theory of the uses, methods and purpose of history. He compares large, sweep-

ing, generalized history works to "theatrical films," p. 128. See also John Berger, *Ways of Seeing* (London: Penguin, 1972), which criticized traditional "high cultural" aesthetics by exploring the latent ideologies embedded in visual imagery.
176. Lorna Hardwick and Christopher Stray (eds), *A Companion to Classical Receptions* (Oxford: Wiley-Blackwell, 2007), p. 13.
177. Op. cit., p. 1.
178. Wyke (1999), p. 1.
179. Maria Wyke, *Projecting the past: ancient Rome, cinema, and history* (New York: Routledge, 1997), p. 8, explaining the view she criticizes.
180. Bernard Knox, *Backing into the Future: The Classical Tradition and Its Renewal* (New York: W.W. Norton and Co., 1994), p. 305. This idea is also echoed in Allan Bloom, *The Closing of the American Mind* (New York: Simon & Schuster, 1987), p. 344.
181. Wyke (1999), p. 1.
182. Wyke (1997), p. 10, for the mixed reception of early mass-market cinema in Italy and America.
183. Walter Benjamin "The Work of Art in the Age of Mechanical Reproduction," in Hannah Arendt (ed.), *Illuminations*, trans. Harry Zohn (London: Pimlico (or. pub. 1968), 1999), pp. 211–224, and Tom Gunning, *D.W. Griffith and the Origins of American Narrative Film: The Early Years at Biograph* (Illinois: University of Illinois Press, 1994).
184. Quentin D. Leavis, *Fiction and the Reading Public* (London: Pimlico (ori. Pub. 1932), 2000), pp. 224–225.
185. Arthur Lindley, "The ahistoricism of medieval film," *Screening the Past*, VI (1999), published online at http://tlweb.latrobe.edu.au/humanities/screeningthepast/firstrelease/fir598/ALfr3a.htm
186. Storey, p. 15.
187. Eliot (1973), p. 92.
188. Vachel Lindsay, *The Art of the Motion Picture* (New York: Macmillan, 1919), p. 177.
189. Umberto Eco, *Faith in Fakes: Travels in Hyper-Reality*, trans. William Weaver (New York: Mariner Books (ori. Pub. 1986), 1995), p. 217.
190. See Leo Braudy and Marshall Cohen (eds), *Film Theory and Criticism* (London: Oxford University Press (ori. Pub. 1974), 2009) for an anthology of critical writings on the subject.
191. Robert A. Rosenstone, "The Historical Film as Real History," *Film-Historia*, V (1995), pp. 5–23.
192. Beard and Henderson, p. 107.
193. Martin M. Winkler, "Introduction," in Winkler (1991), p. 11.
194. Catherine Edwards (ed.), *Roman presences: receptions of Rome in European culture, 1789–1945* (Cambridge: Cambridge University Press, 1999).

The book declares its focus to be on the "strange and often unexpected places where Roman presences have manifested themselves in recent times," p. xi.
195. Jon Solomon, *The Ancient World in the Cinema* (New Haven: Yale University Press (ori. Pub. 1978), 2001). See also Elley (1984).
196. Wyke (1997), pp. 73–110.
197. Martin M. Winkler (ed.), *The Fall of the Roman Empire: Film and History* (Oxford: Wiley-Blackwell, 2009).
198. Martin M. Winker, "Fact, Fiction and the Feeling of History," in Winkler (2009), p. 175, which states that, "I will argue, as it were, the case for the defence of serious and committed fiction based on history as exemplified in the genre of epic cinema ...."
199. Howells (1994), p. 8.
200. Knox, p. 305 highlights this attitude.
201. Howells (1994), p. 10.
202. Winkler (2009).
203. Wyke (1997), p. 9
204. Kracauer (2004), p. 5.
205. See for instance Mark Shiel, *Italian Neorealism—Rebuilding the Cinematic City* (Brighton: Wallflower Press, 2005).
206. David Spring and Richard Taylor (eds), *Stalinism and Soviet Cinema* (London: Routledge, 1993).
207. Wyke (1999), p. 1.
208. Wyke (1997), p. 24.
209. Cited in Martin M. Winkler, "A Critical Appreciation of the Fall of the Roman Empire," in Winkler (2009), p. 8.
210. James Monaco, *How to Read a Film* (Oxford University Press: New York (ori. Pub. 1981), 2000), p. 211.
211. Geoffrey Richards, *Hollywood's Ancient Worlds* (Winchester: Hambledon Continuum, 2008).
212. For the demand of historical accuracy in historical cinema, an excellent summary of the arguments made is provided in Robert A. Rosenstone, "The Reel Joan of Arc: Reflections on the Theory and Practice of the Historical Film," *The Public Historian*, XXV (2003), pp. 61–77.
213. For introductions on the debates about accuracy in academia and its importance see Marnie Hughes-Warrington, *History Goes to the Movies* (London: Routledge, 2007), Pierre Sorlin, *The Film in History: Restaging the Past* (Oxford: Barnes and Noble, 1980), Robert A. Rosenstone, *Visions of the past: the challenge of film to our idea of history* (Massachusetts: Harvard University Press, 1995), William Guynn, *Writing History in Film* (New York: Routledge, 2006) and Marcia Landy, *The Historical Film: History and Memory in the Media* (London: Athlone, 2001).

214. For more on this see Howells (1994), p. 144, which describes the Titanic myth as a modern reworking of the Hellenic themes of hubris and nemesis.
215. Andrew Pulver, "Adaptation of the Week no. 44: The Name of the Rose," *The Guardian* (5th February, 2005).
216. Gideon Bachman, "*The Name of the Rose*: interview with Umberto Eco," *Sight and Sound*, LV (1986), p. 130.
217. See David Salo, "Heroism and Alienation through language in *The Lord of the Rings*," in Martha Driver and Sid Ray (eds), *The Medieval Hero on Screen: Representations from Beowulf to Buffy* (Jefferson: McFarland, 2004), pp. 23–37.
218. *Intolerance* consists of four intercut vignettes, two of these set in Antiquity, detailing the fall of Babylon and the mission and death of Christ.
219. For some good accounts of this principle see William Drew, *D. W. Griffith's Intolerance: Its Genesis and Its Vision* (Jefferson, New Jersey: McFarland & Company, 1986), and Robert M. Henderson, *D. W. Griffith: His Life and Work* (New York: Oxford University Press, 1972).
220. David Williams, "Medieval Movies," *Yearbook of English Studies*, XX (1991), pp. 1–31.
221. The word "ideology" here is not intended to carry the loaded meanings of the Frankfurt school, though the cultural context of the observation is very similar.
222. As is highly evident in Cleopatra (Paramount Pictures, 1934) and both his versions of The Ten Commandments (Paramount Pictures, 1923 and remade 1956). For more on the director's style see Robert S. Birchard, *Cecil B. DeMille's Hollywood* (Lexington: University Press of Kentucky, 2004) and Katherine Orrison, *Written in Stone: Making Cecil B. DeMille's Epic*, The Ten Commandments (New York: Vestal Press, 1990).
223. Roland Barthes, "The Romans in Films," in Roland Barthes, *Mythologies*, trans. Annette Lavers (London: Vintage Classics (ori. Pub. 1972), 2009), pp. 26–28.
224. See Andrew Higson, *Film England, Culturally English Filmmaking Since the 1990s* (New York: I.B. Tauris & Co, 2011), pp. 227–229 for the description of "historical myopia."
225. Derek Elley sees epic cinema as a whole as being necessarily set in the pre-modern past, but not all are so—for example Victor Fleming's *Gone with the Wind* (MGM, 1939). See Elley (1984), pp. 12–16.
226. Lindley (1999), p. 1.
227. Rosenstone (2000), p. 35.

CHAPTER 3

# The Fall of Rome and Ideas of Decline

### THE TRADITION OF DECLINE

In order to approach the subject of the decline and fall as a representational tool, I firstly have to consider what, historically and culturally, the term "decline", and related concepts of decadence and corruption, have signified.[1] The idea of decline contains within it a theory about the nature and meaning of time and temporal change; as does the countervailing notion of "progress", which receives vastly more discussion in academic literature on historiography and the philosophy of history. Much more has been written on the idea of progress than on notions of historical decline: the origins, forms, and significance of the myth of the decline and fall have attracted considerably less attention. This may be an indication that progress is the more distinctive conviction of "the modern mind"—or at least that academic representations of the concept have been built around this idea. Studies of the idea of progress constitute a proper, coherent field, complete with its "classic",[2] its later revisions, and schools of thought on both. Such work as there is on historical pessimism and ideas of decay or decadence remains quite fragmentary, without conventional boundaries or, usually, a common title.[3]

Yet the two ideas and traditions are two sides of the same coin. Every theory of progress contains a theory of decline—seemingly inevitable historical laws, whether secular or supernatural, can just as easily reverse as move forward; or embody the metaphor of the ever-revolving wheel. Lurking underneath a theory about decline is usually one about progress, and vice versa. As Theodor Adorno and Max Horkheimer describes it, "The curse of irresistible progress is irresistible regression."[4] Yet the academic focus is not necessarily suggestive of its wider significance or appeal. Randolph Starn put the point across thus:

> The most systematic student of "the idea of progress" has found it not only very widespread in Western thought; he has also ventured to suggest that almost all Western theories of decline turn out to be theories of contingent progress. One conclusion follows from the other.

The result of this principle, then, is the ubiquity of decline narratives:

> Neither beliefs in progress nor historical relativism seem to make much headway against commonplace talk of political, economic, or cultural "decline" and of "decadent" morals, literature, or art. Doubt has ways of springing quite as eternal as hope; and the belief in progress may actually encourage it, since criteria for measuring progress can easily be turned around to detect decline.[5]

Where this discussion finds a special purpose in this book is that the prototype of these narratives tends to be found, wholly or partly, *in the representation of the later history of Rome*. If the heights of classical civilization concealed or indeed fostered a slow inner decline, if the achievements of the ancients produced the means for their own destruction, and if decadence and decay proved inescapable and fatal, then surely, this logic goes, modern society, or the "modern" world of an author contemporary to it, could be in danger of walking down the same road. It therefore presents one of the most powerful, and creatively pliable, counters to a theory of progress—with an example of how such apparent progress can go wrong. It is worth noting the above point Starn makes about the popular appeal of such ideas, regardless of academic or intellectual trends; or, again to invoke Strauss, the "latent" and buried qualities present in representations of progress. Starn suggests that the very language of decline itself invites historical comparison:

> In a static sense the logic of "de-cline" posits disjunction from some norm. It implies comparison and contrast between higher and lower or normative and "other" points. Applied to history, this suggests or even forces comparison and contrast in time or type between republican and imperial Rome, for instance, or between Augustus and his successors.[6]

One can lead this observation into a much broader insight: that the language and idea of decline, specifically when tied to the Roman example, have comparison so deeply embedded in their meaning, origin, and continued usage that the process has become fundamental to the very idea of the fall. Virtually every social and cultural author and commentator who discusses the theme falls into a comparison with their own period, whether unconsciously or through explicit intent. In an academic and cultural context, the word *myth* is by far the most appropriate term to describe this.

Neither the belief in progress nor postmodern and relativist trends in history and culture have made much impact against the presence in high and popular culture, of political, economic, or cultural decline, and of decadent morals, literature, or art. From Hesiod and Thucydides to St Augustine and Orosius, Montesquieu and Gibbon, Bruni and Machiavelli, Spengler and Toynbee, some of the most significant historical speculation and narratives, influential far outside their original academic and intellectual field, have been phrased in terms of decline.

The word "decline" is not necessarily one that covers everything historical (and cultural) decline may imply. The "decline and fall" is by far a smaller subset of this idea. Furthermore, it is only one familiar term for many approaches in historical discourse. The concept of historical decline, like most historiographical themes, cannot be contained so easily within neat academic territories. As a term, it has a logic which lends itself to speaking about historical experience, and on a deeper level, latent value assumptions and ideologies. While it can be either secular or theological in final form—or a complex mix of the two—it typically resembles the trappings of a "theology" in its sense moral authority and teleological purpose.

This logic relates to networks of ideas, concepts and images. The language, ideas, and schemata of historical decline may be connected in turn with the situations and needs of individuals and groups using them. If the theme has several levels, then a variety of strategies should be deployed in trying to understand it—lending the concept, even when taken in a highly specific form, to the frame of interdisciplinary study.

Essential to defining the scope and field of the relevant material underlying this myth is an age-long cultural tradition around the decline and fall that connects Augustine to Gibbon to *Gladiator*. It takes a multitude of connected forms, many very localized in theme—such as the political decline of Rome, and its relevance to the contemporary world of the author, whether Machiavelli or Anthony Mann—and others that are more overtly universal in scope. Decline as an idea draws a long arc through history, and some conception of a decline and fall exists through most creationist and other stories of theological origin. Views of a cosmic decline from grace are an ancient component of theological narratives of the cosmos. They are present in the classical schema of Hesiod, in the now dead myths of Platonists, Manicheans and Persian Zoroastrians, and countless other religious traditions, the Hellenic timeline of four "ages", each worse than the last—Gold, Silver, Bronze, and then an Iron Age of universal wickedness. Both the Old and New Testaments outline a narrative of history from creation to the foreseen second coming. Godfrey Goodman's *The Fall of Man, or the Corruption of Nature Proved by the Light of our Natural Reason* (1616) describes how "nature now beginning to decay, seems to hasten Christ's coming," and provides extensive and detailed examples of this decay from ancient and more contemporary times to justify the continuing cosmic fall from grace.[7] Religion and even secular authorship so frequently harken back to a lost "golden age" that the idea has been readily imbibed in literary and cinematic production.[8]

Ancient and medieval sensibilities on decline took a number of forms. Firstly, there is the idea of *cosmic* decline: the slow decay of the universe, the old age and unwinding of the world. Such ideas are seeded throughout Judaeo-Christian theology and profoundly shaped the concept of the decline and fall of Rome; an idea with latent theological dimensions, even when taking secular form. This is both directly—as in the comparisons of Augustine, discussed below—and through precedents and archetypes. The Bible provides us with the fall from Eden,[9] Daniel's prophecy of four empires,[10] and the apocalyptic end times foretold in Revelations. Roman Catholic biblical exegesis affirms the fall of man as a primeval event, the beginning of the history of man that forever defined it.[11] This first and original sin was transmitted by Adam and Eve to their descendants, causing humans to be "subject to ignorance, suffering and the dominion of death, and inclined to sin."[12] "Although the state of corruption, inherited by humans from the primeval event of Original Sin, is clearly called "sin", it is understood as a defect inherited in the unity of all humans through the descent from Adam, rather than as the product of personal responsibility. Even children, therefore, share in the guilt and shame of Adam; but not in its responsibility, as sin is always a personal act."[13]

Morality is deeply involved in this type of religious framework, and in that vein is the tradition of flood myths—moral purges of decadence by the divine will—that originated in Mesopotamia and spread to Greece.

However, ideas of moral decline also have a secular dimension. The transition from a life of simplicity and virtue to one of luxury and decadence is frequently lamented. The corruption of the simple life, and the Roman nobility, features prominently in Tacitus.[14] The Humanist Leonardo Bruni in the fifteenth century followed Tacitus in ascribing the decline of the Roman Empire to the loss of liberty, and consequent decline of virtue and morals, following the end of the Republic: a threat he saw in danger of being repeated in his own time.[15] Gibbon, too, saw the universal value in his analysis of the corruption of Rome.[16]

The decline of Rome therefore became a paradigm for interpreting the decline of other states. In doing so, its authors could argue for a powerful re-evaluation of present institutions and their claim to authority, in any form. If Rome had declined, then the model of the Roman Empire could *not* be thought of as the sole or primary precedent on which medieval and modern foundations were to be built or justified. It thus deprived agencies which had claimed continuous authority from Rome in later ideals of political and social order—notably, but by no means exclusively, the Papacy and Holy Roman Empire—of some of their mystique.[17] This revisionist model proved just as useful for criticizing the later claims of post-Enlightenment Britain and the USA.

As an eschatological and prophetic myth, the belief in the imminence of end times is one of the oldest theological traditions, one the persistent failure of the world to end did little to diminish. Traditional notions of cosmic decline have been rewritten to accommodate new realities, often political and social. Salvian, a Christian ecclesiastical writer of the fifth century, blames the miseries befalling the Western Roman Empire in its last decades on the neglect of God's commandments and the terrible sins now endemic to every class of society. Slaves are depicted as thieves and runaways, wine-bibbers and gluttons—but the rich are even worse.[18] It is their brutality and greed that drive the poor to join the Bacaudae, and flee for shelter and safety to the barbarian invaders.[19] As he says, "Everywhere taxes are heaped upon the needy, while the rich escape comparatively free."[20] Contemporary historians do not deem this a reliable social account: Salvian is a writer concerned with telling a moral tale, where the empire has been ruined by a slew of vices, including its love of debauchery and public entertainment.[21] However, its themes and judgements are precisely those which have cropped up so often since.

The most important scheme of history here, with regard to the perceived providential fortunes of the Roman Empire, was the Six Ages of the World, described in Augustine's *De Catechizandis Rudibus* (On the Catechizing of the Uninstructed), XXII, and in more general terms in *De Civitatas Dei* (City of God). Mirroring the six days of creation, the sixth age denotes the time from the coming of Christ to the end days, making the current period also "end times" and a presage of the eschatological finish.[22]

Augustine's approach to the empire plays a fundamental role in shaping the moralistic and spiritual critique of the later Roman Empire.[23] Notably, in *City of God* he attacked the Christian eschatological myth of an eternal Roman Empire, and reduced its providential significance to that of any other human power, which on the cosmic scale were always fleeting and ephemeral. Augustine refused to accept Rome's moral qualities as having been any better than their predecessors. True virtue is impossible without true religion, as, "What kind of mistress over the body and the vices can a mind be that is ignorant of the true god, but instead is prostituted to the corrupting influences of vicious demons?"[24] And so the Romans, blind to the one god, were led astray by philosophers given over to idle speculation, and the temptation of demons.

While deeply influenced by the major Classical historians such as Tacitus and Sallust, Augustine sees the rise of Rome primarily as the result of a simple, abstract law governing the rise of every earthly state, namely a rough balance of virtue over vice that produces an expansionist mentality: thus he compares the ascendancy of Rome with the earlier successes of the aggressive Assyrians. Consequently, the continued existence of Rome was not a necessary precondition to the triumph of Christianity on earth. He condemns the citizens of the early Empire for embracing polytheism, and suggests that its later decline is due to surviving pagan elements in society (i.e. as in the fact that Rome, still a bastion of the old faith, was a sacked rather than "purged" city such as Carthage or Constantinople): Christianity has to survive independent of the continued existence of Rome, because the empire is too morally degenerate to carry the torch of the true faith forever.[25] Such an approach grants Augustine his relevance to later, Gibbonian representations of this subject. It is entirely possible to draw on the human (if not secular) and moral aspects of his judgements, separate from the strict Christian philosophy. Indeed, Augustine did not perceive the religious failings of either the pagan or Christian empire as the reason for their doom, or as necessitating divine purpose in their downfall. The mind of God, we are told, is too mysterious to be reduced to such a simple human causation.[26] When compared with other classical, pagan historians, Augustine's work strips Roman history of its mythical aura; he attempts to "secularize" our understanding of the Empire and regards it as a finite, flawed state whose function within God's plan is not absolute or eternal.[27]

While these approaches above are predominantly theological narratives, the emphasis on imperfection, decadence, and decline also functions as a universal theme—a spiritual and moral subsurface to even ostensibly secular accounts. Christian writers added excited visions of the Apocalypse to Roman moods and terms.[28] Reaching for an antiquity he intensely perceived as now lost, Petrarch reworked or ignored medieval chronologies of continuity, or Augustine's six ages of universal history. He saw a more meaningful break between the Roman Republic and the Empire as the seeds of a "decline and fall"—then between the classical world, encompassing both these, and the period of darkness extending to his own time in the fourteenth century. Petrarch could not only sense historical discontinuity; his sensibility gave him historical perspective for a new periodization of history which disconnected the condition of the present with the past.[29]

With respect to "decline", Petrarch helped foster the notion that European culture had stagnated and drifted into what he now called the "Dark Ages," since the fall of Rome in the fifth century—represented both physically by the loss of priceless classical texts, but also in the corruption of the language and culture of contemporary discourse and debate.[30] Petrarch's division was not based on theology, but purely on a perception of Roman cultural and political decline—ideas which proved critical to the evolution of this myth, and whose core characteristics remain central to it.[31] His intellectual successors formalized the insight, applying an explicit vocabulary of decline, and suite of associated concepts, to Roman history and to what they began to see as the Middle Age coming after it.[32] Such an idea could also be extended to the expanding spatial horizons of the Renaissance. When humanists set a decline between themselves and the ancients, classical or Late Antiquity could become quite as much a new and "other" world as the Americas. European imaginations persisted in transforming new-found peoples into the classical barbarians, noble savages, and virtuous or vice-ridden Romans of classical literature.[33]

The decline of Rome from its material and spiritual zenith also lends itself to the idea that such virtues, while lost in the empire's moral decay, could nevertheless be somehow revived. Rome's (often self-purported) successors and imitators took up the mission of establishing, re-establishing, or at least reimagining a universal empire or culture that would be global and harmonious. The idea is present in that central Christian image of Christ on Judgment Day, the "king of kings" into whose universal and permanent empire all previous and present ones would be dissolved. To Christians of Late Antiquity, Rome's universal empire had seemed to presage Christ's *katholikos* or "universal" Church. In the words of Prudentius, the Roman Christian poet from the fourth century, "What is the secret of Rome's historical destiny? Is it that God wills the unity of mankind? God has taught the nations to be obedient to the same laws and to all become Romans ... This is the meaning of all the victories and triumphs of the Roman Empire: the Roman peace has prepared the way for the coming of Christ."[34]

## GIBBON'S DECLINE AND FALL

The most important single source for the decline and fall myth comes from Edward Gibbon. Not only does he represent its most influential and iconic formulation, but the historian is frequently and directly invoked by intellectuals or filmmakers throughout the period relevant to this book, right up to the present day. Exactly *what* his theory of the decline and fall constitutes therefore warrants considerable attention.

Before Gibbon, the chief emphasis in much Late Antique and Medieval historiography had been on the *translatio imperii*, the "transfer of rule," or the passing on of the heart of civilization: from pagan to Christian Rome, and from *pax Romana* to Charlemagne and the Holy Roman Empire of the Middle Ages.[35] In this philosophy, Roman history and culture had changed, developed, even declined from its highs; but it did not necessarily collapse into oblivion and ruin. A variation on this idea for the Eastern Empire is found in the "Third Rome" myth: namely, that after the collapse of the Byzantine Empire, the Muscovite Tsars supposedly took over the mantle as the inheritors, not just of Orthodox Christianity, but of the entire East Roman tradition—a burden seamlessly passed on to the Russian Empire, the (formally atheist) Soviet Union and subsequently even to the Russian Federation."[36]

Gibbon, however, initiated a new phase in the moralizing, didactic interpretation of the Roman Empire and its fate. It is in his writing that the decline and fall myth emerges in its consolidated, coherent form—and one with a clearly comparative purpose. In the *Decline and Fall of the Roman Empire* he wrote a prose epic, one in which the panorama of historical experience is viewed on a universal, yet highly subjective scale. The title of his work reflects the concerns of the time: it is less a work of "history" in the narrow or descriptive sense than a broad treatise on human nature, its triumphs and failings, and highly notable for how much it is indicative of contemporary concerns, rather than the remote past it describes.[37] Gibbon took as his theme the central episode of the apocalyptic, Augustinian view of history—the fall of the Roman Empire—with the caveat that where Augustine was the pre-eminent theologian of the early Christian Church, Gibbon's vision was decidedly secular.

It is a testament to Gibbon's extraordinary historiographical influence that the term "the decline and fall of the Roman Empire" has become a standard expression since his time. As Bowersock said, "it is Gibbon … who dominates discussion of the subject today … our modern obsession with the fall of Rome not only began in the eighteenth century but also, as most of us have known it, bore the Gibbonian stamp."[38] But the concept and study of the decline and fall of Rome itself also has a long history—one that stretches back to the ancients themselves, in the writings of Sallust, Tacitus and Augustine. It has been stated by Walter Goffart that Gibbon's problem was "discovered" when an observer such as the sixth-century historian Zosimus could put Rome behind him as past history.[39] The record of fairly explicit usage of this comparison, in relation to classical decline, begins in later medieval encounters with the Roman past and present. The twelfth-century chronicler Otto of Freising, generalizing from the example of Rome, reflected on the decline of worldly empire as an immutable cycle in the metaphor of a turning wheel: "if it is at its height, soon it will need to decline."[40] Physical ruin, historical fall and universal fate were linked as early as the famous epigram by Bede: "*Quandiu stabit coliseus, stabit et Roma; quando cadit coliseus, cadet et Roma; quando cadet Roma, cadet et mundus.*"[41] This idea of the rise and fall of states and societies was an integral part of ancient theorizing about the cyclical nature of history and the fate of states—revived in Renaissance historiography by authors such as Leonardo Bruni and Flavio Biondo.[42]

Such discussions tied in with the matter of Rome's fall and speculation as to its causes. In the 1500s, Niccolo Machiavelli, who coined the term the "the five good emperors" for the reigns of Nerva, Trajan, Hadrian, Antoninus Pius and Marcus Aurelius, marked the transition to hereditary succession as the ruin of the empire, stating that, "From the study of this history we may also learn how a good government is to be established; for while all the emperors who succeeded to the throne by birth, except Titus, were bad, all were good who succeeded by adoption, as in the case of the five from Nerva to Marcus. But as soon as the empire fell once more to the heirs by birth, its ruin recommenced."[43] In the early eighteenth century, Montesquieu famously expressed it in his *Considerations on the Causes of the Greatness of the Romans and Their Decline*. Montesquieu emulates the Roman historian Sallust in emphasizing "corruption" (though he discussed economic factors in mirroring it with the decline of Spain in the seventeenth century). His is a work Gibbon knew well, and whose influence on the man is well documented.[44]

It is important to note in this context the historical periodization of the "Dark Ages," one emphasizing the cultural and economic deterioration in Europe following the supposed decline and fall of the Roman Empire. The label employs Manichean light-versus-darkness imagery to contrast the darkness of that period with both earlier and later ages of light, in respect to their culture and civilized values.[45] The term itself mainly derives from the Latin *saeculum obscurum*, applied by Caesar Baronius in 1602 to a tumultuous period from the ninth to the eleventh centuries after the fall of the Carolingian Empire.[46] It is rarely used by historians nowadays because of the value judgement it implies—though sometimes meant to suggest that little was known of the period, making it "dark" and hidden to historians, it's more common, pejorative usage is to denote a period of intellectual darkness and barbarity.[47] It also echoes a disdain for the medieval world, and—as is especially important to note—a need to both emphasize and account for the Roman decline that preceded and enabled it. Robert Bartlett describes how "Disdain about the medieval past was especially forthright amongst the critical and rationalist thinkers of the Enlightenment. For them the Middle Ages epitomized the barbaric, priest-ridden world they were attempting to transform."[48] Gibbon expressed contempt for the "rubbish of the Dark Ages."[49]

By contrast, from the late seventeenth century onwards, Enlightenment ideas had secured the belief that civilization was finally progressing beyond the achievements of the classical world.[50] This allowed for history to be seen as a teleological train of progress that began after the collapse of antiquity, continued through the Middle Ages, gathered momentum in the Renaissance and reached its pinnacle in the Enlightenment and Age of Reason. The problem, therefore, of what brought the ancient world to ruin haunted many of the philosophers and historians of the Enlightenment.[51] Imperial nations from the eighteenth and nineteenth centuries onwards were driven to social and cultural self-examination because, in their eyes, it appeared hard to blame anyone except the Romans themselves for the collapse of their great empire and civilization.

Consequently, the final fate of the Roman Empire fortified an anxiety in Gibbon and successive writers that in their civilization's greatest moments of triumph lay the seeds of its own destruction. Of the 71 chapters, 38 are devoted to the decline of the "primary" empire, up to 476 AD, and discuss different kinds of decline operating at different speeds. In his "General Observations"—which, while featuring half-way through the work, was written before the publication of the first volume[52]—he contemplates whether or not Enlightenment Europe could fall into a political and cultural nadir.[53] Earlier in the text, he suggests that, "This awful revolution [of the decline and fall of Rome] may be usefully applied to the instruction of the present age."[54] To Gibbon, the history of Rome was of universal significance and possessed a profound symbolic value. It was an event so momentous, so revealing of profound truths of human nature, that it was applicable to other societies at other times. Hence, he began his mammoth work by stating, in the opening paragraph, that the fall of Rome was "a revolution which will ever be remembered, and is still felt by the nations of the earth."[55] It is not purely or even primarily an account of the Roman Empire, but a lesson for British and European society in the failings of a past civilization; comparable at least in part in its greatness, yet still undone. The work is a series of *moral judgements* about how society should be ordered, and how it falls into *dis*order when its rules, principles and values come undone. Such judgements, we will see, rise up again and again in representation of decline and fall. This theme, and moral lesson, is what stitches together a narrative that spans 1,000 years of history and almost 2 million words; a delineation of Gibbon's personal conception of history and human nature, in respect to the historical processes that both engender and result from Rome's decline and fall.[56]

The combination of the monumental size and reputation of his work, coupled with its provocative and judgemental tone, is precisely what has made it such an ideal text and reference point for later authors and commentators.[57] It purports to be "history" in the strict, technical, academic sense, and bears the weight of such a reputation—but at the same time, bears all the hallmarks of a moral and ideological myth or story, in the terms I have defined. This contrast between its appearance, image, and reality make it a powerful source for comparing the fall of Rome to the perceived iniquities and failings of the present. Gibbon is a philosophical historian in the semi-heretical tradition that can be traced back to

Giannone and Machiavelli. His work is full of contemplative judgements of human affairs that show the author as a man of the Age of Reason; he is a polished and derisive sceptic who uses his skill with humour and wit to subtly convey highly controversial notions and opinions, particularly concerning Christianity: both as an ideology and in its historical role in the fall of Rome. In this sense he carries on the offensive against Christianity begun by Voltaire and the Parisian tradition, by fashioning a conception of history built around his own humanist, empiricist, and moral ideals.[58]

In the first 15 chapters of the *Decline and Fall*, Gibbon is preoccupied with setting the scene for what he sees as the irreversible stages of the late fourth and fifth centuries by outlining the political, cultural and geographic reality of the classical empire and the discord of the third century. From this emerges the administrative reorganization of Diocletian and, most important to Gibbon, Constantine and the adoption of Christianity as the official religion of the empire. Throughout this part of the book the author has a clear overall scheme, purpose and objective; he is not writing blind, but fashioning a grand narrative in which clear reasons are delineated for—and lessons learnt from—the decline of the empire that preceded its fall. The five Antonine dynasty emperors who ruled from AD 96–180—Nerva, Trajan, Hadrian, Antoninus Pius, Marcus Aurelius—he identified for the starting point of his account, arguing, "It is the design of this, and of the two succeeding chapters, to describe the prosperous condition of their empire; and afterwards, from the death of Marcus Antoninus [i.e. Marcus Aurelius], to deduce the most important circumstances of its decline and fall ...."[59]

This long period of grace is described as the highest state, not merely of the population of the empire, but of mankind as a whole, for, "If a man were called to fix the period in the history of the world, during which the condition of the human race was most happy and prosperous, he would, without hesitation, name that which elapsed from the death of Domitian to the accession of Commodus."[60] He goes on to outline in idealized terms:

> The vast extent of the Roman empire was governed by absolute power, under the guidance of virtue and wisdom. The armies were restrained by the firm but gentle hand of four successive emperors, whose characters and authority commanded involuntary respect. The forms of the civil administration were carefully preserved by Nerva, Trajan, Hadrian, and the Antonines, who delighted in the image of liberty, and were pleased with considering

themselves as the accountable ministers of the laws. Such princes deserved the honor of restoring the republic, had the Romans of their days been capable of enjoying a rational freedom.

The peak state of classical civilization, however, also proved to be the catalyst of its undoing. The summit of prosperity attained by the Antonines is considered to contain within it the seeds of its own decay; the very peace and prosperity that the system had created bred a corruption and complacency that sapped the strength of the empire. Thus:

> The long peace, and the uniform government of the Romans, introduced a slow and secret poison into the vitals of the empire. The minds of men were gradually reduced to the same level, the fire of genius was extinguished, and even the military spirit evaporated. The natives of Europe were brave and robust ... their personal valour remained, but they no longer possessed the public courage which is nourished by the love of independence, the sense of national honour, the presence of danger and the habit of command.[61]

The eventual consequence of this is discussed much later in Chapter 38, in his "General Observations of the Fall of the Roman Empire in the West." He says:

> The decline of Rome was the natural and inevitable effect of immoderate greatness. Prosperity ripened the principle of decay; the cause of the destruction multiplied with the extent of conquest; and, as soon as time or accident and removed the artificial supports, the stupendous fabric yielded to the pressure of its own weight. The story of the ruin is simple and obvious: and instead of inquiring why the Roman Empire was destroyed we should rather be surprised that it has subsisted for so long.[62]

For Gibbon the paradox was political; the decline of Rome the natural result of this "immoderate greatness." This criticism is worth emphasizing because it is so often a fundamental feature of representations of later empires and powers that seek to question or undermine their place in the world—with reference to the Roman example. The idea of a simple life or virtue, corrupted by luxury, features prominently in Sallust and Tacitus, is expounded on by Ammianus, and enshrined with Judaeo-Christian theology by Augustine.[63] Gibbon, as did Machiavelli before him, saw the transition from a politically moderate Republic to the era of Imperial tyranny as fatally corrupting Rome's spirit—the ease and luxury of the age of the Antonines "introduced a slow and secret poison into the vitals of the empire."[64] Such a view is not uncommon amongst other writers of the Enlightenment. Adam Smith referred to the danger to the civilized world coming from "the natural superiority" in military terms of the barbarian militias over those of a civilized nation.[65] Rousseau reversed the poles of civilization and barbarism, his praise for primitive man reiterated in his strictures of how civil society weakened mankind. Those innovations his predecessors had praised he frequently subjected to a harsh, critical analysis; the hallmarks of progress were not driving mankind forward, but enfeebling it, and his discourses specifically mention "the dissolution of morals" and "the corruption of taste."[66]

Such is the process of decline that produces the eventual "fall". Its decay, in this account, resembles those (earlier, and later) ideas of the inevitable cycle of civilization, and the internal pressures that cause it to expand and, later, contract. Gibbon sympathized with the Roman's own moral analysis of the causes of decline: namely luxury, decadence and the corruption of behaviour and manners.[67] This produced both a degenerate and self-indulgent populace and a corrupt political class greedy only for power in the moment: thereby rendering the empire so vulnerable to outside invasion.[68]

At the same time, however, Gibbon attributed more novel and specific forces to the process of internal corruption, and deals in particular with the corrosion of the empire's moral and intellectual spirit by the influx of new belief systems. It is here that his idealization of the cultural merits of a lost classical age comes out in force, intertwined with an emerging pejorative image of the more "medieval" characteristics of Late Roman civilization. In particular—and unsurprisingly, considering his humanist, atheistic, and Enlightenment values—Gibbon attacked the cultural and intellectual traditions of Christianity and Neo-Platonism as "dire superstitions" that ruined the Hellenic tradition of reason and rationality. Neo-Platonism comes under criticism for its wholly abstract character, devoid from logic or empirical reason. Gibbon writes:

> The decline of learning and of mankind is marked ... by the rise and rapid progress of the new Platonists ... Ammonius, Plotinus, Amelius, and Porphyry ... by mistaking the true object of philosophy ... contributed much less to improve than to corrupt the human understanding. The knowledge that is suited to our situation and powers, the whole compass of moral, natural and mathematical science, was neglected by the new Platonists.[69]

Having argued that Platonic rationalism neglected the only meaningful aspects of (natural) philosophy, Gibbon proceeds to mock the achievements, and delusions, of the Neo-Platonists, in their slide into superstition and mysticism,

> Consuming their reason in deep and insubstantial meditations, their minds were exposed to illusions of fancy ... The ancient sages had derided the popular superstition; after disguising its extravagance by the thin pretence of allegory, the disciples of Plotinus and Porphyry became its most zealous defenders ... The new Platonists would scarcely deserve a place in the history of science, but in that of the church the mention of them will very frequently occur ... by a very singular revolution, [they] converted the study of philosophy into that of magic.[70]

As a consequence of this intellectual trend in the empire, Gibbon argues that Christianity—to him, a primitive superstition that replaced the spirit of the secular intellectual inquiry of the ancients—made the populace less interested in the spoiling condition of the human world, because it was happier to wait for the rewards of heaven.[71] He remarks in the opening sentence of his notoriously anti-Christian 15th chapter of the *Decline and Fall* that, "A candid but rational inquiry into the progress and establishment of Christianity may be considered as a very essential part of the history of the Roman Empire."[72] Gibbon argues that the ideology of Christianity and the organization of the Church stifled public spirit and freedom, and thus the advancement of knowledge in a pluralistic society. He sees it as inheriting the "inflexible perseverance" and "zeal" of the Jewish world, but then disastrously imposed, not on a small ethnic group, but the empire as a whole; thus it was "armed with the strength of Mosaic law, but delivered from the weight of its fetters."[73] Institutional Christianity therefore poisoned and polluted society. It was responsible for the outrages of religious intolerance and warfare, and the violent destruction of so much of the culture of the ancient world.[74]

Such an approach was repeated in the fortunes of the Eastern Empire after 476 AD, an entity perceived as medieval, repressive, and religious in its character. As he writes:

> From the time of Heraclius, the Byzantine theatre is contracted and darkened ... the subjects of the Byzantine Empire, who assume and dishonour the names of both Greeks and Romans, present a dead uniformity of abject

vices, which are neither softened by the weakness of humanity, nor animated by the vigour of memorable crimes.[75]

Gibbon further emphasizes this stifling of freedom and its effects by creating a comparison with Homer, "The freemen of antiquity might repeat, with generous enthusiasm, the sentence of Homer, 'that, on the first day of his servitude, the captive is deprived of half his manly virtue.'"[76] Such statements display the arc of his thesis for the decline and fall of the classical world—not just that of the Roman Empire, but civilization as a whole—into the stagnation of the Middle Ages, until the revival of the Renaissance and the triumphs of the Enlightenment. Indeed, he closes his vast account of the history of the Eastern and Western Empires, up to the fifteenth century, with the words, "I have described the triumph of barbarism and religion ... the ruin of Ancient Rome."[77]

Such is the story of the decline and fall, in the version that crystallized in popular and intellectual consciousness. The true value of this tale—and hence its role and purpose as a myth—comes not purely from the historical and ideological narrative, but its applicability to the wider, and often (if even implicitly) contemporary horizons of the author. Gibbon's tireless emphasis on this dramatic *fall* from grace, a major reason for the unified tone of the *Decline and Fall*, is reinforced by his use of contrasts and comparisons through time.[78] It is used to describe the Roman Empire, the city itself, the successor "Byzantium", and the Islamic Caliphate. He uses the dramatic potential of these far-flung associations to create striking comparisons; comparing, for instance, Alaric's sack of Rome with the careers of Hannibal and Charles V.[79] Many of his most powerful contrasts juxtapose the Roman Republic with the empire to emphasize decline. As the narrative progresses, the mighty early empire, especially under Augustus' rule, serves as a contrast to the ruin and decay of later centuries: "A territorial acquisition, which Augustus might have despised, reflected some lustre on the declining empire of the younger Theodosius."[80] Such juxtapositions render a sense of the living past—the echoes in the present of a better time, tragically and irretrievably lost.[81]

A particular and notable instance of this can be highlighted for my purposes. Rome and the USA have served as powerful comparisons for contemporary writers, and this extends as far back as Gibbon. What is very clear in the *Decline and Fall* is the impact that the American Revolution left on his prose. One can see the presence of the "American issue" in his extant collection of letters. In almost half of his published letters from 1775–83, Gibbon mentions the American conflict. In the prose of his second and third volumes, written after these letters, and focusing explicitly on the narrative of the demise of the Western Roman Empire, civil disturbances and taxation problems play a much greater and more central role in accounting for its downfall. For example, the language and imagery used in his account of the fifth-century revolt of Armorica, modern Brittany, can be seen as a parallel with America: "The Armorican provinces ... were thrown into a state of disorderly independence ... and the Imperial ministers pursued with proscriptive laws and ineffectual arms the rebels whom they had made." Gibbon ties the disturbance with the Armoricans' refusal to send customary tribute, and later refers to "the slight foundations of the Armorican republic."[82]

For many scholars, the comparative iconography conjured up by Gibbon can typically be written off as his irony, the artful rhetoric of his prose.[83] Pocock in particular downplayed the significance of the American Revolution on his thought.[84] Whether the loss of the American colonies was a catalyst for Gibbon's historical approach is subject to debate, but also irrelevant to this study; the very *fact* that Gibbon makes explicit reference to America—whether in the context of irony or serious analogy—is, in itself, a clear indication that his perception of the present day infiltrated his own writing. This is noted by Christopher Highet in *The Classical Tradition*, who refers to the *Decline and Fall* as a symbol of the "interpenetration" of the Roman and modern world.[85] Similarly, Glen Bowersock, otherwise critical of the book's surviving relevance or importance, nevertheless argues that its stated purpose was to "connect the ancient and modern history of the world", a task which Gibbon "ultimately achieved," meaning that: "The very idea of connecting the ancient and modern history of the world under the heading of the decline and fall of the Roman Empire is something that should give us pause."[86] Visions of an empire doomed to destruction by its own success had a powerful and profound impact on the modern historical and cultural imagination: suggesting that all great empires and civilizations reach an end point of no return. The "course of empire" embodied a cycle of growth, decay, and destruction. History seen like this is not static, but forever in motion; stagnation invites not a final state of being, but the threat of terminal decline. Gibbon intimated this notion when he stated in an epigram musing on the fortunes of the empire: "that all that is human must retrograde if it does not advance."[87]

## Gibbon and Concepts of Decadence

Political and cultural decline of the sort discussed by Gibbon could also be interpreted as *decadence*, and from the sixteenth century and especially the eighteenth, this usage appears to have been fortified and widely accepted; with the original prototype of the Roman Empire very firmly in mind.[88] "Decadence", literally meaning "falling away," became often inseparable from the notion of decline—an idea had been used by the Romans to describe the loss of an early norm or standard of excellence, and was later interwoven with the image of the fall of the Roman Empire. Decadence in the post-Enlightenment lexicon brimmed over with ideas, principles and metaphors which the ancients had previously used against themselves.[89] In particular it implies a decline in moral standards, of ethics or other qualities of character.

For eighteenth-century and nineteenth-century critics the idea of decline was, in the Roman tradition, an attack on any lapse from the perceived proper classical norms—to which the Renaissance had aspired—but it also introduced the critic into the present as the bearer and arbiter of balance and order, and the mediator of these "proper" classical ideals in a corrupted present. Such an idea reflects the role of this myth as a bridge between antiquity and the contemporary human horizons of the author.

Like the older term "decline" (and together with it), "decadence" in the eighteenth-century and nineteenth-century lexicons refashioned, in more modern cultural language, images the ancients had previously turned against themselves.[90] The new version of decline, arrived at in this period, allowed for an attack on any lapse from proper classical norms. It accorded authority to the author as watchman of cultural, moral, and intellectual standards. A powerful example of this is elaborated by Carl Jacob Burckhardt, the Swiss art and culture historian of the nineteenth century, described as one of the first figures of his age to rise beyond the idea of history narrowly defined as "past politics." Burckhardt therefore acted as a pioneer for an idea which featured widely in critical discourses on social and political decline in the twentieth century: particularly those that use the Roman model of decline *and* fall. His similarity to Gibbon is borne out both by his use of cultural themes to argue for universal trends and patterns, and by the significance of the concept of Roman decline to his thesis. This is despite not sharing quite the same positive attitude to progress itself, or the pejorative outlook on the Middle Ages.

Burckhardt argued that the vitality of a people or a race did not determine the health of a society, but the other way around: a challenge to the social fabric could lead to the enervation and exhaustion of a people. What matters is the state of the larger social order; on whether it is still growing and developing, or on whether it had achieved overripeness, and featured the "inward degeneration and decrease of life" that marks the end of the old and the beginning of the new. Though most famous for his account of the high cultural achievements of the Renaissance,[91] Burckhardt described his preference not for the radical cultural and social changes of that period, but the organic unity and community of the Middle Ages.[92]

All societies and civilizations, Burckhardt argued, are a dynamic balance of three social elements or powers. The two traditional elements were religion and the state with the third being culture: "that process by which the spontaneous and unthinking activity of a race or nation is transformed into considered action."[93] Each element follows a course of "growth, bloom, and decay," or a rise and fall of social groups and forces over the passage of time.[94] Consequently, "During epochs of high civilization, all three powers exist simultaneously at all levels of mutual interaction."[95] However, when they collide or conflict with each other, "a crisis in the whole state of things is produced," which affects entire societies and civilizations as a whole.[96] Burckhardt's history does not present us with a smooth path for the progress of human forces and movements, but instead with a recurring tension between its three elements that flares up in periodic, destructive crises.

The fall of the Roman Empire was one such crisis. Burckhardt's first extended historical work, *The Age of Constantine the Great* (1852), described the flaw in the Roman imperial state being that it had expanded at the expense of other social institutions, to the point that *civilization itself* broke apart. While the form his cycle takes, and his emphasis on culture as the driving force in history, are somewhat particular and specific to his approach, Burckhardt falls in line with the stereotypical notion that the barbarian invasions did not "cause" the fall of the Roman Empire; they simply exacerbated a crisis that was already under way in Roman society itself. Such a decline is evidenced mainly in the cultural and artistic subtleties apparently obvious to Burckhardt—"the decline of plastic art and painting," the "decline of beautiful form in architecture,"[97] which "contributed no less to the final dissolution of the structural system inherited from the Greeks," and even, in a chapter entitled "Physical Degeneration," the decline in the physical beauty of man, as witnessed in "the average as presented in classical art"[98]—evidence, he assumes, of a general decline in the standard of living, the "neglect of agriculture" and the "ravages of disease."[99]

The result of this process is the destruction of the empire itself, and its replacement with a vital new cultural and social force. As Burckhardt puts it, the "youthful peoples across the Rhine"[100]—literalizing by this contrast the metaphor of a dying, aged empire—broke through a weakening and vulnerable imperial defence, prompting a series of ruthless military emperors to seize power and accelerating the spiral into decline. It was these emperors and their legions, not the German tribes, who destroyed the ancient world's civilization as its rulers tried to prop up their own tyrannical dominion. As a result, another power—religion, or the institutional Christian religion founded by Constantine—rose up to replace the state, and the new Church dominated European affairs and civilization: until it, too, became unbalanced and eroded from within, resulting in a new historical force to topple its previously unchallenged might—the Reformation.[101]

Such, then, is the perceived cycle between the primacy of the Roman Empire and the supremacy of the Christian Church. Where this becomes pertinent to this book is in the *purpose* of this account of Rome's fall; namely as an expression of a universal, revolving trend found in civilization and cultures. Burchkardt believed that in his own time, European civilization was undergoing another similar crisis—a cultural crisis in origin, brought about by the movements and ideals, notably radicalism, democracy and socialism, unleashed in the nineteenth century, particularly in the revolts of 1848. Men hoped "to find salvation in demolishing and rebuilding the whole (social) structure" in the name of progress and reform, an impulse for them to escape their own natural station, and resulting in them imposing their own mediocrity on society as a whole.[102] Such a selfish desire for pay and privileges beyond those appropriate would lead to chaos, and out of the vacuum, to tyranny and absolutism.[103]

Burckhardt's conclusion that democracy inevitably gives way to dictatorship is as old as Plato and Aristotle, and common with political theorists such as Machiavelli. Where he gains particular relevance to this book, in his account and analogy of the fall of Rome, is his role in imagining the triumph of a debased and growing mass culture coming to dominate society; one which disrupts the organic balance of institutions, values and ideals.[104] Burckhardt described a border between the Classical and Medieval so he could then project it onto the transition between the medieval and the

Renaissance. He anchors those epochal boundaries in the ruin of Rome, as an emblem for an eternal historiography of violent ruptures with the past.

This response to the question of the decline and fall was far more active and explicit than that of Dano-German scholar Theodor Mommsen: Burckhardt's contemporary, and arguably the most prominent classical historian of the nineteenth century. Mommsen published three iconic volumes of *Roman History* covering the rise and fall of the republic. However, he never wrote a history of the empire—and strongly implied that the reason why he did not continue his *Study of History* through the imperial period was that he was never able to make up his mind what it was that brought about the collapse of the Roman Empire and the downfall of Roman civilization. Highet puts it that to describe history after the Republic, "Mommsen would have had to show that the Roman Empire was happier, more virtuous, and more powerful than the Roman republic. And this he could not do." Any comprehensive history of the Roman Empire must face the problem of its eventual collapse. Mommsen could not face this problem because he shrank from applying it to the German empire, then just approaching its birth, the conclusions to which his answer must lead. He did, however, suggest that the decline of Rome saw a transfer of strength to the provinces, and eventual Germanic inheritors of Rome, with this statement about the capital in his *Introduction* to *The Province of the Roman Empire*: "The Roman state of this epoch resembles a mighty tree, the main stem of which, in the course of its decay, is surrounded by vigorous offshoots pushing their way upward."[105]

## Notes

1. On this see Ernest Tuveson, *Millennium and Utopia: A Study in the Background of the Idea of Progress* (Berkeley: University of California Press (ori. Pub. 1949), 1972), Quentin Skinner, "Meaning and Understanding in the History of Ideas," *History and Theory*, VIII (1969), pp. 5–53, and Robert A. Nisbet, *Social Change and History: Aspects of the Western Theory of Development* (Oxford: Oxford University Press, 1970).
2. John B. Bury, The *Idea of Progress: An Inquiry into its Origin and Growth* (USA: Project Gutenberg (ori. Pub. 1920), 2000).
3. For one of the few—focusing primarily on language—see Randolph Starn, "Meaning-levels in the theme of historical decline," *History and Theory*, XIV (1975), pp. 1–31, especially pp. 1–2, which highlights this point in detail. Some of the classic works that do deal with this theme include Cyril E. M. Joad, *Decadence: A Philosophical Inquiry* (London:

Harthorpe, 1948), Henry Winthrop, "Variety of Meaning in the Concept of Decadence," *Philosophy and Phenomenological Research*, XXXI (1971), pp. 510–526, and Peter Burke, "Tradition and Experience: Ideas of Decline from Bruni to Gibbon," *Daedalus: Edward Gibbon and the Decline and Fall of the Roman Empire*, CV (1976), pp. 137–152. More recently there is Hermann, *The Idea of Decline in Western History* (London: Simon & Schuster, 1997), a book with a popular rather than a purely academic focus, which provides an overview of authors who dealt with decline since the Renaissance.
4. Max Horkheimer, "The Concept of Enlightenment," in Theodor Adorno and Max Horkheimer, *Dialectic of Enlightenment: Philosophical Fragments*, trans. Edmund Jephcott (Stanford: Stanford University Press (ori. Pub. 1944), 2002), pp. 1–34.
5. Starn, p. 1.
6. Op. cit., p. 8.
7. Ronald W. Hepburn, "George Hakewill: The Virility of Nature," *Journal of the History of Ideas*, XVI (1955), pp. 135–50, quote on p. 136.
8. Mann's *The Fall of the Roman Empire* (1964) draws on Gibbon in this way, as discussed in Chapter 4.
9. Genesis 3:14–24.
10. Daniel 2:31–40, 38–44. The prophecy Jerome perceived as completed in his own time: see Gleason Leonard Archer (trans.), *St. Jerome, Commentary on Daniel* (Oregon: Wipf & Stock Publishers, 2009). pp. 15–157.
11. Highet (1949), pp. 783–4 refers to those Humanist and Enlightenment authors who discussed decline on a cosmic scale, such as Godfrey Goodman, and sixteenth-century French Humanist Louis Leroy, who "discussed what he called the vicissitudes of empires, languages, and other human creations."
12. Elizabeth A. Livingstone, "Original sin," *The Oxford dictionary of the Christian Church* (Oxford: Oxford University Press, 2005), pp. 1202–1204. See also Catholic Church, *Catechism of the Catholic Church: with modifications from the Edition Typica* (New York: Doubleday, 2003), p. 390.
13. Op. cit., pp. 404–5. Eastern Orthodoxy, by contrast, rejects the idea that the guilt of original sin is passed down through generations.
14. In the *Agricola*, 2.1, 3.1, Tacitus contrasts the liberty of the native Britons with the tyranny and corruption of the empire, and rails against the greed of Rome.
15. Hugh Baron, *The Crisis of the Early Italian Renaissance* (Princeton: New York, 1966), p. 461.

16. Gibbon (1993), I, p. 3. See also John Robertson, "Gibbon's Roman Empire as a Universal Monarchy: The *Decline and Fall* and the Imperial Idea in Early Modern Europe," in Rosamond McKitterick and Roland Quinault (eds), *Edward Gibbon and Empire* (Cambridge: Cambridge University Press, 1997), pp. 247–270.
17. Starn, p. 1.
18. Salvian of Marseilles, *De Gubernatione Dei*, trans. E.M. Sanford (New York: Columbia University Press (ori. Pub. 1930), 1966), IV. 3.
19. Op. cit., V. 5–6. On the Bacaudae see also John F. Drinkwater, "Peasants and Bacaudae in Roman Gaul," *Classical Views*, III (1984), pp. 349–371.
20. Op. cit., V. 7.
21. Op. cit., V. 5–7.
22. The theory is found in Jewish tradition, but has an important precedent in Peter. The theory originated from a passage in II Peter 3:8: "But of this one thing be not ignorant, my beloved, that one day with the Lord is as a thousand years, and a thousand years as one day." The criticism of a Platonic and cyclical view of world history is found in City of God, XII. 14, and XII. 18 defends this linear conception of history within the context of a divine purpose.
23. For the definitive biography of Augustine see Peter Brown, *Augustine of Hippo* (University of California Press: California (ori. Pub. 1967), 2000). See also Henry Chadwick, *Augustine of Hippo: A Life* (Oxford: Oxford University Press (ori. Pub. 1986), 2010), and James J. O'Donnell, *Augustine: A New Biography* (New York: ECCO, 2005).
24. City of God, XXV. 1.
25. Op. cit., XIX. 6.
26. Op. cit., X. 8, X. 17.
27. Op. cit, XIX. 6. Augustine refuses to regard Roman history as privileged and sees its rise primarily as the result of a simple, abstract law governing the rise of every earthly state, namely a rough balance of virtue over vice that produces an expansionist mentality; thus he compares the ascendancy of Rome with the earlier successes of the aggressive Assyrians. For more detail on this see Brown (2000), Chaps. 23–27, 29.
28. Paul J. Alexander, "Medieval Apocalypses as Historical Sources," *American Historical Review*, LXXIII (1967), pp. 997–1019. See also twentieth-century historian Ernest Tuveson, who argued that the modern idea of progress sprung from Christian doctrines of the millennium and the return of Christ's kingdom; and therefore that progress, even in the form of atheistic Marxism, is a secularized version of the Apocalypse. See Ernest L. Tuveson, *Millenium and Utopia: A Study in the Background of the Idea of Progress* (Berkeley: University of California Press (ori. Pub. 1949), 1972), pp. 1–22.

29. Theodore Mommsen, "Petrarch's Conception of the 'Dark Ages'," *Speculum* (1942), XVII, pp. 226–42. See also Charles G. Nauert, *Humanism and the Culture of Renaissance Europe: Second Edition* (Cambridge: Cambridge University Press, 2006). On Petrarch's humanist approach to the "decline and fall" see Morris Bishop "Petrarch", in John Plumb (ed.), *The Italian Renaissance* (New York: American Heritage, 1961), pp. 161–175.
30. Mommsen, pp. 226–42.
31. Op. cit., pp. 236–7.
32. More generally, Leonard Bruni and Flavio Biundo developed a three tier outline of history composed of Ancient, Medieval and Modern. The Latin term *media tempestas* (middle time) first appears in the late fifteenth century, with the term *medium aevum* (Middle Ages) first recorded in 1604. "Medieval", an anglicized form of *medium aevum*, first appears in the nineteenth century. See Martin Albrow, *The global age: state and society beyond modernity* (Cambridge: Stanford University Press, 1997), p. 205.
33. For background context see Roberto Weiss, *The Renaissance Discovery of Classical Antiquity* (Oxford: Blackwell, 1969).
34. Prudentius, *Contra Symmachum*, II, pp. 634–6, as quoted in Christopher Dawson, "Edward Gibbon and the Fall of Rome," in Christopher Dawson, *The Dynamics of World History*, ed. John J. Mulloy (New York: Sheed and Ward, 1956), p. 332.
35. From the historian Orosius in the fifth century to Bishop George Berkeley in the eighteenth, it was often suggested that the empire had a tendency to move westward, from Persia and Mesopotamia to Greece, Rome, and finally Britain and America. The idea is particularly prominent in George Berkeley, *A Miscellany, Containing Several Tracts on Various Subjects, by the Bishop of Cloyne* (London: J. and R. Tonson, 1752), pp. 186–7, as quoted in Antonello Gerbi, *The Dispute of the New World* (Pittsburgh: University of Pittsburgh Press (ori. Pub. 1955), 2010), p. 137.
36. A cause aided by a blood claim—Ivan III having married Sophie Paleologue, a niece of Constantine XI, the last Byzantine emperor. For more on these claims see Ken Parry and David Melling (eds) (1999). *The Blackwell Dictionary of Eastern Christianity*. Malden, MA: Blackwell Publishing. p. 490. In his speeches, Mussolini imagined his Fascist Italy as a "Third Rome", or a new "Roman Empire", for which see Martin Clark, *Mussolini: Profiles in Power* (London: Pearson Longman, 2005), p. 136.
37. Hugh Trevor-Roper writes at length on its relevance to contemporary concerns in his introduction to a recent edition of Gibbon's work, see Gibbon (1993), pp. liii–xcvii.

38. Bowersock (1996), p. 30 and pp. 36–37.
39. Walter Goffart, "Zosimus, the First Historian of Rome's Fall," *American Historical Review*, LXXVI (1971), pp. 412–442.
40. In the Latin, "Si in summo fuerit, mox eum declinare oportebit," *Gesta Federici Imperatis* in Lombardia, I.4, cited by Walther Rehm, *Der Untergang Roms im abendländischen Denken* (Darmstadt: Buchgesellschaft (ori. Pub. 1930), 1966), p. 20, meaning "if it has reached the summit, soon after its decline will be necessary."
41. "As long as the Colossus stands, so shall Rome; when the Colossus falls, Rome shall fall; when Rome falls, so falls the world," Howard V. Cantor, "Venerable Bede and the Colosseum," *Transactions and Proceedings of the American Philological Association*, LXI (1930), pp. 150–164.
42. See in particular Romilly, p. 199.
43. Niccolo Machiavelli, *Discourses on the First Decade of Titus Livy*, trans. Thomas N. Hill (Gutenberg Project: Public Domain, 2000).
44. Montesquieu, *Considerations on the Causes of the Greatness of the Romans and Their Decline*, trans. David Lowenthal (Indianapolis: Hackett (ori. Pub. 1734), 1999). See also Robert Shackleton, "The Impact of French Literature on Gibbon," in Glenn W. Bowersock, John Clive, and Stephen R. Graubard (eds), *Edward Gibbon and the Decline and Fall of the Roman Empire* (Cambridge: Harvard University Press, 1977), pp. 207–218. Charles N. Cochrane, "The Mind of Edward Gibbon," *University of Toronto Quarterly*, XII (1943), pp. 1–17, especially page 9, describes Montesquieu as an anticipation and forerunner of Gibbon, almost a "précis" of his more elaborately developed ideas.
45. See in particular Mommsen (1942), pp. 226–242. It is worth noting that Mommsen, one of the most prominent classical historians of the nineteenth century—and though he published three volumes of Roman history covering the rise and fall of the republic—never wrote a history of the empire as a whole, stating that he was unable to explain the collapse of the empire and the downfall of Roman civilization, as cited in Highet, pp. 474–5. This, however, is the uncommon and contrarian approach to the decline and fall.
46. John C. Dwyer, *Church history: twenty centuries of Catholic Christianity* (New Jersey: Paulist Press, 1998), p. 155.
47. See also Graeme Dumphy, "Literary Transitions, 1300–1500: From Late Mediaeval to Early Modern," *The Camden House History of German Literature*, IV (2007), p. 43, which describes how, "A popular if uninformed manner of speaking refers to the medieval period as the dark ages."

48. Robert Bartlett, "Introduction: Perspectives on the Medieval World," in Robert Bartlett (ed.), *Medieval Panorama* (London: Oxford University Press, 2001), p. 12.
49. Gibbon (1993), VI, p. 9.
50. Op. cit., VI, p. 664.
51. Jeremy Bentham, who wrote voluminous critiques of the French, British, and Spanish empires, described the "denial of justice, oppression, and despotism" in their colonies as signs of the failings of empire and portents of their own internal doom. See Jeremy Bentham, *Colonies, Commerce, and Constitutional Law* (Oxford: Clarendon Press (ori. Pub. 1820–22), 1995), p. 225. By contrast, John Stuart Mill thought imperialism served a *qualified* purpose, to educate "barbarians" as long as it "provided the end by their improvement", for which see John S. Mill, *On Liberty and other Writings* (Cambridge: Cambridge University Press, 1989), p. 13.
52. Edward Gibbon, *Memoirs of My Life and Writings* (London, Penguin Classics (ori. Pub. 1792–3), 1984), p. 129.
53. Gibbon (1993), IV, pp. 117–127.
54. Op. cit., I, p. 121. See also Dawson, p. 335 and p. 337.
55. Op. cit., I, p. 3. See also John Robertson, "Gibbon's Roman Empire as a Universal Monarchy: The *Decline and Fall* and the Imperial Idea in Early Modern Europe," in Rosamond McKitterick and Roland Quinault (eds), *Edward Gibbon and Empire* (Cambridge: Cambridge University Press, 1997), pp. 247–270.
56. Equally vast is the weight of scholarship that has grown up around the work. Interpretations of his work have been made from a range of angles, from sociological models to literary analysis and Freudian-themed elucidations of its psychoanalytical meaning. William Buck, for instance, even goes so far as to dub Rome a metaphor for Gibbon's own unresolved Oedipal conflicts—a "subliminal sexual drama;" William R. Buck Jr., "Reading Autobiography," Genre, XIII (1980), pp. 477–98, quote on p. 485.
57. In a letter to Gibbon in 1788, William Robertson expressed this reaction to Gibbon's scope: "Indeed, when I consider the extent of your undertaking, and the immense labour of historical and philosophic research requisite towards executing every part of it, I am astonished that all this should have been accomplished by one man. I know no example, in any age or nation, of such a vast body of valuable and elegant information communicated by any individual." For this see John Lord Sheffield (ed.), *The Miscellaneous Works of Edward Gibbon* (New York (ori. Pub. 1814), 1971), p. 424.

58. For more on how this intellectual backdrop informed Gibbon's writing see Harold L. Bond, *The Literary Art of Edward Gibbon* (London: Greenwood Press (ori. Pub. 1959), 1976).
59. Gibbon (1993), I, p. 3.
60. Op. cit., I, p. 43.
61. Op. cit., I, pp. 65–66.
62. Op. cit., IV, p. 119. See also VI, p. 620.
63. See Glenn W. Most, *Hesiod: Theogony, Works and Days, Testimonia*, Loeb Classical Library, LVII (Harvard: Harvard University Press, 2006), and Bartlett (2006), pp. 177–205. See also Barry J. Gordon, *Economic analysis before Adam Smith: Hesiod to Lessius* (New York: Barnes and Noble, 1975), and Romilly, p. 199, for the links between this and early political and economic thought.
64. Gibbon (1993), I, p. 65.
65. Adam Smith, *The Wealth of Nations*, V, (London: Penguin Classics (ori. Pub. 1776), 1992), p. 68.
66. Jean-Jacques Rousseau, "Discourses on the arts and sciences," pp. 18–19, in *The Social Contract and Discourses by Jean-Jacques Rousseau*, trans. G.D.H. Cole (London: J.M. Dent and Sons, 1923), pp. 132–4.
67. Gibbon (1993), IV, p. 119–120. John Julius Norwich blames Gibbon for the lack of interest in the Byzantine state shown in the nineteenth and twentieth centuries, as a result of the endurance of this damning critique, for which see John J. Norwich, *Byzantium: the apogee* (London: Viking Press, 1991).
68. Gibbon (1993), IV, pp. 117–27.
69. Op. cit., I, p. 433.
70. Op. cit., I, p. 434.
71. Op. cit., IV, pp. 120–121.
72. Op. cit., I, p. 487. The chapter as a whole covers pp. 487–567.
73. Op. cit., I, p. 491, p. 494.
74. Op. cit., I, pp. 487–567. The indictment of Christianity as essential to the downfall of the empire is repeated at VI, p. 620. For more on Gibbon and Christianity see Patricia B. Craddock, *Edward Gibbon, Luminous Historian 1772–1794* (Baltimore: Johns Hopkins University Press, 1989), Ramsay MacMullen, *Christianizing the Roman Empire* (AD 100–400) (New Haven: Yale University Press, 1984) John G. Pocock, "Gibbon and the Primitive Church," in Stefan Collini, Richard Whatmore, and Brian Young (eds), *History, Religion and Culture: British Intellectual History, 1750–1950* (Cambridge: Cambridge University Press, 2000), pp. 48–68. While the large part of Gibbon's caustic view of Christianity is in the notorious Chapters 15 and 16 of the *Decline and Fall*, he rarely neglects to note its destructive influence through the entirety of the text.

75. Gibbon (1993), V, p. 82.
76. Gibbon (1993), V, p. 83.
77. Op. cit., VI, p. 624.
78. John B. Black, *The Art of History: A Study of Four Great Historians of the Eighteenth Century* (New York: Methuen and Co. Limited (ori. Pub. 1926), 1965), p. 165.
79. For Gibbon's use of temporal and geographical juxtaposition see Leo Braudy's, *Narrative Form in History and Fiction: Hume, Fielding and Gibbon*, (Princeton: Princeton University Press, 1970), p. 244 which discusses "the themes of narrative control, time, and place."
80. Gibbon (1993), III, p. 368.
81. Says Gilbert Highet, "In a sense one could argue that the key differences between humanist and earlier responses to Rome lay in a much heightened sense of disjuncture, a conviction that antiquity had died and so needed to be brought back to life again, together with an increased preoccupation with its physical remains," Highet, p. 247.
82. Gibbon (1993), III, p. 465, IV, p. 60.
83. David Wootton, "Narrative, Irony, and Faith in Gibbon's Decline and Fall," *History and Theory, XXXIII* (1994), pp. 77–105.
84. John G. Pocock, "The Ironist," *London Review of Books*, XXII (2002), pp. 13–17.
85. Highet, p. 344.
86. Bowersock (1996), p. 30.
87. Gibbon (1993), VI, p. 619.
88. Starn, p. 6. He cites as examples of this "Bossuet as universal historian" and "Boileau as arbiter of literary taste."
89. See on this Peter Gay, *The Enlightenment: An Interpretation* (New York: W.W. Norton & Co. (ori. Pub. 1968), 1996).
90. Peter Gay, *The Enlightenment: An Interpretation* (New York: W.W. Norton & Co. (ori. Pub. 1968), 1995), Frank E. Manuel, *The Eighteenth Century Confronts the Gods* (Cambridge: Harvard University Press, 1967).
91. Carl J. Burckhardt, *The Civilization of the Renaissance*, trans. Samuel G.C. Middlemore (London: Penguin Classics (ori. Pub. 1860), 1990). The Swiss historian and modernist art and architecture critic Siegfried Giedion accounted for Burckhardt's legacy in the following terms: "The great discoverer of the age of the Renaissance, he first showed how a period should be treated in its entirety, with regard not only for its painting, sculpture and architecture, but for the social institutions of its daily life as well." Siegfried Giedion, *Space, Time and Architecture: The Growth of a New Tradition* (London: Harvard University Press (ori. Pub. 1941), 2008), p. 3.

92. Burckhardt, p. 32, also saying, "The Middle Ages are not responsible for our present decline! It was a time of natural *authority*."
93. James H. Nicolls (ed.), *Force and Freedom: An Interpretation of History by Jacob Burckhardt* (New York: Meridian Books, 1955), pp. 229–31.
94. Burckhardt, p. 124.
95. Op. cit., p. 92.
96. Op. cit., p. 96.
97. Carl J. Burckhardt, *The Age of Constantine the Great* (Berkeley: University of California Press (ori. Pub. 1852), 1983), p. 228.
98. Op. cit., p. 227.
99. Op. cit., p. 221.
100. Op. cit., p. 72.
101. These themes are found throughout the book. Op. cit., p. 109 and p. 299 on the barbarians, pp. 344–5 on the fall, and p. 117 and p. 353 on Christianity and the Papacy.
102. Carl J. Burckhardt, *On History and Historians* (1965), trans. Harry Zohn (New York; Harper and Row, 1965), p. 220.
103. Nicolls, p. 263, p. 265. See also Burckhardt, p. xvi.
104. Theodor W. Adorno, *The Culture Industry: Selected Essays on Mass Culture*, ed. J.M. Bernstein (London: Routledge Classics, 1991), pp. 85–6.
105. Theodor Mommsen, *The Province of the Roman Empire* (London: Macmillan, 1909), pp. at 4–5.

CHAPTER 4

# Roman Decline and the West in the Modern Age

## ROME AND REFLECTIONS ON TWENTIETH-CENTURY SOCIETY

In the early part of the twentieth century, there were numerous ways that Americans and Europeans could talk about time, change, and history. There was the myth of the original Golden Age, and a countervailing awareness of the relentless decay of time. There were invocations of universal empire, together with their critics. At the same time, the affirmation of decline and decay might serve to explain present troubles, re-synthesize the intense meditation on historical mutability so widespread in Antiquity and the Middle Ages; and, in the end, suggest a solution. In doing so, they helped to recharge classical images of historical decline which would have a profound impact on the broader culture, and the perceived "underworld" of modern thought—those ideas and philosophies which critique aspects of the modern world.[1] Theories of time such as this ultimately remain pessimistic about the fate of the world. There was awareness that each stage of a civilization's advancement required a destruction of what came before. In criticizing these ideals of Progress, they betrayed the same basic notion—that societies and civilization had a fixed lifespan and function, and that the form of their decline and fall followed a shared and comparable path.

In the growing sense of cultural and political crisis in the interwar years, writers from Britain, the USA and Germany found parallels with the decline and fall increasingly relevant to their concerns. Walther Rehm, in a study on the theme of the decline of Rome in Western thought, commented that the subject of Rome's decay was an especially insistent one: "when an age was itself stirred and disquieted by a sense of decadence, when it desired to obtain certainty about the historical position it occupies in its life."[2] Oswald Spengler's *The Decline of the West* (1932) and Arnold Toynbee's *The Study of History* (1934–61, written in 12 volumes) are an attempted summary of all the meaningful history of mankind. These both comprised the best-known assessment of Western civilization's overall place in "world history." Spengler and Toynbee both took as their symbol of the peak of Western civilization the modern British Empire, and both were driven by the conviction that its guiding place in History was coming to an end. For them, the decline of the classical world served as the prime precedent, both to compare to the fortunes and future of Britain, and to suggest a more general set of rules at work in the process of decay.

Inspired by the sight of a volume in a store entitled *The Decline of Antiquity*, Spengler conceived of his theme and title as *The Decline of the West*. Spengler believed he had moved to a whole new level of historical thinking, in "predetermining history."[3] This approach would, for the first time, relegate Classical and Western culture to its proper, diminished place in the overall story of mankind.[4] Relying very heavily on the discussed tradition of cultural criticism, the work summed up a long period of historical and cultural pessimism and discontent. For Spengler, Europe had reached this sterile winter stage in the nineteenth century, and entered a period that was the common thread of all civilizations—from Buddhist India to Hellenistic Greece to Taoist China—namely, the disturbing of the previous order and harmony.[5] As he says:

> Long ago we might and should have seen in the "Classical" world a development which is the complete counterpart of our own Western development, differing indeed from it in every detail of the surface but entirely similar as regards the inward power driving the great organism towards its end ....[6]

Spengler describes how these entities may exist in stagnation "for hundreds or thousands of years," dominated by "dead bodies, amorphous and dispirited masses of men." Such a state "loses its desire to be ... as in Imperial Rome."[7] The cultural and implicitly moral aspects of this decline receive special notice from him, for "it is one of the most impressive facts of historical symbolism" that the change is manifested in "the extinction of great art ... of great formal thought ... but also quite carnally," and that, above all, this is "a phenomenon not peculiar to ourselves but already observed and deplored—and of course not remedied—in Imperial Rome ...."[8]

The message is made clear here. The modern world is losing its spiritual essence and values, and, through the precedent of other civilizations—of which Rome is the best understood and comprehended example—we learn that the path trodden by mankind is irreversible. How exactly Rome was brought down, in terms of detailed historical mechanisms, is not discussed—but its myth is typically invoked in artful, poetic language, as a universal truism of human nature, one which can be subjectively applied to those qualities of the present the author (here, Spengler) dislikes or abhors.

Spengler's approach to Antiquity was notably criticized by the prominent cultural and historical theorist Theodor Adorno. "If the fall of Antiquity were dictated by the autonomous necessity of life and by the expression of its soul," he wrote in a 1941 essay on Spengler's *The Decline of the West*, "then indeed it takes on the aspect of fatality and by (analogy) ... carries over to the present situation." As a Marxian of the Frankfurt School, Adorno rejects Spengler's historical model of the organic cycle, and the Roman analogizing from which it is largely derived. This is not, however, because of a fault with the analogy itself, but with the purpose to which it is put. Adorno is just as willing to draw on a *Roman* model of decline and fall to make his point, just not a Spengler-ian one that attaches to this process a grand, inevitable cycle. As he says:

> If ... the fall of Antiquity can be understood by its unproductive system of latifundia (landed estates) and the slave economy related to it, the fatality can be mastered if men succeed in overcoming such and similar structures of domination. In such a case, Spengler's universal structure reveals itself as a false analogy drawn from a bad solitary happening—solitary in spite of its threatening recurrence.[9]

Consequently, the decline of Rome is perceived as a prophetic warning, not an eternal and inevitable process. *Universal* decline may not be inevitable, if the *Roman* example is heeded. Conversely, to "deny the decline is to become even more firmly caught in its fatal coils." It is still invoked as an abstract historical force. Drawing on another comparison to the fall of Rome, Adorno suggests that to avoid this fate, the "barbaric element in culture itself must be recognized," and those societies which survive must "challenge the idea of culture as well as the reality of barbarism." Furthermore, decay itself, as it is produced by an oppressive system, provides an opportunity to escape from the "dictatorship of culture" through the "forces released by decay." As he concludes on the matter, "What can oppose the decline of the west is not a resurrected culture but the utopia that is silently contained in the image of its decline."[10] Though these are two very different thinkers, they are invoking a comparable model of decline, with the same, Roman, frame of reference. As put by Northorp Frye, "The decline, or aging, of the West is as much a part of our mental outlook today as the electron or the dinosaur ... and in that sense we are all Spenglerians."[11]

It is clear in these writings that while the idea of an eternal and irrevocable pattern of decline is intended to hold a universal value, the precedent for that abstraction is specifically the Roman myth. As Spengler says, "Rome ... will always give us, working as we must by analogies, the key to understanding our own future."[12] The potent, poetic imagery of Roman ruin and fall is evoked, not in military and political terms, but through the broader idea of inward collapse. Notably, this overall criticism of civilization as a whole, and the value systems it evolves through its life cycle, incorporates concepts of degeneracy into the ideologies of *any* such civilization, as they are perceived to manifest in its advanced stages. In this way, the temporal and universal elements of the story are connected. It is in this fashion that Spengler attacked liberalism as the outdated, bankrupt ideology of a dying civilization, and described imperialism as "civilization unadulterated."[13] Drawing inspiration from Hegel and the British "Idealist" tradition,[14] he makes it clear that it was up to the free thinkers remaining in the Western world to refurbish and redefine it as a spiritual community of shared moral values, accepting of its eclipse, and not defined by its material, political, or imperial base.[15]

The same building blocks are present in these stories of the downward path of civilization. The example of Rome is extrapolated beyond a simple comparison, and into the grander language of a universal framework, organism, or cycle: an objective and recurring constant of human nature. At the same time, the *specific* details described reflect the subjective prejudices and preoccupations of the author, even when they are couched as objective features of the system. The history, or comparative history, demonstrated in these examples is laced with a specific ideology and borders on personal "propaganda"—just as it does with the other authorial voices discussed here. Yet the underlying *values* of the myth, the belief in internal decline and decay fatally weakening the empire and its culture, such that it "destroyed itself from within," is constant and immutable, whatever the historical record or advances in the field of study.[16] To invoke Strauss's analogy of the score, the harmony—or *latent* content— stays broadly the same, even as the melody, or narrative, is localized to its time and audience.[17]

This conceptual structure is equally evident in Toynbee's 12-volume *A Study of History* (1934–61), a collection intended to cover the entire history of mankind, from Hammurabi to Hitler. Toynbee came from an intellectual tradition quite different from that of Spengler, namely nineteenth-century English liberalism. Nevertheless, they both took as the symbol of the modern West the British Empire. In exploring the growing sense of social and cultural crisis in the inter-war years, they found the decline and fall of Rome increasingly meaningful.[18]

Toynbee represented a generation of disenchanted intellectuals who dominated the English scene in this period, and who feared that industrial growth had impoverished the working class, socially, culturally and morally. For Toynbee, the Industrial Revolution was "a period as disastrous and terrible as any through which a nation ever passed."[19] Such a disaster he compared to the decline of a "creative minority" in Late Antiquity.[20] This statement echoes Leonardo Bruni when, creatively re-interpreting a passage of Tacitus on the exclusivity of brilliant historical minds, he said that, "After the Republic had been subject to the power of one man, the brilliant minds vanished."[21] The modern tradition of liberal English pessimism had many of its roots in Matthew Arnold's *Culture and Anarchy*. In Arnold's view, the nation lacked any cultural compass, and he worried that an upwardly mobile, overly commercial middle class would pollute the wellspring of culture.[22] These barbarians would "rule by their energy, but they will deteriorate it [Britain] by their low ideas and want of culture."[23]

The decline in intellectual and moral standards could therefore be related to the process of larger social and/or economic changes. Arthur Balfour, the Conservative writer and politician, outlined in 1903 how Roman history revealed that in "an ancient but still powerful state, when the reaction against recurring ills grows feebler, enterprise slackens and vigour ebbs away ...." He concludes his observation with the remark that there must be "present some process of social degeneration, which we must perforce recognize," and that "those who are most reluctant to admit that decay, as distinguished from misfortune, may lower the general level of civilization ...."[24]

Clearly these authors concerned with culture and the industrial world shared the same central conviction and attitude: that Western civilization was in crisis. The ruin of the classical world, and the circumstances of that tragedy, were entirely relevant to understanding this crisis and its likely path, if unchecked. In criticizing these ideals of progress, they betrayed the same basic notion—that societies and civilization had a fixed life span and function, an organistic notion of society (as opposed to a progressive one) dating back to ancient Hellenistic and Roman notions of decline.[25] Writing in the period after the Second World War, Catholic historian Christopher Dawson, in an observation and reflection on Gibbon's *Decline and Fall*, wove it into a concept of the cosmic order at large, and drew from it an image of universal decay:

> All earthly things are subject to mutability. Growth and decay, life and death, are the law of states as well as of individuals ... this conception only needs to be interpreted in a vitalistic sense in order to become an organic theory of social development. And though such theories are often regarded as characteristically modern, they were by no means unknown in Gibbon's day .... In reality, the Roman Empire fell not by war or political incapacity but because of a process of sociological decay which destroyed the foundations of its strength.[26]

Dawson references modern theories of sociology, yet reiterates the very same precepts found in virtually all iterations of this myth—that the empire was finally corrupted from within, a victim of its own hubris. In this way, the historical analysis is ultimately beholden to a much broader narrative. Such an approach to the cycle of civilization is reiterated in writer Francis Neilson's *The Decline of Civilizations* (1945), which again, pulls out the Roman precedent to fortify an example:

> We can no longer ignore the manifestation of cycles and repetition of growth and deterioration. Spengler suggests that this civilization is dying of an overdose of history. It may very well be that the historian of the future, in comparing what is now taking place in the world with those events that brought Rome and Greece to the winter of their despair, will say that the only difference is in the fact that the tragedy of our day covers a greater area, goes deeper, and that the outlook for us is more hopeless ... [that] we have entered

our winter, according to the findings of Adams, Spengler, and many others, is a fact no amount of optimism can hide.

The repeated reference to the ancient world by these authors is, according to Neilson, evidence in itself of the "winter" of civilization. Any possibility of optimism is challenged by relating it to the misguided attitudes of past ages, including the somewhat spurious and convenient comparison of ancient prophets to the radio:

> And, yet, those who wish to be deceived scarcely ever pause to reflect on what happened to the optimists of other ages. The soothsayers of Greece and Rome were no different from those who use the radio morning, noon and night. Before anyone here realized the coming of this catastrophe, I wrote: Those who imagine that this civilization is proof against decay disregard the warning which is present in the history of the decline of every people that has passed. They seem to be under the impression that inventiveness and machinery or, to use the much-worn phrase, scientific approach, will enable us to escape what other nations suffered before their fall. There were always, however, optimists in every civilization who took just exactly the same attitude.[27]

Again, the argument here is generalized in its scope, and seeks to convey a universal truth—the fall of the classical world is *not* simply a unique historical event, but part of an eternal process that speaks as much to the present as it does its own time. The perceived faults and failings of the modern world reflect this fundamentally very similar path to destruction. Historical cycles, and organistic notions of society, lend themselves to the central paradox of negative classicism—that out of progress and achievement come inevitable decline and fall; and that the classical forges a path to the medieval.

This castigation of the developments of Western society is hardly unique to the literary record of the early twentieth century. Cecil B. DeMille makes the comparison between past and present achingly explicit in *Manslaughter* (Paramount Pictures, 1922), where images of debauched flappers are juxtaposed with flashbacks to orgies in ancient Rome; conveying a similar message and moral tone about the dangers of decline. It finds a particular resonance with the rise of a new medium of entertainment in the middle of the century. From its commercial beginnings in the late 1940s, television has been accused of causing cultural and political decadence—in its varyingly suggested forms—more than any other visual medium aside from cinema; and, unlike cinema, has benefited from less enthusiastic defenders. Anything it broadcasts is apt to be deemed antithetical to the spirit and purpose of high culture. As the apparatus for automated barbarism, it lends itself easily to analogizing with Roman decadence and decline. Milton Shulman, writing in 1952, described public political opinion as mediated over the TV set to "the electronic equivalent of the mobs in the Roman colosseum being asked to give a thumbs up or a thumbs down sign about the fate of an intended victim."[28] In an account of the influence of television on the 1965 "Watts" rebellion, John Dunne wrote in the *New Republic* magazine, "television turned the riots into some kind of Roman spectacle, with the police playing the lions, the Negroes the Christians."[29] More recently, Anthony Quinton described the inclusion of popular culture—including the study of television drama and fiction—in educational syllabi as "comparable to the fall of the Roman empire, and its replacement by the barbarian kingdoms," and criticized "cultural studies" in which "the simple mental fare served up by the entertainment industry will be scrutinized for its political content."[30]

These are not original ideas about mass or popular culture, despite the topics in question, namely the advent of television and visual mass media, being a comparatively new and novel form. The Romans did not have TV sets, yet the advent of TV is seen to somehow *make* us more like the Romans—in precisely the wrong ways. Something of this notion of commonality is addressed by David M. White, who defends the medium precisely by pointing out the frequency of this depiction: "The mass culture critic always insinuates that in some previous era the bulk of men were rational, pacific, and learned. The good old days—like the Roman Empire under Nero? Admittedly, the Romans didn't have a television set to massacre various unwilling guests during the coliseum half-time shows."[31]

In these examples, the identification of the decline, corruption and downfall of the Roman world is assumed to be obvious; despite, that is, the wildly different technologies, the historical and cultural context of ancient rituals and practices, and the rise of modern media culture. While the specific subject of criticism may vary, there is little difference in the ideological necessities of the approach, or its moral tone. To invoke Strauss, one can say that the melody of the story changes, but the essential harmony remains the same.[32]

## Roman Narratives and the Cold War

Just as it proved vital to authors engaging with the consequences of the First World War, the decline and fall have proven a powerful model for describing social, cultural and political trends from the middle of the twentieth-century. The impact of the Cold War functioned as a crucial mechanism for such comparison. Gilbert Highet, writing in *The Classical Tradition* (1949) soon after the beginning of the Cold War, describes the post-Roman Dark Age as an era characterized as a "scarcely civilized" era of "the raiding savages, the roaring criminals, and the domineering nobles."[33] Highet mourns the consequences of the age following the end of the Western Roman Empire, and Sidonius Apollinaris's apparent ignorance of their consequences.[34] In particular he compares the emerging Cold War of the late 1940s and its sundering of far-reaching trans-national intellectual horizons to the Dark Age surrounding Sidonius. He talks of the supposed end of the Renaissance from the sixteenth to the nineteenth centuries, and breaks out into emotive, poetic language as he equates the tragedy of Sidonius' time with his own:

> Are these shadows on so many of our horizons the outriders of another long night, like that which was closing in on Sidonius? Modern scholars must regret that they have to work in a time when ... it is becoming more and more difficult to exchange opinions across the world ... and to feel oneself part of a world-wide structure of art and learning, greater than all the things that divide mankind: nationalities and creeds, fear and hate.[35]

The lesson Highet wants to pass on in his writing, and the focus of his fears, is clear; that the "dark age" that consumed Rome is a constant and universal threat, in this and every culture, including his contemporary world. He warns:

> ... we are so accustomed to contemplating the spectacle of human progress that we assume modern culture to be better than anything that preceded it. We forget also how able and how willing men are to reverse the movement of progress: how many forces of barbarism remain ... still powerfully alive, capable of not only injuring civilization but of putting a burning desert in its place ... but two or three generations of war and pestilence and revolution destroy culture with appalling rapidity.[36]

Gilbert Highet suggests that the consequence of the Industrial Revolution was that "most of the great nineteenth-century writers hated and despised the world in which they lived," and that "it is difficult to think of any other period in which so many talented authors have so unanimously detested their entire surroundings and the ideals of the people among whom they were forced to exist." This means that, instead, "they look to other lands and other ages ... they admired the cults of antiquity as free, strong and graceful." Cited by Highet as evidence of this tendency is the periodical *Parnassus*, a symbol for the nineteenth-century idealism which loved Greco-Roman culture.[37]

Aside from the literary record, it is in cinema that, implicitly or explicitly, the connection between a dwindling Roman Empire or culture, and the modern world becomes a dominant trait in the epic Hollywood movies of the Second World War period. These frequently compare and contrast the character, fate and fortunes of the Roman Empire and the USA.[38] The prologue to Cecil B. DeMille's *The Ten Commandments* (Paramount Pictures, 1956), the hugely successful remake by the same director, makes clear the film's relevance to the Cold War; DeMille offers a choice between the law of God and the whims of the dictator—whether that may be Ramesses or Stalin.[39] Those more "Christian" stories—*The Robe*, *Quo Vadis*, *Ben-Hur*, and *The Sign of the Pagan*—describe the possible rise of a better, *Christian* empire, out of the rubble of a pagan and decadent Rome; with clear analogies to their contemporary world, and a Christian America. At the end of Mervyn LeRoy's *Quo Vadis* (MGM, 1951) Marcus Vinicius, its hero, and his friend reflect on the fates of empires from Babylon to Rome, and their seemingly inevitable decline. With heavy Christian overtones, the friend offers hope for "a more permanent world ... or a more permanent faith." Vinicius answers, to the sounds of a heavenly chorus singing "*Quo Vadis, domine?*" that "One is not possible without the other." In Henry Koster's *The Robe* (1953), which describes the rise of Caligula and the persecution of Christians, the hero and his beloved are condemned to death, but through the use of special effects they walk straight up to heaven. Gore Vidal, novelist and a screenwriter for Wyler's *Ben-Hur*, accounted for his work on a series of historical novels—for an American audience—with the overarching title *Narratives of Empire* in this way:

> I had been taken to task by *Time* magazine in a review of my first book of essays .... *Time* wrote that I had dared to refer to our minatory global presence as "an empire" which of course it could *not* be as we were, in the Luce

publications, Christian goodness incarnate. It seems I had ... said the unsayable too soon. I was subversive.[40]

Hollywood's Roman epics from *Quo Vadis* to William Wyler's *Ben-Hur* (MGM, 1959) and Stanley Kubrick's *Spartacus* (Universal Pictures, 1960) typically presented the Romans as ruthless and ambitious warmongers, as inhumane and oppressive slave-owners, or as degenerates obsessed with spectacle and orgies. Judah Ben-Hur argues with his former Roman friend Messala with the words "I warn you! Rome is an affront to God! Rome is strangling my people and my country, the whole Earth! But not forever. I tell you the day Rome falls there will be a shout of freedom such as the world has never heard before!"

The idea of the decline and fall as a historical fact or inevitability is seeded in all these films. In most of them, however, the actual end of Rome is only implicitly touched on, rather than central to their theme. It is suggested as an inevitable outcome of the process of decline, but the detailed process of events is not formally represented or described. The most direct cinematic exception to this (before, less directly, Anthony Mann) is *Sign of the Pagan*, a 1954 historical epic directed by German émigré Dougal Sirk. This is a film which, while set nominally in Late Antiquity, incorporates many "medieval" elements in its content and themes.[41] Sirk was a former film and theatre director in Weimar and Nazi Germany who was steeped in the German concern with medieval visual art—studying art history at the University of Hamburg in the 1920s, and at least "claiming" to have been taught by Panofsky.[42]

*The Sign of the Pagan* sets its drama during a crisis of the fifth-century empire, as it is victimized by the predations of Attila the Hun. This failing state is supposedly replaced by a unified and wholly Christian Roman Empire under Marcian (who never, historically, ruled in the West). At the beginning of the film, Marcian is a Roman centurion sent by the Western Roman Emperor Valentinian to urge Theodosius to stay loyal to Rome in the face of the barbarian onslaught. On his way to Constantinople to meet Theodosius, Marcian is captured by Attila, but escapes and makes it to the city. Attila also rides to Constantinople to make his own demands on the Emperor there. Theodosius rejects Marcian's plea to stay firm and loyal and instead makes a treacherous pact with Attila against Rome. Marcian, however, wins the ear and love of Theodosius' sister Pulcheria, and with the support of a loyal general, Paulinus, they manage to expose

Theodosius' treachery, overthrow him in a coup, and institute Pulcheria in his place.

Marcian then sets off to protect Rome against Attila's invasion. Valentinian flees the city, leaving him in charge. Attila has assembled his troops to march on the city but he hesitates, as he and his seers are plagued by portentous visions. Meanwhile, Attila's daughter, Kubla (not in any way, shape or form a historical figure), who has fallen in love with Marcian and secretly converted to Christianity, covertly informs the Romans of Attila's portents of doom. Enraged, Attila kills her, but abandons the attack. Marcian arranges an ambush in which Attila's retreating troops are wiped out and Attila is killed by Idilko, his long-suffering prisoner and wife. The film ends with Marcian marrying Pulcheria and becoming, in a historical fabrication, the Emperor of both the Western and Eastern Empires.

I have discussed the role that the decline and fall plays as a source of portent and judgement in the literary record, and such also applies to its presence in the cinematic tradition. The power of prophecy plays a vital part in *Quo Vadis* (1951)—the title itself a proverbial phrase from the Bible, meaning "Where do you go?" or "Whither goest thou?"[43] It takes a more secular form in Anthony Mann's *The Fall of the Roman Empire*, with the doom-laden warnings of senators about the threat to Rome. *The Sign of the Pagan* is a film itself riddled with omens and portents. Attila is undone by his inability and unwillingness to deal with the numerous visions and signs he receives of his impending fall. A seer falsely prophesies to him that Rome will fall that autumn, and is then crushed by a biblically appropriate thunderbolt that hits an overhanging tree. Attila, a pagan, is unable to comprehend the value of this warning, and so imagines that his god intended the seer's greatest prophecy to be his last. Similarly, he rejects Kubla's portents concerning his death, treating the account she gives of his blood being spilled as *her* (and therefore family) blood. Throughout the film, Attila demonstrates this inability to comprehend abstract and spiritual truth, and is instead lost in his appreciation of the purely material. As he tells Theodosius, "What are words? A little noisy breath, spoken and forever gone. Your gold has greater security." Marcian, aware of the weakness of his word, mocks Theodosius' conviction that the barbarians will honour their agreement and not attack Constantinople, and for thinking he is "safe behind a shield of parchment." In this vein, Attila refers to the Christian cross as merely a "symbol" of their faith, as he describes it to two pilgrims. He believes that the symbolic, religious culture of the Romans cannot compete with his raw displays of strength—but he retreats in horror from the image of a cross floating in a church (though it is carried by a priest, hidden by the dark), and, as he retreats—too late to save him—from his campaigns against Rome, is finally cowed by the power of Pope Leo. The supernatural elements of the movie are justified by their *Christian* context—it is the spiritual power of the faith that triumphs over the earthly, barbarian might of Attila (and this bears easy comparison to the spiritual victory of Christian Roman values in *Quo Vadis* and *King Arthur*).

Sirk's analogy to the geopolitical climate of the 1950s is an easy one to make. In *The Sign of the Pagan* (1954), where Attila's hordes threaten Rome, the Empire can readily be taken to stand for the USA, and Attila for the USSR. The film's consequent message is that unity in Christian ideals is necessary to resist the "barbarian" threat from the East. This reflects the broader portrait of the faith reflecting liberty and humane, moral value, as suggested in the common cinematic stories of this period that concern persecuted Christians. Nevertheless, the Christian empire Sirk depicts is fundamentally corrupted. Emperor Valentinian is a coward—Theodosius, selfish and treacherous. Marcian, a true Christian, is the closest thing we have to a hero (aside from the distant spiritual presence of the Pope), but as with Livius in *The Fall of the Roman Empire*, he is surrounded by human corruption: appropriately enough, on the eve of the fall. The film therefore suggests the survival of Christian spirituality and values, past that of the wasting and decadent body of the empire; in this way, the Roman Empire may be dying, but the Pope saves the city of Rome itself, and its spiritual legacy. Such a model fits with the typical suggestion of the USA as a *superior* empire to Rome, precisely because it better embodies those values. One is reminded, therefore, of the end of Mervyn LeRoy's *Quo Vadis* (1951), where the protagonist Marcus Vinicius and his friend contemplate the fate of empires from Babylon to Rome. In heavy Christian overtones, the friend desires hope for "a more permanent world ... or a more permanent faith." Vinicius answers that, "One is not possible without the other." Such a statement is not made explicitly in *The Sign*, but neither is it overtly needed.

Such a positive appraisal of the redeeming power of Christianity, and its role in the rise of a new and better order out of the ashes of Rome (or at least a thousand years later, in the New World), may appear to sit at odds with the traditional, Gibbonian narrative of the decline and fall. But Christianity, despite its prominent place in Gibbon's critique and invective, is *not* at the core of this myth. It is not a necessary property of its structure or form. Christian authors from Augustine to the modern era have been cited above who use it in its varying forms. Anthony Mann, discussed below, self-consciously articulates a version of Gibbon without any of the religious criticism present. Indeed, it must be remembered that Gibbon himself did *not* merely attack the religiosity of the Christian faith—he condemned the Roman populace at large for its broader slide into superstition long before the advent of that creed. The adoption of Christianity was merely *one* aspect of the degradation of rational thinking and Roman moral values.[44] Removing that content does not alter its underlying principle.

The decline and fall can function both as a secular and a theological narrative. The core property of this myth is not in the attributed specifics of its cause, which vary, but the *process* itself. What remains strikingly common in all these representations, by different degrees direct or implicit, is the type of moral and value judgements that can be placed on this process. A great empire must and can only fall because it is morally corrupted from within, whether in its political, social, cultural or religious dimensions. It is through understanding such truths that the final story of Rome can be related to the modern world as a moral tale. Such are the axioms out of which this myth is necessarily constructed.

## Mann, Hollywood, and Historical "Truth"

It is in this context that the particular significance to this book of Anthony Mann's *The Fall of the Roman Empire* (1964) must be made clear. Firstly, it is the only epic film of this era that directly discusses the theme of the decline and fall of Rome—and, furthermore, in a way which deliberately and consciously invoked the historical record. At least partly because Mann's film is an intermediary between Gibbon and *Gladiator*, the great old historian of the Roman Empire, who originally wrote for an upper-class British audience in the late eighteenth century, continues to exert his influence in a corner of modern and mass culture where most people would not think to look for it. Secondly, of interest here is the content of the critical attention, mostly academic, that the film has received. Despite the flaws, distortions, inaccuracies, and simplistic moral judgements presented to the viewer (which will be outlined in detail below) the film's reception—for its accuracy and historical merit, not simply its creative qualities—has been almost universally positive. Indeed it is perhaps the "epic" film most lauded for its factual accuracy, profound thematic qualities, and historical relevance. Thirdly—and reinforced by its discussion in the above criteria—*The Fall* is a revealing instance of my "integrated regime of historical representation," to paraphrase White,[45] and a prime example of the intersection of high and popular culture involved in creating and perpetuating the myth of the decline and fall. Historians, and particularly historians of cinema, have written about the links between Gibbon and Mann, but not discussed the broader cultural and historiographical significance of what this means—just taken it as a given that this was an "accurate" or "appropriate" model to represent the past. Here, instead, Mann will be related to Gibbon in the context of the study of the myth paradigm—a more appropriate avenue for its appreciation—then through a judgement of its merits as a historical account. While the tools conveying Gibbon and Mann's image of Roman decline are, on the surface, very different, the underlying message still strikes a common critical chord.

To properly examine the place of the *Fall of the Roman Empire* in the intellectual tradition of the decline and fall, it is necessary to discuss the film's academic reception, on which much has been written. *The Fall* has typically been praised for its value and contribution to cinema: not simply as a piece of art or entertainment, but as a faithfully effective recreation of history for popular audiences. Derek Elley, who in *The Epic Film: Myth and History* provides one of the earliest and most influential academic appreciations of the film, praises its mediation of an essential Roman spirit, calling a particular senate scene "one of the most thoughtful sequences ever placed on 70mm film." He also, pointedly, values the film for the *truth* and depth of its portrayal: for Mann and his associates "examine Roman thought at its most civilized peak ... breaking new ground."[46] *The Fall* is given positive treatment in Jon Solomon's defining work on film and antiquity, *The Ancient World in the Cinema*.[47] Martin Winkler, a classicist and staunch defender of the reputation of *The Fall of The Roman Empire*, argues on academic and artistic grounds, "the case for the defence of serious and committed fiction based on history as exemplified in the genre of epic cinema, with special focus on Anthony Mann's *The Fall of the Roman Empire*."[48] The film is worthy of these laudations because it so effectively "delivers the excitement, spectacle, action, and romance audiences expect from their epics, but it transcends them. The film articulates the meaning of historical cinema with greater eloquence, passion, and conviction than any other ancient epics have managed to do."[49] The significance of this positive assessment can, it is hoped, be applied more broadly, for it "can provide a test case, a kind of *apologia pro pellicula historiographica*, that can be applied to other historical films."[50] The key analysis in this context is provided by Elenora Cavallini, who praises the apparent truthfulness of the film on these grounds:

> It is based on the historically plausible assumption that the primary causes of the epoch-making phenomenon referred to in its title can be traced back less to the barbarian invasions than to the weakening of Roman institutions and the ascent to the imperial throne by a series of mentally unstable and megalomaniac princes, who were incapable of, or uninterested in, their governing responsibilities.[51]

This holds that its account of the causality of the decline and fall is a plausible and perceptive analysis. Its historicity, whatever liberties are taken with events, is thereby cause for great respect. Furthermore, "*The Fall of the Roman Empire* ought to be appreciated for its attempt to undertake an analysis of Roman society. The results may be sketchy, but they are not too distant from historical reality, at least in some respects."[52] Allen M. Ward echoes this with the words, "What makes *The Fall of the Roman Empire* a worthy film is how seriously its director, producer, and screenwriter approached the history they portrayed."[53]

The immediate problem with these assessments is that they are primarily concerned with proving and promoting the intellectual integrity of historical cinema—particularly that of the ancient world—and their value as methods to mediate history to the public. In this respect, it is very reminiscent of that ideology of the "Classical Tradition," retooled for this medium of delivery. To examine all these attitudes in their proper context, one needs to return to the aims and intentions of *The Fall*, and see why they have found such a resonance with this scholarship. Mann's thesis can be elaborated both by looking at the content of the film (in terms of its overt and latent or implicit meaning), from the essay "Empire Demolition" that he wrote in the same year as *The Fall* to discuss its themes and purpose, and from additional interviews he provided on the subject.[54] His asserted aim is to "dramatize how an empire fell."[55]

The thesis presented runs thus. Rome is an advanced civilization and the basis of Western culture, enlightenment and prosperity. Its fall presented a calamitous setback to peace and prosperity for mankind. This fall is not the consequence of a material defeat by outsiders, or an actual process of political, military, or territorial collapse, but a tale of decline and corruption at the centre of the Imperium; a tragic genre narrative of folly and hubris that deserves repeating as a cautionary tale for future generations to avoid these mistakes.

This thesis of Mann achieves its final fruition at the close of the film. Right before the credits roll, the film finishes pointedly—in AD 193, almost 300 years before the actual "end" of the Western Empire in AD 476 —with the narrator, returning for the first time since the opening scene, quoting William Durant to say, "This was the beginning of the Fall of the Roman Empire. A great civilization is not conquered from without until it has destroyed itself within." The rest of the Durant line, as it was originally published, summarizes the fall of Rome in this way: "The essential causes of Rome's decline lay in her people, her morals, her class struggle, her failing trade, her bureaucratic despotism, her stifling taxes, her consuming wars."[56] Aside from trade and bureaucracy—difficult subjects for a feature film to tackle—all of these factors are explored in the film, and mark the stated beginning of the process of "decline and fall," and thereby the fundamental reason for the end of the Roman Empire and an era of civilization: which, as we learn, originated in the tumultuous and self-destructive reign of Commodus.[57] The film shows how these enervating processes were first set in motion—the "First Cause" of the eventual fall, unseen here, 300 years ahead in the future, yet still deemed inevitable by the close of events.

It is here that I need to turn back to the influence on this film of Edward Gibbon. Both Mann and Gibbon desire to communicate a certain philosophical truth to their audience, through their own respective media, and we need to remind ourselves of what exactly that intended "truth" is. They equally mourn the death of the "heroic spirit of the Romans."[58] To both of them, the history of Rome was of universal significance and possessed symbolic value: it was something momentous, both something that had to be understood and also whose lessons were applicable to other societies in other ages.

In Mann's *Fall of the Roman Empire*, Roman civilization is represented as becoming subject to a moral paralysis which prevented its citizens, consumed by apathy and hubris, from averting its decline and downfall. Its people no longer believed in it; they felt that their government did nothing for them, and so they did nothing in return to help it. Consequently, not only did Rome fall, but, on a more philosophical level, this fall was a both morally inevitable and justified result of the processes set in motion by the reign of one mad ruler, Commodus, 300 years earlier.

Gibbon wrote in the opening of the first chapter of the the *Decline and Fall* that the fall of Rome was "a revolution which will ever be remembered, and is still felt by the nations of the earth." Gibbon's influence on the film was heavily reinforced by the participation of William Durant, a widely read US historian, whose Roman history *Caesar and Christ*, deeply influenced by Gibbon, Mann appeared to have held in high regard. In a message to Durant, a mutual associate at Samuel Bronston's production company called Mann "a disciple of yours."[59]

Ironically, Durant was cognizant of the film's historical weaknesses when asked to become a consultant for it. His comment on first reading the script was that, though it was "brilliantly done" and dramatically effective, "it took so many liberties with history that I felt I had better withdraw from any connection with the film." The particular divergences he cites are centred on the portrayal of Commodus. Factually, he disliked the manner of the notorious emperor's death—and thematically he felt that the "character and reign" of Commodus were "comparatively minor factors in the fall of Rome."[60] However, Durant finally relented, citing concessions provided by Mann, and an account of its popular context. It should, however, be noted that whatever the *surface* details of the story that Durant criticized, its core themes, of decline, enervation, and the loss of some ineffable Roman spirit were still entirely at play; and consequently it is no surprise that the historian was, as his biography makes clear, quickly brought on board.[61]

The general respect accorded to William Durant is indicated not only by the quotations that bookend the film, but also by the prominent identification the man receives in the film's opening credits as historical consultant. Mann claimed to have read much of Gibbon and Durant—together with ancient sources such as the *Historia Augusta*—in preparation for this film.[62] This is aside from the significant artistic influence of German Expressionist cinema in general on the project; characterized as it is by tales of corruption, doom and decline.[63]

This concern with the causal processes of Rome's fall, together with a melancholia that transpired from this, sets *The Fall* apart from its contemporary screen epics in some ways. It is a key reason for the movie's rehabilitation as a more serious, thoughtful, and somehow more "worthy" piece of historical filmmaking. *The Fall of the Roman Empire* is widely considered an "intelligently" made film and the most accomplished screen representation of Ancient Rome. Historians generally think highly of *The Fall* but criticize *Gladiator*: for example, Eleonara Cavallini argues that in contrast to the more limited and sensationalist approach of *Gladiator*, Mann's film "focuses on the *mechanisms* that underlie historical events."[64]

While *The Fall* is explicitly acknowledging its place in the cinematic tradition of the Roman epic, it is clearly and consciously attempting to be a very different kind of film to the contemporary epics of its time. Instead, in *The Fall* viewers are invited to identify with the Romans as bringers of peace and civilization, as personified by a philosopher and ruler capable of resisting the corruptions and temptations of absolute power—unlike, tragically, his son Commodus. Rome at its best is still a symbol of great virtue—almost, in the form of Marcus, a progressive ideal—even though, at its worst, it mirrors the decadence of an epic such as *Quo Vadis*. In its initial voiceover, Mann's film declares a significant distance between itself and the earlier Cold War narratives of Christianity triumphant[65] over the decadent and immoral body of Rome. Notably, its historical pretensions are revealed in the opening narration, which repeats almost word for word the first paragraph of Durant's epilogue to *Caesar and Christ*, "The two greatest problems in history are how to account for the rise of Rome and how to account for her fall. We may come nearer to understanding the truth if we remember that the Fall of Rome, like her rise, did not have one cause but many and was not an event but a process spread over three hundred years. Some nations have not lasted as long as Rome fell."[66] Implicitly, this also emulates the famous statement by Gibbon: "*instead of inquiring why the Roman Empire was destroyed we should rather be surprised that it has subsisted for so long* (emphasis added)."[67]

All this is a very deliberate attempt to stand outside the Hollywood traditions of the genre, in an apparent quest for some greater historical truth. It is a self-conscious challenge to the entrenched Hollywood style for representing Rome. This serves its purpose as a contrast to the triumphalist Roman religious epics of the time, such as that found in *Ben-Hur* and *Quo Vadis*; whose glorious message of rebirth, and allusions to American supremacy, it replaces with a cautionary message of the threats of overextension, imperialism, and the moral decay of a great society. The primary concern of the film, therefore, appears to be using the narrative and visual techniques available in contemporary cinematography to tell a tale of the events which set the "decline and fall" in motion—and, more indirectly, to relate it to the problems and issues of the contemporary world of its audience.

Despite the trappings of novelty and cinematic radicalism, this supposedly radical challenge to the conventions of Hollywood, for which the film has received very positive attention, is, at least thematically, nothing new.[68] While *The Fall* is frequently cited as a bold, historically minded departure from filmmaking traditions, its whole purpose has actually been one very fundamental to epic, historical, and ancient cinema. Mann observed in "Empire Demolition" that meaningful historical epics should differ from common spectacle films, and that he wanted to distance himself from the common approach.[69] This purpose was suggested 40 years earlier by DeMille, who wrote in an article published in *The Ladies' Home Journal* in 1927, "The Public Is Always Right," that "spectacle, for spectacle's sake, is not only not worth what it costs, but it can be a positive detriment if it is not hooked up with human action."[70]

While many of its academic proponents have argued for the film's concentration on the "mechanisms" of history, the content and narrative direction of Rome's fall, as presented in this film, are rather simple. For all the talk by the opening narrator of a vast scale and subtle exploration of historical causation, the bulk of the story is woven around the tale of a simple contest of leadership between Commodus, and his entirely fictional rival Livius—an archetypal contrast to the villain, and an idealized representation of Roman virtue. The cinematic conventionality of this rivalry is demonstrated in its similarity to the antagonism between Roman and Jew in Ben-Hur.[71] Pointedly in fact, Stephen Boyd—who had played Ben-Hur's rival Messala in that 1959 film—is this time cast as the hero Livius. Rome "destroys itself from within,"[72] with its final and inevitable downfall quickly and rapidly set in motion after the loss of Marcus Aurelius—even if, implicitly, that doom may take centuries to be finally realized. One is reminded, in fact, of Gibbon: "… *the decline of Rome was the natural and inevitable effect of immoderate greatness … the story of the ruin is simple and obvious.*"[73]

This point is driven home in the film's final scene. As Livius honourably refuses the throne of the now hopelessly decadent empire, corrupt senators, greedy for that power, outbid each other with offers of increasingly huge bribes to the soldiers who could help them seize the throne. These closing moments highlight Gibbon's major theme: the inability of the empire's political class—neutered both by authoritarian powers of the emperor and their own corruption—to provide the leadership necessary to preserve Rome's greatness, thereby contributing to the rot at the heart of the decline and fall.

Consequent to all this, it is critical for us to highlight a conspicuous absence from the film, and one that receives little attention from its academic criticism—namely, that the movie, whatever its purported merits, deficiencies, academic or artistic values aside, *does not actually describe the fall of Rome*. By this I mean that, in strict historical and "factual" terms, it does not chart the collapse of the Western Roman Empire over the course of the fifth century AD. It does not narrate the actual end of the empire, which persisted for another 300 years in the West—at least in nominal terms—to 476, and in AD 400 was still nearly at its full geographic extent relative to the time of the death of Marcus Aurelius in AD 192.[74] The film, instead, perfect exemplifies the moral and thematic archetypes of our myth. While it *purports* to be concerned with an "authentic" recreation of history, it actually has very little to do with history at all. Even the events, dates and people it describes have nothing to do with the actual end of the Western Empire, but are connected to it only in the most tenuous fashion, and through a causal leap across almost 300 years.[75]

This brings us to the heart of the film's ideological stance. Rather than actually analyse or narrate the end of the empire as a historical event, *The Fall* elaborates a universally applicable moral and political theory of *decline*: as demonstrated through a very loose historical narrative about the accession of Commodus, for when the empire supposedly, and with little offered evidence, doomed itself to eventual, unavoidable destruction. This hypothesis is deemed to be applicable outside this time frame and to issues of the present day. It is precisely through this logic that the decline and fall acts as a vehicle to paint a view of the present. As Mann himself says,

> The reason for making *The Fall of the Roman Empire* is that it is as modern today as it was in the history that Gibbon wrote: if you read Gibbon, like reading Churchill, it is like seeing the future as well as the past. The future is the thing that interested me in the subject. The past is like a mirror; it reflects what actually happened, and in the reflection of the fall of Rome are the same elements in what is happening today, the very things that are making our empires fall.[76]

Mann acknowledges a debt to the historical record, and suggests objectivity in his essential approach. The efforts of the film supposedly represent a balance between historical fact and an imaginative recreation of the past. When examined in detail, however, his use of history is tenuous and replete with very obvious factual or thematic problems. The director prided himself on his use of historical sources.[77] *The Fall*, for one of its great narrative "twists", draws on the rumour from the *Historia Augusta*, a Late Roman biographical collection, that Commodus was the son of a gladiator, not Marcus Aurelius—providing in the film for a very dramatic revelation scene, near the climax of the action, where Commodus kills his birth father upon this revelation in a moment of mad rage.[78] This fabrication has no real factual basis. Rumours of Aurelius' wife Faustina's adulteries do feature in the *Historia Augusta*, which appears to seek a narrative explanation for why Commodus had a character quite so different from his stoic, austere father.[79] However, more than a century of criticism on, the *Historia* has shown the text to be extremely unreliable at best, and that it often veers into the imaginary and invented. The content of the *Historia* varies from simply inaccurate, to deliberately misleading and fraudulent: it contains some "primary" documents, such as the speeches of senators, but almost all of these are now rejected by historians as fabrications. The true authorship of the work, its date of production, and intended purpose, have long been matters of academic controversy.[80] Modern scholarship is largely dismissive of these stories of Commodus.[81] Nor for that matter is it seen in the more reputable history of Cassius Dio.[82] Gibbon, otherwise a frequent inspiration for Mann, does not see fit to legitimize or even discuss the possibility. The *Historia Augusta* also shows its influence in the depiction of the manner of Marcus Aurelius' death according to Mann, killed by conspirators who wanted to secure the succession of Commodus for their own political interests. The blind advisor Cleander tricks Marcus into eating the poisoned half of an apple, cutting it in full view with a knife that is smeared with poison only on one side; a clever plot device that very closely follows the description in the *Historia Augusta* of Marcus killing Lucius Verus, his former co-emperor, in the same way.[83]

Mann's Commodus still remains very close to the Commodus of the Gibbonian tradition—a self-mythologizing maniac and psychopath who tried to drown every revolt in blood; and who, above all, proved utterly unable to hold on to the reins of the empire.[84] But most of the details narrated to support that image are wholly fictional. The two major events depicted in *The Fall* that catalyse the ruin of the empire—the great Eastern revolt and civil war, and the punitive taxation policy by Commodus that fuelled them—are both fictions.[85] They are possibly inspired by the rebellion of Queen Zenobia of Palmyra in AD 270, who seized the Near East, Egypt and part of Asia Minor, putting her efforts on a scale similar to the rebellion shown in this film. These are the only major precedents, but they had very different causes, and no connection to Commodus' reign and policies.

The man's follies, too, are largely invented. In that respect, they echo the tradition of ancient historiography on the ruler, which often exaggerates his faults to mythic and fantastical proportions,[86] while retaining the same broad depiction of the man as debauched, psychotic, and incompetent. The *Historia Augusta* paints Commodus as a man so consumed by his depravity that he did not hesitate to sign compromising peace treaties with the peoples his father earlier had defeated, in order to devote himself more fully to his dark pleasures: "He abandoned the war which his father had almost finished and submitted to the enemy's terms, and then he returned to Rome."[87]

It is no accident that Mann draws so heavily on the tales and legends of the *Historia Augusta*, despite its dubious and greatly disputed record. *The Fall of the Roman Empire* is the product of fantasy. As with almost every film or imaginative text set in ancient and medieval Rome, it has little to do with known historical realities.[88] Its grand thematic pretentions should not make it immune from these observations. *The Fall* introduces to us an array of fictionary characters, and factually unsubstantiated or implausible details. The decline of the empire is shown primarily in moral terms. *The Fall* puts much greater emphasis on the dramatic and philosophical implications of its story—that of Commodus and his clash with the fictive hero Livius—than on historical authenticity or probability. The narrative is ostensibly about the fall of the Roman Empire and yet the Roman Empire here does not "fall"; it is not split apart, or defeated on the battlefield, its tyrant is removed and its external and internal threats are all dealt with by the end. Yet the closing scene makes it very clear that the fall of Rome, in AD 193, regardless of any future events, has now become inevitable; not for material or military reasons, but due to the *moral* decay—that it has, it is suggested, "destroyed itself from within."

It should be evident that *The Fall of the Roman Empire* is not a work of history in any recognizable scholarly sense, nor a remotely accurate approximation of the events it describes, despite the array of defences that has been offered in this respect. Rather, it combines fact and fiction to create a purportedly accurate feeling of history. *The Fall* interweaves the public—characters from history—with the private—invented characters interacting with historical figures. Mann's film is organized in a form closely resembling a historical novel, in which imaginary characters are mixed in with real ones to allow the author to shape his narrative in a specific way: thus in *The Fall*, Livius provides a binary counterpart to the vice-ridden despot Commodus.

This type of narrative device has its roots in Romantic literature, in particular the novels of Sir Walter Scott.[89] Romantic alienation itself promoted a nostalgic fascination with the Middle Ages, and Scott's influence on historical recreations, in print or on the screen, have played a decisive role—particular in relation to Gibbon's approach to history. Trevelyan in particular noted the thematic links between Scott and Gibbon:

> Gibbon's cold, classical light was replaced by the rich mediaeval hues of Walter Scott's stained glass .... No doubt Scott exaggerated his theme, as all innovators are wont to do. But he did more than any professional historian to make mankind advance towards a true conception of history .... The great antiquarian and novelist showed historians that history must be living, many-coloured and romantic if it is to be a true mirror of the past.[90]

He further argues for the essential value of Gibbon's style in communicating history, for, "If Gibbon had taken as little trouble about writing as later historians, his volumes would have been as little read, and would have perished as quickly as theirs."[91] It is these "artistic" qualities of his history that explain much of his impact and appeal in our wider culture. Trevelyan referred to the "genius" of Gibbon as being his ability "to unite accuracy with art."[92] Bowersock acknowledges this significance by saying: "Gibbon shaped his truth as if it were fiction, preserving thereby the animation of human history and the art of the novelist."[93] As discussed previously, the literary function of historiography is intimately connected with historical films as visual texts. Henryk Sienkiewicz's nineteenth-century novel was the basis for *Quo Vadis*. *Ben-Hur* was heavily based on the nineteenth-century novel. Such a connection with preceding literature and its traditions is highly evident in *The Fall*.[94]

While one can consider Mann's film a piece of imaginative storytelling, and the representation of an earlier literary myth of decline, rather than history of a purer standard, this does not mean that the inferences from the historical record are entirely inaccurate, or irrelevant to the content. Sometimes a more scrupulous accuracy *does* appear to have actually been the goal—where, at least, this interpretation better coheres to the presented conception of decline. In this respect, notable in *The Fall* is the desire to create an entirely *secular* account of the decline of Rome. Christianity—in an era when most ancient epics such as *Quo Vadis*, *The*

*Robe* and *Ben Hur*, possessed profoundly religious themes is instead conspicuous by its absence.⁹⁵

This also involves a departure from the line of its most important literary source, Gibbon. Derek Elley attempts to justify this by saying that "the film-makers found a suitable soulmate: Gibbon also placed little importance on Christianity, preferring a broader view of the reasons for the collapse of the Empire, and he too was apt to let strict chronology fall victim to his overall plan."⁹⁶ But Gibbon ascribed a very considerable amount of blame to the faith, and he and Mann have little in common in this regard. Furthermore, that "strict chronology" of a fall is *exactly* what Mann depicts in this film. The doom of Rome is written by the closing credits—the empire "destroyed itself from within." Furthermore, Gibbon never actually describes the decline and fall as being brought about by the reign of Commodus, and the developments in that period—only that it signalled an end to the fabled "Age of the Antonines," and the beginning of a long, but not permanent period of strife. No deeper inference is present on the period; whereas the whole of Chapter 15 of the *Decline and Fall* is devoted to the impact of religious superstition on undermining the mental and moral foundations of Roman rule.

Christianity, and religion in general, is almost entirely exorcized from Mann's film. Marcus mentions the Christians only once, as he meditates on death, where he expresses a mild aversion to their theatricality.⁹⁷ The only other exception to their absence is a visual allusion in the *chi-rho* pendant worn by the Greek philosopher Timonides.⁹⁸ Faith is much more prominent in *The Fall*'s unofficial remake, *Gladiator*—though even that film keeps its presence relatively subtle, in comparison to the Christian Roman epics of the 1940s and 1950s. Christianity even plays a much greater role in the novelization of *The Fall* than the film, with meditations by Marcus Aurelius and Timonides on Christian doctrine.⁹⁹ In his novel *Marius the Epicurean* (1882)—a literary source of inspiration for the film—Walter Pater repeatedly reminded his readers of the spread of Christianity under the Antonines, especially during Marcus' reign.¹⁰⁰ This represents the second strand of Christianity noted in this study, in reference to representations of Rome and her fall—one is the triumphalist ideology (as present in *Quo Vadis*, *Ben-Hur*, *The Sign of the Pagan*, and their associated literature) of eventual Christian supremacy; the other, typically secular narrative directly associates it with the decline of the empire, and owes much to Gibbon and the humanist tradition.

But here the script presents the decline in purely Roman terms: not as the conflict between paganism and Christianity which Hollywood producers almost exclusively commissioned at the time.[101] Mann criticized those films that "gave the impression that the Christian movement was the only thing the Roman Empire was about," claiming instead that it was a "minor incident" in the history of Rome, and that he and his writers "wanted to tell the Roman story and not the Christian story." The other, implicit purpose in this approach is that the inherently more positive and prominent presence of Christianity in the contemporary American epic would not accord with the director's central theme; it is a film about decline and fall, *not* resurrection or rebirth. Contradicting himself a little, Mann concedes that Christianity *is* important in the later empire, primarily in preserving the ongoing legacy of Rome; for in his words Durant, doing something "Gibbon couldn't do," treated Christianity as "the resurrection of the Roman empire, because out of it came the Papacy and Rome today is as alive as it was in those days.".[102]

In this respect, Mann does attempt to reinterpret one aspect of the historiography that otherwise deeply informs and defines the film. Gibbon was intensely critical of the role of Christianity in undermining the virtues and character of Ancient Rome, and catalysing her eventual downfall, a factor he cited at length. By contrast, William Durant was less savage in his criticism of the faith, but, echoing Oswald Spengler, saw the decline of a civilization as a culmination of tension and strife between secular and spiritual intellectualism—the apex of the cycle of decline and fall.[103] The triumph of such spirituality catalysed the downward motion of the cycle, and the slide into unreason and chaos. Finally, out of these ashes, civilization can be "born anew." The process is described in these terms:

> ... a certain tension between religion and society marks the higher stages of every civilization ... The intellectual classes abandon the ancient theology and—after some hesitation—the moral code allied with it; literature and philosophy become anticlerical .... In the end a society and its religion tend to fall together, like body and soul, in a harmonious death. Meanwhile among the oppressed another myth arises, gives new form to human hope, new courage to human effort, and after centuries of chaos builds another civilization.[104]

On the theme of Christianity, it should be noted that Mann rejects the depiction of conflict, so common in the epic films of this era, between

Rome the imperial oppressor, and a Christianity that represents moral values and liberty. For this the film has drawn considerable academic praise, as a more authentic and accurate interpretation of events.[105] Strictly speaking, this *is* a more "accurate" approach to the period, in that one very specific sense, and it adds to the veneer of historical authority around the project. Thematically, however, the effect of this revisionist approach to Christianity in the decline, and the moral evaluation of its causes, is barely altered at all. Mann's film maintains a *religiously* moral outlook, just as earlier versions of this myth do. Its tone and content may be avowedly a-theological, but such an undertone makes it an easy step for Ridley Scott's *Gladiator* to introduce a more overtly spiritual subtext.

## THE FALL AND CONTEMPORARY DISCOURSES OF EMPIRE

It should be no surprise that, crafted in the context of American epic cinema, *The Fall of the Roman Empire* has a great deal to say about the world of 1964: whether in an overt and deliberate fashion, or buried in its latent insinuations. Mann's own approach to this question reflects a desire to situate the events of the second century AD in a modern context, particularly in light of the Cold War. Despite its stated intention to accurately and meaningfully depict the essence of the downfall of Rome, it is an *American* film, made with modern US themes and concerns in mind. *The Fall* focuses on themes of peaceful coexistence, and the social and political integration of new, initially hostile, ethnic groups into the empire's boundaries. This message is embodied in his use of particular narrative tools. Typically the theme is stated right at the outset in a montage, or a speech, or some images which let us know that what we are about to witness are great public issues at stake. In an early scene, Marcus Aurelius states to his general Livius, his chosen successor and the protagonist of the film, "It is time we found a peaceful way to live with those you call barbarians." In his speech to the assembled leaders of the senate, the emperor declares, "You do not resemble each other .... Yet ... you are the unity which is Rome. Wherever you live, whatever the colour of your skin, when peace is achieved, it will be to all ... the supreme rights of Roman citizenship... No longer provinces, or colonies, but ... a family of equal nations."[106] The parallels are crafted to give them as much contemporary as historical relevance. The speech of an elderly senator supporting the proposal to grant citizenship to barbarians closely echoes that which the Roman historian Tacitus put in the mouth of Claudius before the assembled Senate, where he used the example of Sparta and Athens being ruined because they did not incorporate the conquered into the body politic.[107] Arguments in modern US debates about and against large-scale immigration—a running issue in US society and social and political debate throughout the twentieth century—can echo that voiced here by Commodus and his allies.

The past/present thematic interweaving of *The Fall* recalls the historical parallels between the classical past and US present set up by the religious epics of the 1950s. *Ben-Hur* (1959), *Quo Vadis* (1951) and *The Robe* (1953) had frequently been interpreted by the press as providers of moral and political lessons of the Cold War—both the threat posed to American and Western "freedoms", and the likely positive outcome of the struggle of ideologies itself. The contemporary cultural and political resonance of *The Fall*, though particularly buried and implicit for a historical epic of the time, was picked up immediately by critics and the media upon the film's release. The *Motion Picture Herald* plucked from this a message of the film that the Roman Empire fell because it lacked an essential feature of modern peace and stability: a United Nations.[108] "Progressives" of the 1960s appeared anxious to prevent the dangerous posturing of rival superpowers from escalating into a nuclear holocaust and the worldwide collapse of civilization.[109] Anthony Mann and Samuel Bronston (as producer) had recently made films on similar themes, as peoples and nations that had been rivals united to create a peaceful and prosperous world order: Mann and Bronston with *El Cid* (1961) and Bronston with director Nicholas Ray on *55 Days at Peking* (1963). Presenting the audience with the flipside of this logic, at the very end of *The Fall*, the narrator intones Durant to tell us that *civilizations*, not empires, have to first destroy themselves from within before they can be taken down from the outside. Consequently, a less "liberal" and positive reading of the film's use of historical analogies than that found in the *Herald* would see the film not as an account of the inevitable victory of the USA, but a warning of the impending possibility of its decline and fall; not just as an international power, but in the very fabric of its culture and values.

Paradoxically, the commercial machine overlooked and sidelined the film's aspirations, and the attempted radical reinterpretation of the epic; instead representing it as a flawed blockbuster, a failed attempt to follow in the great tradition of Cecil B. DeMille and his successors. Notably, contemporary critics offered it unflattering regard, treating it as a muddled, inferior, but otherwise typical example of an overdone genre: the *New York Herald Tribune*, in particular, described the film as "all pomp and poppycock."[110] Numerous reviewers saw the film as a dilution and misappropriation of Gibbon's work, an accusation that prompted the director to defensively reply:

> Now I guarantee you there is not one person that had read Gibbon .... From Bosley Crowther on down or up. And for them to start to say: "This isn't Gibbon"—well, this is a lot of crap! Because all we were trying to do was dramatize how an empire fell. Incest, buying an army, destroying the will of the people to speak through the Senate, all these things ... were in the film ... it had more truth than untruth.[111]

The reference to the components of this overall "truth": "incest, buying an army, destroying the will of the people," fits the frame for both the shape of this myth as a whole, and Mann's portrayal of history through it. "Truth" is suggested here to lie not so much in the wholly accurate depiction of events, or even an appropriate timeline (as events here are set 300 years before the "fall" of Rome in any historic sense), but in distilling the essential and meaningful qualities of a story for the audience. Past events have been mined for a dramatic moral tale, which is justified as good history on the grounds of this loose interpretation of the notion of truth.

In light of its poor critical reception, *The Fall of the Roman Empire* was overlooked during the Academy awards, save for a sole nomination for Best Score by Dimitri Tiomkin. Yet the film had its defenders: the critic for the *Daily Express* in Britain called it "an epic to make one cheer rather than cringe" and the *Evening Standard* declared it "one of the best all-round epics I have ever seen."[112] After its critical and commercial failure, the film quickly became synonymous, ironically, with the decline of Hollywood's long empire of Roman epics,[113] though the causes of this trend are complicated, involving spiralling production costs, and a generational trend shift in consumer tastes—both of which challenged the studio system in general—amongst other reasons. As Elley says, "It is a convenient, though nonetheless true, fact that *The Fall of the Roman Empire* is synonymous with the Fall of the Historical Epic."[114] International epic filmmaking, however, continued, in varying forms.[115] The revival of antiquity in epic cinema, however, did not come till the turn of the twenty-first century, in a cultural and political climate that renewed its relevance.

## NOTES

1. A general observation on this note is made by Starn, p. 12: "The exposure of decline carries the conviction of probing in depth and truth. This may explain in part why observers of historical decline have appeared so often in mantles of prophecy or of science ... prophets and scientists are equipped to seek out design and underlying meanings in history; and both are ready to expose deviation from some proper norm. It does not follow that this stance is "anti-historical," at least in its effects. Opting out of easy acceptance of actuality may force critiques of experience which move from myth toward historiography." Of course, the use of the word "myth" here is different to mine—denoting falsehood—but the overall suggestion is that decline appeals to those authors concerned with uncovering "deeper" meaning, and universal patterns and laws.
2. Rehm, p. vii, cited in Edwards, p. 2.
3. Oswald Spengler, *The Decline of the West*, trans. C.F. Atkinson (New York: Oxford University Press, (ori. Pub. 1932), 1991), p. 21.
4. Op. cit., p. 18 and p. 24.
5. Op. cit., p. 360.
6. Op. cit., p. 22.
7. Op. cit., p. 28, p. 106. A fuller and more detailed account of this process is described as such, glancing at a range of "decaying civilizations" before settling on Rome: "... the Culture suddenly hardens, it mortifies, its blood congeals, its force breaks down, and it becomes Civilization, the thing which we feel and understand in the words Egypticism, Byzantinism, Mandarinism. As such they may, like worn-out giants of the primeval forest, thrust their decaying branches towards the sky for hundreds or thousands of years, as we see in China, in India, in the Islamic world .... The dwindling powers rise to one more, half-successful, effort of creation, and produce the Classicism that is common to all dying Cultures. The soul thinks once again, and in Romanticism looks back piteously to its childhood; then finally, weary, reluctant, cold, it loses its desire to be, and, as in Imperial Rome." Op. cit., I, pp. 106–7.
8. Op. cit., p. 359.
9. Theodor W. Adorno, "Spengler Today," *Studies in Philosophy and Social Sciences*, IX (1941), pp. 305–325, as quoted in Theodor W. Adorno, *Prisms: Studies in Contemporary German thought*, trans. Shierry W. Nicholsen (Massachusetts: MIT Press (ori. Pub. 1967), 1983), p. 71.
10. Op. cit., p. 72.
11. Northrop Frye, "The Decline of the West by Oswald Spengler," *Daedalus*, CIII (1974), p. 7.
12. Spengler, p. 26.

13. Op. cit., p. 28.
14. Hegel broke down the history of any given civilization into four phases: birth and original growth, maturity, old age, and dissolution and death. In the example of Rome, this is seen as: its foundation to the second Punic War, to the Principate of Caesar, to conversion to Christianity, then from the third century to the fall of Byzantium. See White (1973), p. 123, for more on this theory.
15. Theodor Adorno published an essay entitled "Spengler after the Decline" in 1950, in which he praises many of his ideas around decline in relationship to contemporary events, such as the Second World War, and argues for a more progressive interpretation of these "reactionary" concepts. See Adorno, "Spengler after the Decline," in *Prisms* (1983), pp. 51–72.
16. The quote is from Durant, p. 665. The statement is then echoed in Anthony Mann's *The Fall of the Roman Empire*, as its closing line, and in Mann, p. 337, where the filmmaker states that, "Our theme, which is essentially that of Durant's book, is that no civilization can be destroyed from without, but it destroys itself from within."
17. Leach, p. 17.
18. Theodore Ziolkowski, *Virgil and the Moderns* (Princeton: Princeton University Press, 1993), pp. 6–26.
19. Arnold J. Toynbee, *Lectures on the Industrial Revolution in England* (London: Rivingtons, 1884), p. 84.
20. Arnold J. Toynbee, *A Study of History* (New York: Oxford University Press (ori. Pub. 1946), 1973), I, p. 578.
21. As cited in Hans Baron, *The Crisis of the Early Italian Renaissance* (New Jersey: Princeton University Press (ori. Pub. 1960), 1993), p. 58.
22. To whom he ascribed the label "philistines": Matthew Arnold, *Selected Prose* (London: Penguin Classics, 1971), p. 211.
23. Op. cit., p. 121. This account of civilized and barbarian culture is further informed by the example of the fall of Rome. In his *Study of History*, Toynbee discusses the fact—surprising, to him—that none of the northern epics describe the greatest warlike achievement of their peoples, the overthrow of the Roman Empire. His explanation is that the barbarians found the Romans too complex to write about. Toynbee also hints that the very process of conquering the empire tended to abolish the urge towards epic literature—it was a success that made them richer and more staid, rather than a heroic defeat against fearful odds that hardened their will. Gilbert Highet adds to it by saying it was too vast, complicated, and took too long to conquer for it to work as a heroic epic told by tribal poets. Highet, p. 27.
24. Jerome H. Buckley, *The Triumph of Time: A Study of Victorian Concepts of Time, History, Progress, and Decadence* (Cambridge: Harvard University Press, 1967), pp. 71–72.

25. It can also be considered as the myth of "The Eternal Return," as espoused by Nietzsche and Heidegger. See Martin Heidegger, *Nietzsche, Volume II: The Eternal Recurrence of the Same*, trans. David F. Krell (New York: Harper and Row (ori. Pub. 1954), 1984), p. 25.
26. Dawson, pp. 326–353, quote at pp. 349–350.
27. Francis Neilson, "The Decline of Civilizations," *American Journal of Economics and Sociology*, IV (1945), pp. 479–497.
28. Milton Shulman, *The Ravenous Eye: the impact of the fifth factor* (London: Collins, 1973), p. 54.
29. John G. Dunne, "A Riot on TV," *New Republic* (11th September, 1965), p. 27.
30. Anthony Quinton, "Clash of Symbols," *Times Higher Education Supplement* (30th April, 1993), pp. 15–16, as quoted in Howells (1994), p. 6.
31. David M. White and Bernard Rosenberg (eds), *Mass Culture Revisited* (New York: Van Nostrand Reinhold, 1971), pp. 13–14.
32. Leach, p. 17.
33. Highet, p. 11.
34. The poet, diplomatic, and literary figure of the late fifth century: see Jill Harries, *Sidonius Apollinaris and the Fall of Rome, AD 407–485* (Oxford: Clarendon Press, 1995).
35. Highet, pp. 471–2. For a similarly enthusiastic comparison of past and present, see Peter P. Witonski (ed.), *Gibbon for Moderns: The History of the Decline and Fall of the Roman Empire with Lessons for America Today* (New Rochelle: Arlington House, 1974).
36. Highet, p. 3.
37. Op. cit., p. 438.
38. Op. cit., p. 46.
39. Cecil B. DeMille, *The Ten Commandments* (Paramount Pictures, 1956). See also Elley (1984), pp. 115–35.
40. Gore Vidal, *Point to Point Navigation: A Memoir, 1964–2006* (London: Little Brown, 2006), p. 123, as quoted in Winkler (2009), pp. 45–46. Americans are generally wary of calling their country an empire, whatever the apparent realities: Niall Ferguson, *Colossus: The Rise and Fall of the American Empire* (New York: Penguin, 2004), speaks at length of an "empire in denial." Several books published or republished since 2001 on contemporary US politics and history discuss the idea of "imperial presidency." See for instance Schlesinger.
41. *Sign of the Pagan* (Universal Pictures, 1954). Whether this film is a "classical" or "medieval" epic is somewhat disputed. Bettina Bildhaeur, *Filming the Middle Ages* (London: Reaktion Books, 2011), p. 105 treats it as a medieval representational work, and cites The Fordham Internet

Sourcebook, a major online medieval source, which includes it as a medieval film, for which see www.fordham.edu/halsall/medfilms.html
42. Halliday (1997), p. 11. Halliday makes clear that Sirk's autobiographical statements cannot always be trusted. However, what is more important here is Sirk's conscious awareness of medieval art, art theory and Panofsky.
43. John 16.5
44. Neo-Platonism and Judaism are especially noted for their harmful impact on the more secular, "Enlightened" values of the earlier empire. See Gibbon (1993), I, pp. 433–4, p. 491, p. 494.
45. White (1973), p. x.
46. Elley (1984), pp. 105–109, quotes at p. 109 and p. 105 respectively.
47. Solomon, pp. 83–92. Martin Scorsese also praised the movie, but this is purely on its artistic merits—as a "lost art" in its sense of "space and drama." Martin Scorsese and Michael H. Wilson, *A Personal Journey with Martin Scorsese Through American Movies* (New York: Miramax Books/Hyperion, 1997), p. 90.
48. Martin M. Winkler, "Gibbon", in Winkler (2009), p. 175.
49. Op. cit., p. 167.
50. Op. cit., p. 175, the Vatican Latin here translating as "an apology for film historiography."
51. Eleonara Cavallini, "Was Commodus really that bad?" in Winkler (2009), p. 102.
52. Op. cit., p. 115.
53. Allen M. Ward, "History, Ancient and Modern", in Winkler (2009), pp. 51–88.
54. Anthony Mann, "Empire Demolition," in Richard Koszarski (ed.), *Hollywood Directors 1941–76* (New York: Oxford University Press, 1977), pp. 332–8. The essay was originally printed in *Films and Filming*, X (1964), pp. 7–8. I have used its reprint in the 1977 compendium *Hollywood Directors 1941–76*. Additional essays and commentaries by the director can be found in, "Now You See It: Landscape and Anthony Mann," an interview with J.H. Fenwick and Jonathan Green-Armytage, *Sight and Sound*, XXXIV (1965), pp. 186–9, Christopher Wicking and Barrie Patterson, "Interview with Anthony Mann," *Screen*, X (1969), pp. 32–54, and in an interview published in Jean-Claude Missiaen, "A Lesson in Cinema," *Cahiers du Cinéma in English*, XII (1967), pp. 44–51.
55. Wicking and Patterson (1969), pp. 32–54.
56. The statement is adapted from a passage of William Durant, *The Story of Civilization: Caesar and Christ: A History of Roman Civilization and of Christianity from Their Beginnings to AD 325* (New York: Simon and Schuster (ori. Pub. 1944), 1980), p. 665. This statement is repeated in "Empire Demolition," where Mann states that "Our theme, which is

essentially that of Durant's book, is that no civilisation can be destroyed from without, but it destroys itself from within." Mann, p. 334.

57. In this respect he differs a little from Gibbon, who points to a weakness in the long period of peace and prosperity under the Antonines. "The long peace, and the uniform government of the Romans, introduced a slow and secret poison into the vitals of the empire," Gibbon (1993), I, p. 65. However, both Gibbon and Mann attach a great deal of significance to the reign of Commodus as initiating the more overt and directly destructive phase of Roman decline.

58. Curtis, pp. 88–89.

59. As quoted in William Durant and Ariel Durant, *A Dual Autobiography* (New York: Simon and Schuster, 1977), p. 355. From a telegram sent to Durant from Samuel Bronstein's production company, October 1962, which states that "Mr Mann, a disciple of yours, voiced a sincere desire to have you associated with [the] film."

60. William and Ariel Durant (1977), pp. 355–6.

61. Op. cit., p. 356. He notes that he was finally convinced because Mann promised in person that "everything would be done ... to bridge the gap between ... script and historic fact," though the screenwriter "had been commissioned not to write history but to fashion a play capable of holding, through three hours, the attention of millions of auditors."

62. Wicking and Pattison, p. 54.

63. In "Action Speaks Louder than Words: The Films of Anthony Mann," a 1967 BBC interview now available in excerpts on the DVD of Anthony Mann's *The Furies* (Paramount Pictures, 1950), the director names German director F.W. Murnau as one of his influences. On the stylistic affinities of Mann's film noir to his early Westerns see Jeanne Basinger, *Anthony Mann* (Middletown: Wesleyan University Press, 2007), pp. 71–79.

64. Eleonara Cavallini, "Was Commodus Really that Bad?" in Winkler (2009), p. 103. See also Andrew Sarris, *The American Cinema, Director and Directions 1929–68* (New York: Dutton, 1968), pp. 98–99, for the film's positive reception as an artistic example of auteur theory in Hollywood.

65. As discussed in relation to *Quo Vadis, Ben-Hur* and *Sign of the Pagan* in this book.

66. Durant, p. 665.

67. Gibbon (1993), IV, pp. 117–127, quote on p. 117.

68. *The Fall* received notable artistic praise from contemporaries: Andrew Sarris, a founding figure in Hollywood auteur theory, highlighted Mann's efforts, along with Douglas Sirk's, for their creative worth amongst the Hollywood mainstream. See Sarris (1968), pp. 98–99.

69. Strongly implicit in this passage from "Empire Demolition": "I found on *El Cid* that Spain is great for locations because there are so many different kinds of country. It is ideal for making a spectacle film. But one must be careful not to let the concept of the spectacular run away with you. In *Fall of the Roman Empire* I have concentrated in the first part on establishing the characters in simple, human terms .... Then the spectacle is done entirely differently to what you would expect ...." Furthermore, Mann states that "I did not want to make another Quo Vadis ... or Spartacus," Mann, p. 333, p. 335.
70. Koszarski, p. 165.
71. One of the earliest sequences, a chariot race between Livius and Commodus (a representation of their rivalry and struggle later in the film), is also an obvious reference to the iconic sequence from *Ben-Hur*.
72. From the closing line of the film.
73. Gibbon (1993), IV, p. 119.
74. The only territorial withdrawal had been from the province of Dacia (in the East) and a bridgehead across the Rhine.
75. Commodus dies in AD 192. The "official", entirely nominal, and retrospective date of the "Fall of the West" is usually given with the deposition of Romulus Augustulus in AD 476 . See Roger Collins, *Early Medieval Europe, 300–1000 AD* (London: Macmillan, 1991), pp. 96–97.
76. Mann, p. 332.
77. Op. cit., p. 332, p. 334.
78. This is a very deliberate intellectual contortion on the part of *The Fall of the Roman Empire* and *Gladiator*; they gloss over the fact that Aurelius, otherwise revered in the productions as an excellent emperor, appears to have willingly chosen Commodus to succeed him.
79. *Historia Augusta*, 19.1–9, see also 23.7, 26.5, and 29.1–3 for rumours of Faustina's adulteries.
80. For this see Ronald Syme, *Emperors and Biography* (Oxford: Oxford University Press, 1971), together with Arnaldo Momigliano, "Review: Ammianus and the Historia Augusta by Ronald Syme," *The English Historical Review*, XXIII (1969), pp. 566–569, and more recently Alan Cameron, *The Last Pagans of Rome* (Oxford: Oxford University Press, 2011), pp. 231–272, on controversies of its authorship and dating.
81. For these kinds of discussions see Ronald Syme, *Emperors and Biography* (Oxford: Oxford University Press, 1971), and Arnaldo Momigliano, "Review: Emperors and Biography. Studies in the Historia Augusta by Ronald Syme," *The English Historical Review*, LXXXVIII (1973), pp. 114–115, and Alan Cameron, *The Last Pagans of Rome* (Oxford: Oxford University Press, 2011) for the most up-to-date outlook. It should be noted that despite the untrustworthiness of the source, it is still

extremely "useful" to historians on a thinly documented period, though its account cannot be taken at anything like face value.
82. See on this Fergus Millar, *Study of Cassius Dio* (Oxford: Oxford University Press, 1964).
83. *HA Marcus Aurelius*, 15.5. Something loosely similar appears in the generally more reliable Cassius Dio, who repeats a story told to him that a group of men who wanted to do Commodus a favour poisoned Aurelius. It is, however, cited as a story, rather than fact. See *Dio*, 71-72.33.4.
84. For Gibbon's depiction see Gibbon (1993), I, pp. 95-116, under the heading "The Cruelty, Follies, and murder of Commodus."
85. On this see Richard Stoneman, *Palmyra and Its Empire: Zenobia's Revolt against Rome* (Ann Arbor: University of Michigan Press, 1992), pp. 155-180, and Alaric Watson, *Aurelian and the Third Century* (London: Taylor & Francis, 2004), pp. 52-53.
86. For example, the account of his birth in the Augustan history—"Faustina, when pregnant with Commodus and his brother, dreamed that she gave birth to serpents, one of which, however, was fiercer than the other. But after she had given birth to Commodus and Antoninus, the latter, for whom the astrologers had cast a horoscope as favourable as that of Commodus, lived to be only four years old." *HA Commodus*, 1.3-4.
87. *HA Commodus*, 3.5.
88. Other such factual inaccuracies abound. Types of military forces are very inaccurately represented—too much prominence given to cavalry, at the time when the Roman army was overwhelmingly an infantry force. However, only the ones of direct relevance to the argument laid out here are worth discussing in detail.
89. James Chandler, "Scott, Griffith, and Film Epic Today," in Gene W. Ruoff (ed.), *The Romantics and Us: Essays on Literature and Culture* (New Brunswick: Rutgers University Press, 1990), pp. 237-273.
90. Trevelyan, pp. 165-6.
91. Op. cit., p. 166.
92. Op. cit., p. 164.
93. Bowersock (1988), p. 10.
94. Lew Wallace, *Ben-Hur: A Tale of the Christ* (Oxford: Oxford World's Classics, 1998). See also Allan Powell, *Jesus as a Figure in History: How Modern Historians View the Man from Galilee* (Westminster: John Knox Press, 1999) pp. 25-26 on its parallels with, and appropriation of, the story of Christ.
95. At the end of *Ben-Hur*, the film's Jesus, dying on the cross, washes away the sins of the world, restoring Ben-Hur to his mother, sister, and sweetheart; curing them of leprosy, and Ben-Hur of his anger.
96. Elley (1984), p. 105, see also pp. 108-9.

97. Historians have noted that persecutions of Christians occurred throughout Aurelius' reign. But to most of the Christian writers of modern times Marcus has been perceived as a soul born to be a Christian. So he appeared to Ernest Renan in the last volume of his vast compendium history of Christianity. See Ernest Renan, *The History of the Origins of Christianity VII: Marcus Aurelius* (London: Mathieson, 1890).
98. Also worth noting is that there is only one single mention of Christianity in the *Meditations*: a disparaging remark about their stubbornness. See Marcus Aurelius, *The Meditations*, trans. A.S.L Farquharso (Everyman: New York, 1992), p. xi.
99. Harry Whittington, *The Fall of the Roman Empire* (New York: Gold Medal Books, 1964) being the novelization. Marcus Aurelius meditates on Christianity and Jesus, p. 31, and Timonides also discusses Christian doctrine, pp. 97–103.
100. Michael Levey, a biographer of Pater, writes as a foreword to this version: "Pater is able to depict an early, pure Christianity, not yet sectarian, authoritarian, or established, which offers Marius a vision which is ideal because untarnished." Walter Pater, *Marius the Epicurean*, ed. Michael Levey (London: Harmondsworth, 1985), p. 17. See also p. 12 for a commentary on his perceived "aesthetic" vision of Christianity.
101. Mann is quite conscious of this distinction and precedent: "I did not want to make another *Quo Vadis*? ... another *Spartacus*, or any of the others because these stories were the stories of the Christ," Mann, p. 332.
102. Op. cit., p. 333.
103. The theme of *Caesar and Christ* is that these two great men defined their age; Caesar the Roman Empire, and Christ the cultural and spiritual "resurrection" of Rome in the form of the Papacy, and the later history of the city. This of course reflects the notion of the *translatio imperii*.
104. Durant, p. 71, describing this cycle.
105. Elley (1984), p. 105, Solomon, pp. 83–85, and Allen M. Ward, "History, Ancient and Modern," in Winkler (2009), pp. 59–60.
106. It is worth noting how much political liberals of the 1960s were anxious to prevent the Cold War rivalry between the USA and the Soviet Union from leading to a nuclear holocaust, especially after the Cuban Missile Crisis. For more on this see Richard Slotkin, *Gunfighter Nation: The Myth of the Frontier in Twentieth-Century America* (Norman: University of Oklahoma Press, 1998), pp. 504–512.
107. Tacitus, *Annals*, 11. 24. For more on the evolution of these conceptions of liberty, see John G. Pocock, *Barbarism and Religion: The First Decline and Fall* (Cambridge: Cambridge University Press, 2003), the most extensive study of Chapters I–XIV of Gibbon's first volume, for an account of its thematic predecessors. See in particular Part III, *The*

humanist construction of *Decline and Fall*, pp. 153–178, subtitled "from translation to declination."

108. *Motion Picture Herald* (1st April, 1964). The comparison may appear at face value to be absurd, but there is a certain narrative logic to it—the UN, as an institution, has been centered on US support from 1945, a crucial difference to the failed League of Nations, and was headquartered in New York, so the institution could easily be equated with more progressive aspects of the international stance of the US.
109. It should be noted that two of the three screenwriters. were politically "transgressive" writers. Barzman was the blacklisted author of several Joseph Losey thrillers, while Yordan had frequently served as a front for other blacklisted authors. See Norma Barzman, *The Red and the Blacklist: The Intimate Memoir of a Hollywood Expatriate* (New York: Thunder's Mouth Press/Nation Books, 2003).
110. The *New York Herald Tribune* (27th March, 1964). See also *The Hollywood Reporter* (23rd March, 1964), and *Motion Picture Herald* (1st April, 1964).
111. Wicking and Pattison, pp. 53–54.
112. The *Daily Express* (1st June, 1964), and the *Evening Standard* (8th June, 1964).
113. Says Derek Elley, "The Fall of the Roman Empire," *Films and Filming*, XXII (1976), p. 18, "It is a convenient, though nonetheless true, fact that *The Fall of the Roman Empire* is synonymous with the Fall of the Historical Epic." Martin Winkler makes the defence that "failure of the film at the box office is, however, not a sign of its artistic failure," in Winkler (2009), p. 21. This is a reasonable observation, though the critical (at the time) and commercial failure of the movie means it failed to communicate its intended message to its audience. He also warned rather presciently that "a story of loss and defeat that stands apart from more common stories either of victory over evil empires and tyrants or of moral or spiritual vindication cannot have been appealing to the masses."
114. Elley (1976), p. 18.
115. For studies on the decline of epic films see Maria Wyke, *Projecting the Past: Ancient Rome, Cinema and History* (London: Routledge, 1997), pp. 183–192, Allen Barra, "The Incredible Shrinking Epic," *American Film*, XIV (1989), pp. 40–43, p. 45, and Vivian Sobchack, "Surge and Splendor: A Phenomenology of the Hollywood Historical Epic," *Representations*, XXIX (1990), pp. 24–49.

CHAPTER 5

# Decadence, Imperialism, and Decline from the Late Twentieth Century

## MASS CULTURE AND ITS CRITICS

The later industrialized world finds an especially appropriate significance in the decline and fall; configuring barbarism with the dehumanization of the mechanized and mass-produced world. Writing in *The Promise of the Coming Dark Age* (1976), Leften Stavrianos says that "the circumstances of the fall of Rome ... are very relevant to the present world."[1] For critics of "late industrial capitalism," the abundance of material production presupposed and required divisions of labour which intensified the divisions of societies and men against themselves. In the decadence of capitalism, as in the "slow poison" of Gibbon's seemingly peaceful and productive second century AD, the fruits of human accomplishment ironically diminished their creators.[2]

For some authors, this phase of industrial society represents the very end of the processes of decline that precede the fall. Robert Sinai, in *The Decadence of the Modern World* (1978), describes how, Almost identically, John Lukacs in *The Passing of the Modern Age* (1970) refers earlier to how, "We live now amidst the ruins of a civilization: but most of these ruins are in our minds." Sinai discusses the decline and fall of the ancient world only indirectly in his account of the problems of modern society. He pays most attention to "mass culture" and "mass civilizations" as the principal causes of the disaster and terminal decay he predicts in the imminent future of the world. The reason for him, as suggested by cultural theorist Marshall McLuhan, is that "the old verbal culture is in decline and there is everywhere a general retreat from the word."[3] Sinai, in a 1979 edition of literary magazine *Encounter*, suggests that visual mass media have followed mass literacy in sabotaging the high cultural elements of a civilization, developed and nurtured only through the leadership of creative elites. The consequence of this is that, "The high culture based on privilege and hierarchical order and sustained by great works of the past" has disappeared; bombarded and disoriented by "a central failure in the arts and in the graces of personal and social behaviour ... modern man is suffused with fears of a new 'Dark Age' in which civilization itself as we know it may disappear ...."[4]

Such a decline can have a significant cultural component to its critique, and a natural target in mass cultural output. In *The Culture of Narcissism* (1979), Christopher Lasch quotes a surfboard enthusiast on the impact of the TV networks on his pursuit, "Television is destroying our sport. The TV producers are turning a sport and an art form into a circus." One word here, *circus*, is enough to invoke the analogy of the corrupting processes of Ancient Rome.[5] The British author and journalist Malcolm Muggerridge, concerned with the indoctrinating power of mass media, quotes Gibbon in conservative magazine *The American Spectator*, namely the words "it was artfully contrived by Augustus Caesar that in the enjoyment of plenty, the Romans should lose their memory of freedom," and draws from it the observation that "in the case of the American dream .... [It is as if] Augustus Caesar read the media and the advertisers who support them."[6] On more exclusively cultural grounds, Bernard James in *The Death of Progress* (1973), citing Toynbee's distinction between external and internal barbarians, writes that:

> Where the external barbarian pounds at the gates of civilization with battering ram and war club, the internal barbarian insinuates values and habits that degrade civilized life from within. I interpret much of the so-called counter-culture we witness about us today as evidence of such internal barbarism. It takes the form of vandals scratching obscene graffiti on the walls of a synagogue or a courthouse; it is a mass of middle-class youth ... knee deep in the rubbish of spent affluence; it is a faddish imitation of primitive dress and body paint.[7]

For James, modern mass culture has produced a decline in society, standards, culture and manners, all of which produces a "decay in meaning."

The analogy with the undoing of Ancient Rome, implicit above, becomes obvious when he describes the significance of this newer type of barbarian, who, in that they "betray gross and alien values," are "evidence that something has gone out of modern Western civilization, that something is insinuating itself through every breach in Western ideals." Their apparent newness betrays a familiar archetype: "They bring to mind images of goatskin-clad Visigoths stumbling among the ruins of ancient Rome, draping themselves with loot, grinning as they urinate at the base of empty temples in the Forum. These symbols of Classical ideals had no meaning to such men."[8]

Contained within this criticism of "faddish" practices is a cherishing of the past—or rather an idealized vision of a distant one—at the expense of the present. Such a view is not confined to conservative authorship. It is mirrored in Daniel Bell's Marxian-inflected *The Cultural Contradictions of Capitalism* (1976), which attempts to identify "the historic cultural crisis of all Western bourgeoisie society." Aside from the familial criticism of hedonism, consumerism and industry, Bell searches for a positive and energizing force by which society may be revived, and accomplishes his goal through a parable of the fall of Rome, and the parallel rise of Christianity. The crisis Bell predicts is similar to those of the past in that it can only truly be resolved "over long historical time-frames." This is because, "It took almost 300 years for Christianity to become established in the Roman Empire, and as Gibbon remarked of the conversion of Constantine, Rome then passed into an intolerable phase of its history, a phase that lasted for 250 years."[9]

It is through the apparent wisdom of this precedent, therefore, that Bell seeks to reverse the perceived decline and fall of the modern world; through, he believes, a "great instauration," or revival of the sacred. What Bell is looking for is some analogue to the rise of Christianity—a "religious answer" to the "shambles of modern culture," elsewhere described by him as "demonic". This is in contrast to the mere "cults" sprouting up everywhere in the modern world contemporary to Bell, sources of hope amidst the decay, but which lack "the superior strength of a theology and organization" of early Christianity.[10] Rome, therefore, was better able to manage and survive her own decline, because she maintained a religious and spiritual vitality that is conspicuously absent from the supposed chaos of modern culture. The superiority of the religious and spiritual values of the classical world is again argued for in Richard Sennett's *The Fall of Public Man: On the Social Psychology of Capitalism* (1977)—a work which first rejects, then embraces, the comparative model of Roman decline. Sennett dismisses the idea that "moral rottenness is supposed to have sapped Rome's power to rule in the west," and that, as a consequent analogy, such rot "is said to have sapped the modern West's power to rule the globe." The dismissal, however, is qualified; partly because the Romans were always decadent, but *also* because this was balanced by their theistic spiritual values; they were still somehow *less* rotten than the secularized mass culture of modern life.[11]

Eschatological and religious language, therefore, deeply informs these representations of decline and their corresponding imagery. That the age and culture of the late twentieth century are somehow apocalyptic in their character is almost a truism in public intellectual criticism. In the words of Walter Wagar, since the First World War "the serious literature of most Western countries" has been "drenched with apocalyptic imagery."[12] Patrick Brantlinger in *Bread and Circuses* (1983) reaffirms the "decadence and barbarism" of the modern world, whilst also offering a vision for "the dawn of a new faith," for currently, "We only have faith that we are declining and falling; we do not yet have faith in our ability to build a new civilization." Instead, he suggests, "We, the newest barbarians, in the midst of this declining civilization, must learn to preserve what we are ravaging … we must learn to change it in ways which are radical, even utopian …. " This analogy is conveyed through a comparative image of the fifth century, for, as Brantlinger quotes William Thompson, "A Roman senator cannot become a Frankish Christian without first dying and being reborn."[13] It is notable, then, for the *spiritual* qualities suggested in this change, couched as it is in the language of Christian rebirth. This highlights, in line with old theological precepts, the *decadence*—the opposite force of spirituality—and moral emptiness that need to be surmounted.

These criticisms can therefore contain a spiritual dimension, just as they have been more narrowly secular or social in character. What they have in common, however, is the myth and usage of Roman decline. The cursory and repeated invocation of some form of a Dark Age in culture, society or politics, provides a narrative model for invoking the decline and fall to engage with a panoramic debate about the modern world. Reflecting on the 1992 riots in Los Angeles, the writer Jack Miles can muse on the comparison in this way: "When the barbarians sacked Rome in 410, the Romans thought it was the end of civilization. You smile—but what followed was the Dark Ages."[14]

Without needing to discuss the historicity of the decline and fall, the story of the fate of Rome can be summoned to buttress the account of the impending doom of Western civilization, by enshrining its teleology with the sanction of precedent. No further details of this period are provided: the very phrase itself, functioning as an archetype, is frequently enough. Indeed the logic here is characteristic of virtually all such social theories and criticism that have been discussed—namely, that if the fall of empires can be *prophesied*, it must also be predetermined. The primary consequence of the Roman example, therefore, is that it means *the steps in this process are known*. The decline of civilization, such as that of the classical world, produces the ignorance and barbarism of the "medieval" Dark Age. In these representations, the classical and medieval function hand in hand.

Such an idea proves a powerful notion when discussing societies and civilizations perceived to be at their peak: and painting it, as Gibbon did with the Antonines, as a paradox. Robert Sinai writes that, "Growing efficacy involves growing degeneration of life instincts," and has produced, in no uncertain terms, "the decline of man. Every progressive impulse must sooner or later become fatigued," and "a culture may founder on real and tangible progress."[15] This paradox of inherent decadence, and internal undoing, present in the arc of progress is painted in similar assertions by other contemporaneous writers. Hans Morgenthau, the historian of international relations, states that "it is one of the great ironies of contemporary history that the moral and material *decline* of the West has in good measure been accomplished through the moral and material *triumphs* of the West [emphasis added]."[16] One is reminded of Gibbon's statement on Rome that "prosperity ripened the principle of decay."[17] Marya Mannes, the author and cultural critic of US life, speculates that the "greatest technological leap known to man" may have produced "a night of the soul, a return to a new form of barbarism?"[18]

The conceptual model of Rome present in these narratives, whether only hinted at (as with Mannes) or declared more explicitly (as by Bernard James), is composed of the same notions about the success of civilization sowing its own downfall. Gibbon, echoing Montesquieu, had declared that Rome fell, first and foremost, due to her "immoderate greatness." Augustine, in the first elaborated account of Rome's decline, emphasizes in more theological terms, pride as both raising the empire to greatness and sowing the seeds of its downfall.[19] Rousseau describes how, "The Roman Empire in its turn, having engulfed all the riches of the universe, fell prey to the people who knew not what riches were."[20] Luxury and prosperity undermine empires and societies. Such is a central premise of this myth; that it represents and describes not a single past event but an archetype of universal application and meaning. It is one usually devoid of many actual *facts*, but suffused in *narrative*. Such a tale is easily fashioned out of this history. A book by George Brauer, published in 1967, was titled *The Young Emperors: Rome, AD 193–244*. It describes the early part of the third century, during which a series of young rulers came to the throne, often with hereditary connections behind their claims. Reissued in 1995, the book was given a new title: *The Decadent Emperors: Power and Depravity in Third-Century Rome*.[21]

A detailed invocation of Roman history to describe the strains faced by the advanced industrial world is made by Joseph Tainter, the American anthropologist and historian, who in *The Collapse of Complex Societies* (1988) fashioned a theory of the inherent vulnerability of complex societies to successfully adapt to their problems. Tainter argues that societies become more complex in order to resolve their internal tensions. Such complexity requires a considerable and growing "energy" subsidy, and when society is confronted with a shortage or difficulty of access to such "energy", it creates new layers of bureaucracy, infrastructure, and class hierarchy to cope with the challenge. Such a process adds so much strain to the system that it invariably leads to its downfall. The decline of Rome functions as a test-case for this idealization of history, as he explained in a documentary interview on economic and energy crisis:

> In ancient societies that I studied, for example the Roman Empire, the great problem that they faced was when they would have to incur very high costs just to maintain the status quo. Invest very high amounts in solving problems that don't yield a net positive return, but instead simply allowed them to maintain what they already got. This decreases the net benefit of being a complex society.[22]

The importance of this example is explored in some detail. As Roman agricultural output is supposed to have declined, per capita energy availability dropped. The Romans supposedly solved this problem by conquering their neighbours to acquire their energy surpluses in the form of raw-material commodities and labour. However, as the empire grew, the cost of maintaining the administration and bureaucracy of the empire, army and state spiralled faster than the benefits of expansion and conquest, resulting in the so-called "crisis of the third century." Intense, authoritarian efforts to maintain cohesion by Diocletian and Constantine in the third and fourth centuries only led to unsustainable pressures on the citizen and serf population. Consequently, the Western Empire, eroding in power and cohesion, crumbled in the wake of its powerful external foes—the East, also weakened but less threatened, succumbed only slowly and by piecemeal.[23]

I have discussed how these approaches to universal and comparative notions of decline more explicitly examine the details of the later Roman Empire, in particular its political and economic configuration. Much of Tainter's analysis sits in stark contradiction to the professional and academic history around the Late Antique Roman Empire—in particular, the size of the bureaucracy and the state of agriculture. This highlights the difference between a factual approach to the past, and the *representation* of it; which can be wildly divergent from this, and beholden to other narrative and ideological concerns. An illusion of professional and "academic" veracity is found in Tainter's analysis, who devotes a chapter of his book to a summary of historic and historiographical notions of the fall of Rome, focusing on a divide between mystical, moral, and socio-economic theories of decline; and notes the value of all of them whilst emphasizing his own preference for the latter, a supposedly more grounded and modern, empirical study.[24] Yet while the tools of his analysis are decidedly secular and contemporary, the core thesis is unchanged—that the empire was worn away by slow, progressive, internal decline, and that, most importantly, it is of the kind that can be extrapolated universally to explain the fates of other societies. Tainter does not confine his form of analysis to Rome, but speculates, in the same book, on Mayan civilization, Chaco culture, and the contemporary world; Roman decline and fall underpins the model that is applied to all of these.

The only alternative thesis to explain the fall of Rome that is seriously considered by Tainter is that of the classical and Late Antique historian John Bagnell Bury, who argued (in Tainter's words) "that there was no general explanation for the fall of Rome, that is resulted from a series of contingent events," as a succession of weak emperors mismanaged the defences of the empire at the time of the significant barbarian irruptions into the empire of the "Visigoths". Bury is one of the few professional historians of the period actually cited, and his argument is quickly dismissed, on these grounds:

Chance concatenation arguments by definition provide no basis for generalization, and so fail to satisfy the need for a global understanding of a recurrent process. Explanation by reference to historical accident furthermore has logical failings. It is argued by some that *all* is chance concatenation of events. This argument goes too far but there is some validity to the notion that random factors influence all processes. To the extent that random factors occur with some statistical regularity over time, they cannot account for a phenomenon far more limited in its occurrence.[25]

It is therefore seen as impossible to describe the fall of Rome through historical contingency, because that would be "random", and random factors occur all the time. This is of course at odds with many of the dominant historical explanations for the events and processes of the fifth century AD. It also makes little logical sense: just because *some* random things occur all the time, it does not mean that the *specific* ones involved in a historical event such as the fall of Rome do. Most importantly for Tainter, contingency is dismissed because it conflicts with the notion at the heart of this work, namely "the need for a global understanding of a recurrent process," and is therefore rejected on principle. In his argument, the Roman Empire had been undergoing a catastrophic loss of complexity from the crises of the third century, and so the specific events or facts of its downfall are simply functions of this broader, inevitable trajectory. Crucially, the modern, globalized world is deemed to be subject to many of the same stresses and strains that brought these ancient societies to ruin.[26] The thesis of spiralling complexity and its eventual implosion is best accounted for in the story Rome, therefore, yet proves to have universal and modern implication.

This discussion brings us onto the point of exactly *what* are the failures, or symptoms of decline, that the writers of the twentieth and twenty-first centuries have seen as represented in Rome's perceived fall that feature in their present horizons. It is here that one can contradict the contention of Glen Bowersock, who in 1996 in *The Vanishing Paradigm of the Fall of Rome* wrote that, "The fall of Rome is no longer needed, and like the writing on a faded papyrus, it no longer speaks to us."[27] Not only is the decline and fall a *living* myth, but it has acquired a particular modern relevance in the tradition of US political and historical thought that compares the rise and zenith of Rome and the USA respectively as superpowers of their age.[28] A long string of "crisis" books have appeared in the run-up to the twenty-first century, and especially with the end of the Cold War; as if to prepare in some way their readers for an approaching period of deep dislocation and uncertainty, with Rome serving to trace the expected path from glory to ruin. Paul Kennedy, in an often quoted work, argued in *The Rise and Fall of the Great Powers: Economic Change and Military Conflict from 1500–2000* (1987) that Americans were poised to share the same fate as the British a century earlier, and, before that, the Romans: their decline as a world power. Kennedy argues that the strength of a Great Power can only be adequately measured in relation to other such powers, highlighting the usefulness of the analogy with even ancient societies such as Rome. The USA, according to Kennedy, was suffering from what he termed "imperial overstretch"—squeezed by its vast military commitments, and confronting a rising tide of economic challengers, it faced an inevitable and irreversible end to its dominance. The best it could hope for in this light was a "managed erosion." The very familiarity of these themes is highlighted by Kennedy in the key point that "too much of what happened then is happening again," and that the future presents us with the approaching struggle of "the West against the rest."[29] Such a position is reminiscent of Arnold Toynbee, who declared in 1962 that the USA "now stands for what Rome stood for," namely the defence of imperial interests against the needs of the poor and the Third World.[30] In a similar vein, T.S. Eliot's *The Waste Land*, described as owing something to the "imperial frontier myth," is explained in these terms by William Vance in *America's Rome* (1989): "Beneath T.S. Eliot's *The Waste Land* lie the history and mythology of imperial Rome, fragmented and transposed to our century in the dying British Empire."[31]

Such ideas of erosion, overstretch and decline have found a particular resonance in the media classes in the USA. American expansionism appeared to endanger the institutions and ethics that the Founding Fathers had sought so keenly to establish and safeguard. Critics of this apparent "American Empire" frequently looked to the decline of Rome as a vision, example and warning for the USA. In *Arrogant Capital* (1995), political analyst Kevin Philips used Kennedy to compare Washington to Late Imperial Rome and nineteenth-century London: the "arrogant" capital of a declining empire ruled by "abusive and entrenched elites." The similarity of this analysis is evident is his usage of the same forms of decline—moral, cultural, political—to characterize the fall of these respective superpowers. In his reasons for this deterioration, Philips cites "an expansion of luxury and moral permissiveness", a lengthy period of "greed"—in his mind, personified by the Reagan era—and the "loss of old patriotism," all judgements and ideas that lend themselves naturally to the universal notions of decline and fall.

Through the use of somewhat circular logic, Philips cites as evidence contemporaries' "complaints of moral decay"—this diagnosis of decline therefore being cited as evidence of the decline itself. The connections to ancient history, and the iconic examples of decline, are made obvious by pointing out the corruption and degeneration of Rome and Athens: "There is no point in mincing words ... aging great-power capitals often become parasitic cultures," and contemporary Washington "is beginning to resemble those wayward governmental centres of previous declining empires."[32] Such a picture is presented in very similar terms by cultural critic Cornel West in *Race Matters* (2001), who appropriates Kennedy's "image of the eclipse of US hegemony in the world" as evidence of a decline and decay in the culture and spirit of the nation. As he says, "cultural decay in a declining empire" had created "rootless, dangling people" and a "powerless citizenry that includes not just the poor but all of us."[33]

Typically in this frame, the mass media are presented as tools of our collective cultural suicide: both the zenith and nadir of progress. They are the forces of "bread and circuses" imperialism, a trend which invariably ends in barbarism, decadence and decline. In *Backing into the Future: The Classical Tradition and Its Renewal* (1994), the classicist and cultural critic Bernard Knox describes a fear that progressive cultural attitudes threatened to "abolish the cultural traditions on which the West's sense of unity and identity is founded," and that "it is only to be expected that in this age of cultural dilution, of plastic substitutes, of mindless television shows ... the genuine article is no longer valued."[34] In the same year, the Noble Prize-winning poet and writer Joseph Brodsky made this comparison between the approaching end of the "golden age" of Marcus Aurelius and his own time: "*Ave*, Caesar. How do you feel now, among barbarians? We are your true Parthians, Marcomanni, and Quadi, because nobody came in your stead, and we inhabit the earth." In considering the legacy of Aurelius, Brodsky concludes on the dark note that, "if *Meditations* is antiquity, it is we who are the ruins."[35]

Putting this outlook into a more strictly economic and class context is Charles Murray's *The Bell Curve* (1994), a widely publicized study that painted a picture of the future of US society fast becoming "two nations"— a detached elite isolated by their more sophisticated culture, wealth and values, and an underclass, impoverished in their reliance on mass culture, and incapable of taking care of themselves. Murray reaches the conclusion that "unchecked, these trends will lead the US toward something resembling a caste society," and, referencing past visions of decline, adds that "like other apocalyptic visions, this one is pessimistic, perhaps too much so. On the other hand, there is much to be pessimistic about."[36]

## *GLADIATOR*, ROME, AND THE USA IN AD 2000

Considerations of the USA's place as a civilization and an empire, at the turn of the twenty-first century, are not confined to the literary record. Ridley Scott's *Gladiator* (Universal Pictures, 2000) is a film about the place of America as a solo superpower; where the challenges and turmoil it must face come not from without but within. As such, both in the period it discusses—the last days of Marcus Aurelius, and the reign of his son—and its theme of imperial troubles, the decline and fall myth plays a prominent, though significantly re-envisaged, role in this story.

Thirty-six years after its appearance, Mann's *The Fall of the Roman Empire* provided the model for *Gladiator*—despite the significant contrasts between the two films—and in this way profoundly influenced the current revival of Ancient Rome in cinema and television. Because Mann's film is now an intermediary between Gibbon and *Gladiator*, the historian of the Roman Empire continues to exert an explicit influence in a significant part of recent modern culture since the turn of the twenty-first century. The link between the two films, however, is poorly credited outside the specific academic study of the former. As Martin Winkler points out, "A noteworthy aspect of all the publicity that studio, star, writer, director, and others advanced to promote this new Roman spectacle, however, was the almost complete silence about an epic film that bears a strong resemblance to theirs. It is unlikely that *Gladiator* would have been possible without *The Fall of the Roman Empire*."[37] In the official literary companion to the film, *Gladiator: The Making of the Ridley Scott Epic* (2000), author Diana Landau offers only a single line on its significance: "Also in the category of interesting failures was Anthony Mann's 1964 film *The Fall of the Roman Empire*, whose plot featured several of the main characters who later appeared in *Gladiator*." The book provides a collection of illustrations of other Roman-themed films, and none of these is *The Fall of the Roman Empire*—a very odd omission considering it is the *only* one which shares the same historical setting and time frame.[38]

The question must be raised of why a genre largely defunct for over 30 years was revived at all. DreamWorks' production head at the time, Walter

Parkes, noted a trend in the box-office success of recent epic "historical" films such as Mel Gibson's *Braveheart* (Twentieth Century Fox, 1995) and James Cameron's *Titanic* (Twentieth Century Fox, 1997) and saw an opportunity for the revival of the toga franchise. But its potential for commercial success is noted by him as running deeper than recent tastes, as "The Roman epic occupies a strange, special place in the heart of moviegoers. We love the good ones like *Ben-Hur* and *Spartacus*, but even the bad ones are guilty pleasures."[39]

Moreover, advances in computer technology allowed the creators of *Gladiator* to display Roman spectacle on a new scale, without being burdened with quite the enormous production costs of its predecessors from the 1960s and earlier. As *New York Times* critic Herbert Muschamp put it:

> Why revive this genre of movie now? DreamWorks, the movie's producer, boasts of special effects made possible by computer imaging techniques. Rome can be built in a day. Just run some paintings by Cole, David and Alma-Tadema through the scanner, et voila! Better yet, feed.[40]

Scott himself described his hopes for grandeur in the days before filming: "I hope to design the film in such a way that when people see it, they'll think, 'Gee. Rome's never been done like this before.'"[41]

But technical innovations alone cannot explain the success of *Gladiator*. An astonishing financial success that netted $450 million at the box office worldwide, on an (unexceptional) $103 million budget, *Gladiator* resurrected not only imperial Rome at the height of its power but also helped to revive interest in a film genre considered to have been dead and buried since the 1960s.[42] The *New York Times* specifically referred to this as the "*Gladiator* effect," saying "in this case, it's the movies—most recently *Gladiator* two years ago—that have created that interest in the ancients."[43]

*Gladiator* presents the audience with much of the imagery and iconography of Roman decadence, and draws heavily on our myth; in particular, the depiction of Commodus in both Gibbon and Anthony Mann's film. It is *not*, however, a representation of the decline and fall. *Gladiator* is a modern counterpoint to this myth; one which recognizes the *threat* of moral and political corruption and decline, but *not* its eventual triumph. It openly challenges the Gibbonian narrative of the Roman path to ruin that followed the death of Marcus Aurelius, and provides a vision of a positive and redeeming alternative. This approach makes absolutely no sense as a historical commentary. Republican Rome was not restored with the death of Commodus—but its meaning is clear if the film is taken as a metaphor for contemporary America. Instead of describing the process by which Rome's dissolution is set in motion, *Gladiator* adapts the myth of the decline and fall in order to express, examine and, finally, extinguish contemporary social and political concerns. The mythology of Rome, in these terms, is elsewhere described by Peter Bondanella as "not so much a relic to be venerated as it is a flexible and limitless source of self-expression, a common heritage which has met the needs of successive generations .... Something in the myth of Rome has helped us to understand our human condition, our world, and ourselves."[44] In this sense, apart from the film's setting in the late second century, it has more in common with representations of Classical Antiquity in general than the specific themes surrounding its apparent decline in Late Antiquity.

As such, while *Gladiator* quietly borrows much of the same material and narrative content as *The Fall of the Roman Empire*, it reveals a striking reversal of perspective, departing from the core theme of Mann's film and indeed from the entire Gibbonian conception of the consequences of the end of the "Age of the Antonines," and its dreadful consequences. The Romans depicted in Gladiator function as a stand-in for perceived US supremacy at the turn of the century, after the Cold War but before 9/11 and the Iraq War came to pose a challenge to the supposition of global dominance. In his review entitled "Throwing Our Anxieties to the Lions," the film was described by Muschamp as "a meditation on the perplexity of the world's sole surviving superpower." Reflecting on the film's themes, Muschamp poses the question, "Where does America go from here?"[45]

The plot of this film begins in AD 180, the last year of the rule of Marcus Aurelius, and shows the ascension and brief, tyrannical rule of his son Commodus. A fictional hero, suitably named Maximus (meaning, as is emphasized in the film, "greatest"), a victorious general and the favourite of an aged Marcus Aurelius for the succession, is betrayed when Commodus murders his father and seizes the throne. His family murdered, and reduced to slavery, Maximus manages to ascend in fame in the gladiatorial arena, first in the province of Zucchabar and then in Rome. His success at the Colosseum in a re-enactment of the Battle of Zama leads to Commodus coming down to personally congratulate Maximus, at which point he publicly reveals his identity, and vows revenge.

The gladiator is so popular with the crowd that Commodus is unable to order his death, and his attempt to have him killed in the arena by paying Tigris of Gaul, an undefeated former gladiator, also fails. Commodus' opponents in the Senate, and his sister Lucilla, plan to bring the emperor down by freeing Maximus and bringing him back to his army. However, the emperor catches wind of the plot, and orders Lucilla to reveal the details by threatening to execute her son. The plotters killed or arrested, Commodus arranges a personal gladiatorial duel with Maximus, but, before the fight begins, stabs him in the side, severely weakening him. Nevertheless, Maximus kills Commodus in single combat, though he is mortally wounded from his earlier injury. Before dying, he asks for the rule of the Senate to be restored, thereby putting Rome back on the right moral and political path.

*Gladiator* poses the very question of the direction and purpose of US cultural and political dominance. It thereby introduces a new geopolitical context for a discussion of Rome's power. The film's sepia-toned prologue, accompanied only by ghostly female backing vocals, informs us that Rome is "at the height of its power."[46] It opens with the empire demonstrating its absolute supremacy in military might along the northern frontier. As Maximus tells the emperor after his triumph, "There is no one left to fight, sire." Yet within days of this statement, the empire is afflicted with crisis. Internal pressures almost sunder it from within, leading very nearly to civil war.

The supremacy of the Roman Empire is crucial to the film's narrative. Victory over the Quadi and Marcomanni is here depicted as a defining and final affirmation of Roman power, across all its lands. There is no mention of the vulnerabilities on the Eastern frontier. *The Fall of the Roman Empire* concluded with the line, "A great civilization is not conquered from without until it has destroyed itself from within." In *Gladiator*, there is no threat from "without", nor any hint of one after the opening act—the dangerous is wholly located within. Unlike in *The Fall*, the new emperor does not have to concern himself with mounting military and civil pressures on his rule, but can fully absorb himself in the decadence extravagance of gladiatorial games.

After its opening act, therefore, the narrative theme of *Gladiator* shifts to represent a conflict between two competing visions of the kind of superpower this newly unchallenged Rome—and, by analogy, the post-Cold War USA—can and should be. Rome, both as a city and a spiritual analogy for the empire at large, is fought over in an ideological battle between despotism and tyranny, as epitomized by Commodus, and a traditional, humanist republicanism by Maximus and his senatorial allies. Ridley Scott presents the empire, in its more despotic aspects, as the oppressor of its inner, purer Republican self. The clash between Maximus, the senator Gracchus, and Commodus is a battle for the soul of Rome, or a Rome as defined by their competing ideologies. The arena resembles the ugly side to Rome's vision military might and power. As Commodus says, "I will give the people a vision of Rome, and they'll love me for it."

*Gladiator* speculates on which of these opposing visions of rule will prevail; and it proves to be the positive and progressive one. Maximus slays Commodus and restores good government and the "dream of Rome." By this innovative plot structure, the film is able to cast the improbable restoration of a form of the Roman Republic upon the death of Commodus. It turns the Gibbonian idea of his accession marking the end of the Antonine high point of the empire into an ahistorical fantasy in which the forces of good and freedom triumph over those of evil and tyranny. It underscores the notion that imperial power, with the right leadership structure and moral imperatives, can be a just and positive force in the world.

The significance of this theme is underscored in the film's ending. *Gladiator* still conforms to the basic pattern as Anthony Mann's film. Maximus kills Commodus in the final duel, just as Livius did in *The Fall*. Stabbed in advance by Commodus, Maximus himself dies, and in death is reunited with his murdered family, whom we see waiting for him in a final vision. But Maximus' death is no tragedy—he has killed Commodus, and so saved Rome. His final commands are to order the release of Graccus, the senator who will form or head a new government that Marcus Aurelius had intended as the means to restore the Republic. Maximus' last words are: "There was a dream that was Rome. It shall be realized. These are the wishes of Marcus Aurelius." Lucilla, as his body is carried out, confirms his crucial role in saving the empire from itself: "Is Rome worth one good man's life? We believed it once. Make us believe it again." There is now hope for the future, and the last view of Rome—a panoramic long shot of the sun breaking through the clouds over the city—confirms the onset of this new dawn for Rome.

In this ending, tyranny and corruption are shown to be a potential threat to society, but inherent *only* in individuals, not in society as a whole or its institutional edifices. The threat, therefore, can be overcome through a noble and virtuous struggle, such as that of the hero Maximus. Once the villains are removed, and the right people are (re)instated, then the condition of society and the body politic will improve; without any necessity for radical changes in the structures of government or society. There has been corruption, decadence, and tyranny at the core of Roman society, as represented by the gladiatorial games, and the rarity of the noble vision of Maximus and Marcus. But there is no inevitable spiral into decline: no suggestion of a coming fall.

It is clear that *Gladiator* is in no way an attempt to portray Roman history authentically. The only notable exception to this is the architecturally exacting representation of the Colosseum.[47] Otherwise, the imagery of the film is drawn from strictly imaginary sources. Scott reverts to idealistic and romantic art as sources for the depiction of the city and empire, notably those that appear in Thomas Cole's set of paintings, *The Course of Empire* (1836). Indeed, Cole's vision of the rise and fall of Rome was intended as an allegorical warning to the USA. Scott also refers to the impact of Jeon-Leon Gerome's 1872 gladiatorial painting *Police Verso*.[48] The film is openly and overtly aware of its own involvement in retelling and reinterpreting the story of Rome. The opening announcer in the first scene at the Colosseum proclaims, "On this day we reach back to hallowed antiquity to bring you a recreation of the second fall of mighty Carthage," highlighting what the film is doing. Less obvious but just as deliberately, the film creates a fascistic comparison between the regime of Commodus and the Third Reich. The depiction of the new emperor's entry to Rome is explicitly derived from one particular visual source, Leni Riefenstahl's *Triumph of the Will* (1935), an account of the 1934 Nazi party rally at Nuremburg. The aerial view of Rome by which Scott first provides a glimpse of the imperial city is a deliberate homage to the opening sequence of that film; namely an aerial shot of Hitler arriving by plane, to the massed crowds, eagerly waiting.[49]

*Gladiator* offers a critique of imperialism and the Roman political system under the empire. At the same time, however, its final vision can be seen as quite a conservative one, born of its classical precedents. The desire to return Rome to the control of the Senate, out of the grasp of emperors and their exploitation of the uglier instincts of the mob, reflects the Republican longings among the Roman senatorial class of the early empire.[50] It is one of the primary themes of Robert Graves's novel *I Claudius*.[51] Indeed, the fictitious senatorial character of Gracchus is played by Derek Jacobi, who has the titular role in that series. Furthermore, there is no great indictment of Roman society or civilization at large—no suggestion, as came in *The Fall of the Roman Empire*, during their festival celebrating Commodus, that the social mores of the population as a whole are in decay. Instead, the dramatic tension in the film is a product of the fact that the new head of state is an irredeemable villain who murdered his way to the purple. Indeed the difference between *The Fall of the Roman Empire* and *Gladiator* is reinforced by the two films' portrayals of their Roman emperors, Marcus Aurelius and Commodus. In *The Fall of the Roman Empire* Marcus is the central figure of the film's first half; the dominant personality who determines how audiences are to respond to the world he rules, and departs from. By contrast, *Gladiator* focuses on Commodus, the villain who rapidly kills his father with his own hands. Marcus is murdered a quarter of the way into the film, after appearing in only four scenes. His brief presence is overshadowed by both Maximus and Commodus, and mostly serves as a dramatic foil to the latter. His role in the film's events is largely passive and conversational, he makes no military or political decisions, and his inspiration is summarized at the end as an inspiring "dream of Rome," rather than a specific reality or practical accomplishment. The film also never mentions the *Meditations*. It does, however, imply an appreciation for learning that contrasts with his son. Returned to Rome as his father's successor to the purple, Commodus is pestered by a senator who is justifiably worried about sanitation in Rome. He retorts that he will not follow his predecessor's example, for: "My father spent all his time at study, reading books, learning philosophy." *However*, this appreciation of his learning is noted but not earmarked for praise. Shortly before his death, Marcus asks his general Maximus: "Will I be known as the philosopher, the warrior, the tyrant? Or will I be the emperor who gave Rome back her true self?" His philosophy is thereby associated with the lesser traits of imperial leadership: something unsatisfying when compared to his final vision of the restoration of Rome.

That vision is instead explicitly invested in the newly invented person of Maximus. Dreamworks, in updating the visual and narrative portrayal of Rome, heralded Ridley Scott's *Gladiator* as featuring a more modern kind of heroism to embody the new millennium. Posters with Russell Crowe in gladiatorial dress declared in the tagline that "A Hero will Rise ... in May 2000 AD." As screenwriter David Franzoni put it, "this movie is about our culture, our society ... Maximus is the hero we all wish ourselves to be; the guy who can rise above the mess that is modern society." The significance of this is that it strengthens the connection between the story's setting and the world of the audience, for, "The movie is about us. It's not just about ancient Rome, it's about America."[52] The kind of hero that Maximus *is* has therefore to be one who fits modern sympathies. As Jon Solomon observed, "Gladiator reveals another twenty-first century bias. Contemporary Hollywood family values interject themselves into the ancient Roman zeitgeist."[53] So, while we see him at the opening as a powerful and aggressive military commander, Scott soon after contrasts this by having Maximus express his desire to the old emperor to return to a peaceful farm life with his wife and child in Spain. This, of course, gives the implicit impression that the Roman army was a volunteer force recruited for a particular war or campaigns—rather than a permanent professional soldiery serving a fixed term.

The film therefore explores as a principle theme the return to traditional ideals of home and family through Maximus—whose ideals manage to save the empire from Commodus and itself. Maximus, a farmer, is a rural working-class hero—an old and popular archetype of American nobility and virtue.[54] The ethics of the simple farmer, and the virtue of his background and values, thereby contrast with the corruption and dangers of the metropolis. In this way, as Solomon states, Scott "superimposed both modern familial sensitivity and ancient Roman Republican virtues" onto the story.[55] The old emperor, concerned with the legacy of his rule and the dangerous prospects of his son, has realized that the countryside is the true "Rome", and the path to saving it—a vision that comes true when Maximus finally kills Commodus.

*Gladiator*, in this way, also recalls the spectacles of corruption and debauchery in earlier Roman epics. While its picture of the moral decadence of Rome is confined to the "bread and circuses" depiction of the Colosseum, there is the suggestion that tyranny goes hand in hand with sexual deviance. Commodus goes on to reveal his incestuous plans for a "pure" heir to his sister Lucilla, thereby connecting transgressive desire with his despotic plans for a permanent, hereditary dynasty of rulers.[56] Maximus, by contrast, is a man of personal religiosity and spirituality; a devoted father and husband who honours the old Roman gods, and whose spirituality leaves him untroubled by the possibility of death. As he says when encouraging his troops before battle, "And if you find yourself alone, riding through green fields with the sun in your face, do not be troubled, for you are in Elysium, and you are already dead!" The loss of his family motivates Maximus through the film, and the image of him reunited with them grants the film a kind of positive resolution in the arc of the protagonist, who is driven throughout by revenge but finally finds peace.

The honour and purity of the early Maximus characterization also highlight his disillusionment and fall from grace in the second act of the film. His skill and courage at battle are transformed and trivialised into bloody entertainment in the arena. He displays his contempt for the crowd by spitting in their view, and, at the conclusion of one fight in the arena in Zucchabar, hurls his sword into the official viewing box for local dignitaries. In this phase of the film, he has scraped off the insignia of the legions—SPQR, or "The Senate and people of Rome"—and is referred to by his captives as a deserter. While technically inaccurate in regard to his situation, this descriptor serves as an apt metaphor: now that Rome is under the grip of a new tyrant, Maximus has excised the Roman part of his identity. When Commodus first asks of his identity in the arena, he refers to himself simply as "gladiator", confirming the extent to which this has subsumed his old self-image. Such a profound disillusionment with the Roman way is also found in Livius in *The Fall*—but, crucially, only at the end, when he is offered the purple and rejects it, publicly suggesting the assembled senators deserve to all hang, and walking off with Lucilla. Maximus, after the same duel in *Gladiator*, has had his faith not destroyed but rekindled, and speaks of Marcus' "dream of Rome." The theme of the final act of Mann's film is suggested in Scott's second act, and then discarded for an alternative and even more ahistorical vision.

*Gladiator* presents an optimistic vision of the future but in this respect is earmarked by its date of release in May 2000. Subsequent interpretations of the film have dwelled as much on its critical elements of the body politic, in light of geopolitical developments. Under the subheading of "The Exhaustion of Empire," Monica S. Cyrino compares the message of the film with the geopolitical developments that followed its release, specifically 9/11 and the "War on Terror," and sees in it an important modern message:

> Washington's policy of brash unilateralism has heightened the general perception that America ignores or disdains international opinion and foreign allegiances. This leaves the United States in the precarious position of a lonely, self-righteous, and determinedly bellicose superpower. The 2003 State of the Union address was delivered on January 28 by a president indifferent to foreign opinion: "The course of this nation does not depend on the decisions of others."

Once such aggressive unilateralism is defined as a feature of the foreign policy of the administration, the comparison to *Gladiator* is made explicit:

Like Commodus in *Gladiator*, who plans to dissolve the Roman senate so that the emperor can from now on act with sole power, President Bush has devalued the United Nations' role in maintaining global accord and pledged that America will act alone, if necessary. It has begun to do so.[57]

Here, in fact, the reception of *Gladiator* has *much* more in common with that of *The Fall of the Roman Empire*—a film with a very different direction and overall message, but in which common ground is found in their portrayal of Commodus and the threat he poses. Film historian and critic Richard Corliss begins a laudatory retrospective on Anthony Mann with these words: "Do you think old movies can't speak to today's concerns? See some of Anthony Mann's films and think again. They speak for their time: they speak to ours." He goes on to compare, via strong and unsubtle implication, the inept and blundering tyrant Commodus to the 43rd President, describing the former as "a weak man with a drunken past who says he was divinely chosen to make war against the Middle Eastern tribes," and noting the line in the film, "You must also let them know they must forget the weakness of my father," and describes Commodus' desire to address "the military flabbiness of an earlier President—sorry, Emperor."[58]

This is a crucial comparison to make. While Ridley Scott's film may not be a direct example of the decline and fall, it possesses enough of the content and ideas imprinted in that narrative, and inherited from Gibbon, Durant and Mann, that such elements can be easily invoked where the priorities of the author and the political context of their commentary call for it. The myth has enough of a latent presence in the structure and sources of *Gladiator* that it can be easily and readily invoked when desired.

## 9/11 AND CRITICS OF EMPIRE

If *Gladiator* contains a more optimistic vision or prospect for the future of the USA, the geopolitical events of the subsequent years reflect a different kind of output: one that adheres much more closely to the decline and fall myth in its traditional form. The extensive pessimism and political and cultural concern documented earlier in this study find a particular focus, in the years after 9/11, on the place and role of the USA as a global empire under threat both without and within. Turning to the idea of "imperial overstretch," one can find the comparison of Roman and US decline by the historian and columnist Chalmers Johnson in *The Sorrows of*

*Empire: Militarism, Secrecy and the End of the Republic* (2004). The author makes this comparison of the rates of decline: "Roman imperial sorrows mounted up over hundreds of years. Ours are likely to arrive at the speed of FedEx." Johnson is not a Roman or medieval historian by background, though he discusses such subjects at length. Rather, his last three works include detailed examinations of the supposed consequences of "American Empire," with particularly attention paid to the Roman example in *The Sorrows*. He goes on in this work to describe these "sorrows" as derived from a form of "imperial overstretch" leading to "perpetual war," the "loss of democracy and constitutional rights," and "bankruptcy". These ultimately stem from the militaristic path pursued by the USA's "imperial leaders," and bear close analogy to the progressive and final fate of the Roman Empire.[59]

Analogies between the Roman and US empires have become a regular part of contemporary political discourse. Notable recent studies of this trend include Harold James, *The Roman Predicament: How the Rules of International Order Create the Politics of Empire* (Princeton: Princeton University Press, 2006), and Charles S. Maier, *Among Empires: American Ascendancy and Its Predecessors* (Cambridge: Harvard University Press, 2006). Once such analogies are brought into the discussion, the lessons of Roman failure serve their purpose. Patrick Buchanan, in *State of Emergency: The Third World Invasion and Conquest of America* (2006), compares the policies of Rome and the USA in regard to the Eastern Emperor Valens' admission of "a great horde of refugees" into the empire in AD 376 . Valens was killed in 378 by the Goths at the Battle of Adrianople, one of the worst field defeats in the history of the later empire. Buchanan concludes: "What Valens had done was the Christian thing to do, but it had never been the Roman thing to do." To Buchanan, the lesson is obvious: religious differences aside, the Roman Way is also the American Way.[60]

Appropriately enough, the first chapter of Harold James's book is entitled "The Model of Decline and Fall." He willingly embraces the notion that "Roman decline" can inform an understanding of the present climate. He begins as follows: "Our predecessors have thought about problems similar to those of the modern globalizing world, and they in turn believed that they could understand their environment by thinking about their own predecessors. Faced with an economic dynamism both driven and divided by the assertion of political power, they saw the Roman Empire as a model for the dilemmas of future ages."[61] Niall Ferguson reinforces this sentiment, stating in a review quoted on the back cover that, "In a glut of books about American empire, Harold James's stands out for its subtlety and erudition. Few other scholars could so elegantly and persuasively relate Edward Gibbon's account of the decline of Rome to the present predicament of the United States."

More self-consciously referential to this very tendency is Cullen Murphy's *Are We Rome?* (2007), an overtly comparative study between Rome's fate and the future of the USA by the editor-at-large of *Vanity Fair*. Murphy points out, quite legitimately, the place of Roman decadence in our cultural tradition, as reflected in some notable and popular linguistic anachronisms: such as the term "bread and circuses," or the way waves of illegal immigrants are compared to "barbarian hordes." However, he readily embraces and accepts the anachronistic nature of his own analysis: "President and Emperor, America and Rome—the comparison is by now so familiar, so natural, that you just can't help yourself."[62] The argument is summarized by him in this fashion:

> Are we Rome? In a thousand specific ways, the answer is obviously no. In a handful of important ways, the answer is certainly yes ... America's impact may be unprecedented in its scope, but the phenomenon itself is one that Rome knew well .... [63]
> 
> Later, he continues:
> 
> [Rome was] no stranger to dislocations caused by worldwide market forces, or to the riotous and unpredictable interplay of ethnicities, cultures and religions. And when it comes to the physical aspects of borders ... the dynamics haven't changed fundamentally in two millennia.[64]

The differences between America and Rome, though discussed, are nevertheless dismissed as minor variations; secondary to the more "important" universal themes. Murphy notes that, "The Roman Empire was not thickly settled; at its height the total population was no more than that of modern France, perhaps 50 or 60 million and skewed towards the East ... " but argues that despite this, "you'll find in EL Paso, on the American side, the same imperial tension between separation and integration, between sepsis and symbiosis.[65] Similarly, while "Rome's economy may have been primitive ... for its time the empire was already a globalized place." Most importantly, the comparison is worthy of attention because "In popular shorthand the long saga of Rome and the barbarians is typically held up as a case study in failure."[66]

Murphy sees a number of key parallels between these worlds: like Rome, the USA is a vast, multi-ethnic and cultural state, burdened with an expensive and overstretched military, and imbued with a messianic sense of its global mission, coupled with an ignorant disregard of alien cultures. It is beset with a decadent and deteriorating national character, with leaders in the grip of a messianic, moralizing religious belief. According to Murphy, the two states share the self-centred behaviour of ruling elites who see the world as revolving around their capitals. He describes the USA as "dangerously overcommitted abroad and rusted out at home, like Rome in its last two centuries."[67] He also notes the privatization, or "feudalization" of public services, which leads in his eyes to much greater corruption, and quotes historian F.L. Ganshof's definition of feudalism: "a dispersal of political authority amongst a hierarchy of persons who exercise in their own interest powers normally attributed to the state," meaning that "public wealth and public spaces fell increasingly into private hands for private gains." For Murphy, this is the perfect analogy for privatization.[68]

The consequence of these trends, therefore, is a decadent, myopic empire: one which displays a growing inability to manage its own sprawling affairs and powers, and whose primary difference with Rome appears to be only the accelerated rate of decline in the modern world. Indeed, Murphy quotes the line by Chalmers Johnson about how Roman sorrows "are likely to arrive with the speed of FedEx."[69] Rome, despite any perceived differences by these authors, is forever constituted as "a world not unlike our own," as was the type of decline suggested by Gibbon and his predecessors. It is paradoxical, therefore, that Murphy is dismissive of the man's influence and legacy—offering a description of him as "a man of his times, blind to many things, and in this case this sort of sweeping historical assessment is out of fashion."[70] This is despite offering exactly the same qualitative type of assessment: an almost unmodified description of Rome, from which can be derived universal and contemporary themes. Like Gibbon, Murphy believes that Rome's global dominion produced a largely bankrupt ruling class, an overdominant yet overextended army, and an imperial throne that had become the plaything of madmen, tyrants and degenerates. He also thinks that these are lessons to be learnt by present generations: "To American eyes, Rome is the eagle in the mirror."[71] While overtly attempting to transcend the mindset of the British Enlightenment historians, and update his ideas for a US audience, Murphy demonstrates little fundamental novelty in the actual content and themes of his work—

even though this is an explicit and stated purpose of his approach. It is suffused with myth, unmodified by its modern context.

A significant contemporary work that offers up a supposedly revisionist approach to Late Antique history is the British historian Adrian Goldsworthy's bestselling *The Fall of the West: The Death of the Roman Superpower* (2009). The stated emphasis of the book is not, at least overtly, to draw on such history to better understand the present, but is more directly concerned with the issue of Rome's fall itself. Goldsworthy proves critical of modern academic historiography. As he argues, "Studies of Late Antiquity stress the great strength of the fourth-century empire," and that, while they are "correct" to do so insofar as "Rome in this period was overwhelmingly stronger than any other nation or people in the known world," what they apparently fail to properly regard is that "it was not as stable as the empire of the second century, nor was it as powerful." As he says, "by 400 the empire was weaker again, and by 500 it had vanished in the west and only the rump was left in the lands around the eastern Mediterranean. A longer perspective is necessary to explain these shifts."[72]

When discussing the flourishing and extensive academic field on the Late Roman Empire that has sprung up in the past two generations, Goldsworthy says that, "The main reason I wanted to write this book was a dissatisfaction with quite a few of the conclusions and assumptions made in these works." This is because,

> There is no generally accepted explanation for the fall of the Roman Empire in the west in the fifth century. "Fall" is not a fashionable word ... many [scholars] talk instead of such things as "transformation", accepting that there was change, but casting it in a gentler light. A few voices have been raised against this rosy portrait, but any suggestion of decline seems tantamount to heresy.[73]

The challenge to the status quo is thus clearly stated. Such a momentous historical event as the fall of Rome requires a much clearer and more powerful explanation for Goldsworthy than simple transformation. Ironically, he actually cites the cultural and psychological impact of its representation as a reason for this: saying that, "every successive generation has turned to the mystery of why Rome fell."[74] And yet, in the face of "sheer common sense," the "historians of Late Antiquity" demonstrate an apparent psychological weakness: "It seems very hard for many people working on Late Antiquity to consider the possibility that anything was declining. Instead they prefer to see change and transformation." Goldsworthy, by contrast, desires such a great historical event to be furnished with an appropriately *meaningful* narrative, for "the reasons for the collapse of Roman power deserve an explanation."

The explanation offered up to explain this dilemma is a very familiar one. Goldsworthy says that though, "The Roman Empire did not fall quickly ... to use this as proof that its institutions were essentially sound is deeply misguided." Instead, the opposite assertion can be made—that Rome is a body "made vulnerable by prolonged decay."[75] To fall, therefore, Rome first had to decline its long life evidence not of strength, but of a slow deterioration. For this author, this decline is most prominently represented in the civil wars he believes ate away at the vitality of the state. They are notable not just for their "physical price" but also, in a *moral* sense, for their impact on "attitudes and behaviour from the emperor down." Rules became more paranoid and authoritarian, the bureaucracy expanded and became more inefficient and corrupt, and the senatorial class was sidelined from civil life.[76] Such an approach is not so much a "revision" as a reversion, unwinding decades of scholarship, all the way back to the arguments of Gibbon, Bury, and Durant.

With his very traditional approach to the fall of Rome in place, Goldsworthy turns to the inevitable comparison between Rome and the present day: "The imagery of ancient Rome has been invoked for its associations with the ultimate heights of power and civilization. It is never long before talk also turns to Rome's fate." The significance of this is that, "Insiders to the modern great power usually see this as a humbling reminder that everything passes, and perhaps as a warning against complacency and corruption." Just as the most natural comparison from Gibbon's time to about a century ago would have been Britain, so it has turned inevitably to the USA. Yet Goldsworthy is insistent, in this regard, that no meaningful historical analogies are to be made between these two worlds, and that, contrary to the grain of writing on the subject, he will stand apart in this respect, stating that, "This not a book about modern America and its place in the world."

*The Fall of the West*, self-described as a modern, academically subversive, revisionist approach to the period, betrays only an old-fashioned, anachronistic set of historiographical standards. Academically speaking, it is a reaction to modern revisionism itself—as in the new perspectives on Late Antiquity found in the field since the 1960s—couched as being revisionism in its own right.[77] Goldsworthy is able to see and acknowledge this tradition, but not escape it. He points out that:

It has always been easy to learn lessons from history, but all too often this is simply the case of using the past to justify modern ideas. Any close look at the Roman Empire will soon reveal massive differences with any modern state, including the United States .... [Rome is] an empire long vanished and from a world where the technology and culture were so very different from today. Understanding that world is the only way to understand Rome's fall.

This means that:

> Filling the pages with constant references to the present day is unlikely to help achieve this. It is more than a little odd to read studies of the Roman period describing the "shock and awe" of the invasion of Britain in 43. It is even stranger when the discussion of the end of a Roman province provides the opportunity for criticism of Bush and Blair and the war in Iraq.[78]

This is effectively a disclaimer for what follows, and despite the intended impression of authorial originality, the book falls into analysing comparative decline. Goldsworthy makes specific, comparative, and concerned judgements between past and present. As he says, "Britain has been a fairly depressing place in the last decade or so," wrapped up in a culture of "corruption or blatant deceitfulness," while "bureaucracy and regulation continue to grow apace" as "the basic efficiency of institutions declines." As in the Roman example, the number of "civil servants rises," while "the size of the armed forces shrinks at the very time they are more heavily committed to serious campaigns," buttressed by the "self-righteous" yet "ineffectual" nature of government decrees.[79] Such criticisms could be taken straight out of the pages of Gibbon or Bury. It is the traditional narrative of decline and fall, and the words "Britain" and "Rome" are effectively interchangeable in these descriptions.

Another such traditional narrative of a Late Antique process, namely the adoption of Christianity, comes to the fore in Charles Freeman's *The Closing of the Western Mind—The Rise of Faith and the Fall of Reason* (2003), in which the reader is treated to a self-described "radical and powerful reappraisal of the impact of Constantine's adoption of Christianity on the later Roman world, and on the subsequent development both of Christianity and of Western civilization," and the decline into superstition that followed, for "the closing of the Western mind is Rome's deliberate persecution of those whose God is the noble syllogism." Freeman's thesis is described thus:

> The first alliance of church and state in the fourth century, marked by the Roman emperor Constantine's conversion to Christianity, and how this decision irrevocably compromised the Roman empire's intellectual tradition of rationalism, paved the way toward a narrow religious orthodoxy, and aided the development of Christian anti-Semitism.[80]

Aside from the comparative historical insignificance of the "anti-Semitism" within the transition described here, one notes in particular the use of the words "a radical and powerful appraisal." The idea that Christianity fostered a decline in Western civilization is not remotely new, and is a central feature of Gibbon's analysis. Nevertheless, Freeman is praised in the *Times Literary Supplement* for having "added a new level of understanding" to these discourses, and enhancing our comprehension of the "darkness" produced, and "lessons" provided, by the "decline of the Roman Empire."[81]

## CINEMA AND THE DECLINE AND FALL IN THE NEW MILLENNIUM

Even as the cinematic classical epic has seen a revival in the twenty-first century, so the fall of Rome and its consequences have been a recurring subject in film. Antoine Faqua's *King Arthur* (Touchstone Pictures, 2004) advertised itself as "The Untold True Story that Inspired the Legend."[82] *Arthur* locates the myth in the fall years of the Roman Empire, when our fragmentary medieval chronicles lay claim to the idea that the Romano-British resisted the Anglo-Saxon invaders with some success.[83] It purports to achieve its claims to "truth" by alluding to modern-day speculation that "Sarmatian" cavalry stationed in Britain may have been a forgotten inspiration for the Arthurian story, and provided the historical basis of the legend.[84] The theory, while briefly popular in some academic circles, is not one that is genuinely accepted to have any real factual basis.[85] Nevertheless, it is the basis for the film's recursive claim to a real "authenticity."[86] It allowed the film to make claims about personal freedom, and its disappearance dooming a declining empire, as symbolized by the (again, unhistorical) execution of the "progressive" theologian, Pelagius—and to drape these anachronistic assumptions with the false veil of authority.[87]

Without delving too deeply into the extensive body of historiography surrounding the Arthurian myths, it should be noted that there are two distinct "King Arthurs" we can identify—one an elusive, hypothesized historical figure from the late fifth/early sixth century AD, the other a legendary medieval hero whose exploits were embellished and invented by the myth-makers of a much later age.[88] *King Arthur* weaves an unsteady and contradictory compromise between these two traditions, the "history"— such that exists—and the "myth" (which in both content and cultural presence overwhelms the former). As the narrative drives us from the late-Roman historical context to the self-aggrandized speculation on "what happened," it cannot help but morph into a New-Age inflected romanticization of Britain's lost "Celtic" past—complete in fact with Boudica-inspired Guinevere. It removes some, not all, of the archetypal elements of the Arthurian story—there is no Merlin, no magical elements, and no Holy Grail, but there are still knights and a re-envisioned Round Table. The attempt to create and visualize a more authentic history morphs into an acquiescence to the *literary* tradition which fashioned such icons, rather than a historical correction of that tradition.

Following a similar approach, Doug Lefler's *The Last Legion* (The Weinstein Company, 2007) connects the last years of the Western Roman Empire with the legend of the missing "Ninth Legion" in Britain—its continuing independent existence once a popular idea amongst historians— and its own self-spun legend about a missing sword of Julius Caesar, now revealed to be Excalibur. The film's tagline summarizes this theme with "Before Arthur, there was Excalibur." In this story, Romulus escapes the fall of the Western Empire, brought down by an alliance between Odoacer and the East, and goes on to sire Arthur.[89] Such an imaginative connection of two unrelated stories is at least vaguely reminiscent of Virgil's origin myth of the Romans in the *Aeneid*.

Both these films, while dealing with the end of the empire, at least imply that something more positive may have followed its destruction. Elsewhere, the theme of civilization facing a Roman-style crisis and an uncertain future has remained at the fore. Both Neil Marshall's *Centurion* (Pathé, 2010) and Kevin Macdonald's *The Eagle* (Universal Pictures, 2011) use the story of the Ninth Legion's supposed disappearance in Britain in the second century to deal with the theme of an empire weakening at the periphery and struggling to hold back the barbarians. But in director Alejandro Amenábar's ambitious and expensive *Agora* (Newmarket, 2009), we see the Roman Empire of the fourth and fifth centuries directly giving way to a new Christian order. While *The Fall of the Roman Empire* attempted to show how the seeds of Rome's collapse were sown under Commodus, *Agora* strives to display, through the individual tragedy of the philosopher Hypatia, how and why classical civilization was actually brought down, and uses this as a parallel for the material and political decline of the empire.

The film begins in Alexandria in AD 391 AD. The opening titles tell us that, "By the end of the fourth century AD, the Roman Empire was on the verge of collapse." This reinforces the conviction offered in the trailer that the film displays "the last days of the Roman Empire ... the fall of civilization." Such is a familiar and easy reiteration of the decline and fall myth, and no further explanation for this assumption is offered. Nevertheless, in this vision, it appears that something worthy of the old order survives, as "Alexandria, in the province of Egypt, still retained much of its splendour," including "the greatest library on earth." This library, we are told, had a dual significance in Late Roman society and the Hellenic tradition, for it "was not only a cultural symbol, but also a religious one. A place where pagans worshipped their ancestral gods."

In is in this context that we are introduced to the arc of the story. The Greek philosopher Hypatia (played by Rachel Weisz) is a teacher at the Platonic school, and daughter of Theon, director of the Museum of Alexandria, where the elite of Roman society are educated. Hypatia is openly pursued by one of her pupils, Orestes, whose advances she spurns. She is also silently admired from afar by her slave Davus, who assists her with her classes. This love "triangle" is set against a turbulent social and political landscape that threatens what survives of both the old faith and classical culture and learning itself. Increasingly fevered debates between pagans and Christians about the righteousness of their respective beliefs spill out into open conflict. From the outset, it is established that Christians have to use aggressive, bullying tactics to advocate their cause. A pagan preacher is forced into a fire by a Christian preacher as he mocks the power of his gods to protect him.[90]

When the Christians start defiling pagan statues and attacking their leaders, a large group of pagans, including Orestes and Theon, organize an ambush—staunchly opposed by Hypatia—to curb their rising influence. In the subsequent clash, however, they find themselves vastly outnumbered by an enormous Christian mob, and, with Theon mortally wounded, flee to the library of the Serapeum with Hypatia. A brief siege, barely contained by Roman soldiers, ends when the authorities declare that, though the pagans are pardoned for their deeds, the library will be opened to the Christians. Consequently, the pagans flee, Hypatia trying to remove as many of her beloved scrolls as possible. Davus, having joined the Christian forces, seizes Hypatia and attempts to rape her, but quickly breaks down and cries, offering his sword to her. Instead, she removes his slave collar and declares him free.

We now advance an undetermined number of years forward (though we could estimate it to be the months prior to Hypatia's death in 415). An intertitle informs the viewer that the majority of pagans have now converted to Christianity; including Orestes, who has become prefect of Alexandria, and maintains a close personal relationship with Hypatia. It also declares that, "The Roman Empire finally split into two parts. Many Christians saw this as a sign of the end of the world and decided to prepare themselves by living holier lives." In Alexandria, this means that the Christian authorities have turned their attentions increasingly to the Jewish community, identified as the murderers of Christ, and other religious dissidents. Hypatia is now preoccupied with her scientific pursuits—namely an investigation into the motions of the Sun, Moon and five "wanderers" in the heavens. Such views prove increasingly unpopular with the Christians, who have banned her from teaching due to her heliocentric sympathies. The Jews suffer increasing violence and harassment, but their objections are largely ignored by the authorities. Cyril, a leader of the Christians, resents Hypatia's influence over the prefect, attacking her both on the grounds of her faithlessness and her womanhood. A former pupil, Synesius, now bishop of Cyrene, comes to her defence, but says he cannot help her unless she embraces their faith. This she refuses to do when her former pupils beg her, citing that she must always doubt what she is told, and cannot believe blindly.

While these forces mount against her, Hypatia makes an extraordinary discovery; she realizes that the Earth orbits the Sun in an ellipse, not a circular orbit, thereby creating a working heliocentric model of the world. But before she can deliver this discovery to the world, Cyril convinces a mob that she is a dangerous heretic and a witch. They capture her, strip her, and are about to flay her alive, but Davus convinces them to stone her instead. Once they go outside to collect rocks, he suffocates her beforehand to spare her the pain. We are told in the final titles before the credits that Cyril became venerated as one of the Doctors of the Church; and that, a thousand years later, Galileo proved Hypatia right.

*Agora* dramatizes the decline of Greco-Roman polytheism and the concurrent Christianization of the Roman Empire. I have discussed earlier how the idealization of the "classical" is interwoven with the more negative image of the "medieval", and this is a film which makes the comparison between these two sets of qualities stark and explicit. It associates the process of the decline and fall—highlighted as an inevitable fact in the opening titles—with a rising conflict between religion and science, and the disappearance of classical traditions of free and rational inquiry into the natural world. The historicity of this account of Late Antiquity and the impact of the rise of Christianity is suffused with anachronism. The film highlights a contrast between reason, as embodied in the sceptical and inquisitive natural philosophy of Hypatia, and religious superstition, represented in part by the more militant pagans, but especially by the fanaticism of the Christian mob and its leaders.

In this way, the film has little to do with the turn of the fifth century AD, the end of paganism, or the fall of the Western Empire. Instead, it uses the decline and fall myth to tell a story of the downfall of the classical traditions of science, philosophy, and reason, and their replacement with a more "medieval" flavour of Christian conviction. At the same time, it highlights the eventual triumph of the former, from the Renaissance, with Hypatia playing a tragic but noble role as visionary precursor to a future age of heliocentric enlightenment.

In respect to its account of the end of the classical world, then, the film has much in common with the Gibbonian tradition. The latter author described her fate in these terms: "the great and justified reputation of this paragon was the cause of her downfall .... Hypatia was not a Christian, and Cyril, who was jealous of the way in which the female philosopher was courted ... took advantage of that fact to bring about her downfall." The problem for her in Gibbon's account was that the city was riven by faction, in particular a bitter rivalry between the "proud and violent Archbishop Cyril, the patriarch, and the prefect who commanded the city." Consequently, a rumour was spread by the latter that she was the sole obstacle in the way of reconciliation between prefect and archbishop. The result was this apparent atrocity:

> ... on a fatal day, in the holy season of lent, Hypatia was torn from her chariot, stripped naked, dragged to the church, and inhumanly butchered by the hands of Peter the Reader and a troop of savage and merciless fanatics: her

flesh was scraped from her bones with sharp oyster-shells, and her quivering limbs were delivered to the flames.[91]

It should be noted that in this description, even Gibbon does not ascribe her death to the bigotries of Christian dogma. Rather, he asserts that such bigotries provided a convenient excuse for Hypatia's removal due to age-old civic factional rivalries. Despite his own Enlightenment predisposition, his avowed contempt for Christianity, and his obvious disdain for Cyril and the mob, Gibbon does not go as far as to cast her death as symptomatic of an ideological war between science and fundamentalism. *Agora*, however, has no such problem. Nor does it skirt away from easy modern analogies, Amenábar himself stating that the material had given him "the chance to make a film about today."[92] Elsewhere, he identifies his target as not explicitly "Christians but ... those who set off bombs and kill in the name of God, that is, against religious fanatics."[93] The mention of "bombs" makes clear the contemporary context of religious terrorism that informs the director's perception of the dangers of blind faith to the supposedly civilized world, whether in Hypatia's time or the present.

*Agora* is a story about the final stages of the decline and fall of the Roman Empire, in a cultural and intellectual rather than material sense. The film attempts to both narrate and comprehend the end of Antiquity, but skirts over any military or political issues, stating simply that in AD 391 it was "on the verge of collapse." Instead, it offers a case study of the decline and fall, positioning the brutal murder of Hypatia by religious zealots as a symbol of the demise of the classical world. The scenes depicted in the film are intended to represent a turning point in the history of civilization for the worse; one, it is implied, only corrected with the discoveries of Galileo and the Renaissance. In this way, therefore, the "medieval" phase of history represents the consequence of the collapse of Greco-Roman culture and intellectual life at the turn of the fifth century, and the rise of a fanatical, intolerant form of Christianity. We see this change literally and physically occur not just through the murder of Hypatia but with the destruction in the Serapeum. While the building was indeed destroyed and levelled to the ground in AD 391, the account presented here is almost entirely fictional. There was no remaining "Great Library" in the sense of the iconic vast, priceless collection.[94] In this version, the Christians leave the building intact, and, aside from toppling a few statues, concentrate on collecting all the scrolls from the library and burning them in a giant pyre in the courtyard, to cries of jubilation at their destruction. Consequently, while this scene is indeed based on a historical event, Amenábar weaves a new version in which the Christian mob was focused on destroying ancient knowledge and learning. In this, he at least appears to have been partly inspired by Carl Sagan's iconic television series *Cosmos: A Personal Voyage* (PBS: 1980), which loosely recounts the death of Hypatia in the thirteenth and final episode, with Sagan stating that the Christians "came to burn down the great library of Alexandria … [and] there was no one to stop them."

It is in the context of these historical liberties that Hypatia is cast as a prophet of a future scientific revolution. She has the wisdom to embrace the heliocentric model, even though she cannot refute objections to it. As well as her invented final "breakthrough" in this field her other achievements are inflated in the film's publicity. Antonio Mampaso, an astrophysicist and one of *Agora*'s scientific consultants, offered this defence of her scientific credibility: "We know that Hypatia lived in Alexandria in the fourth and fifth centuries … only three primary sources mention Hypatia of Alexandria, apart from other secondary ones." He says that although "no works of Hypatia were preserved," it is possible to hypothesize from the secondary sources—notably a letter by Synesius dated to 402 that credits the design of an "astrolabe of silver" to her—that her father, Theon, designed the first astrolabe, and that she both contributed directly to this invention, and came close to achieving it on her own.[95] He also claims that she invented the hydrometer. However, there is ample evidence that the astrolabe was in use at least 500 years earlier.[96] The claim about the hydrometer has been widely repeated, but the evidence for it is limited to this letter Synesius sent Hypatia, requesting the construction of one.[97]

The historical liberties here extend further in the account presented of Hypatia's beliefs. The film strongly hints she is an atheist, a suggestion without any historical support, and which flatly contradicts the fact that she was head of the Platonist school in Alexandria. This school followed the teachings of Plotinus, a thinker who encouraged logic and mathematics in place of empirical inquiry, and whose goal was a mystical union with the divine. Her death did not lead to the end of the teaching of Hellenic philosophy, and its portrayal here completely ignores the influence of such philosophy, and Neo-Platonism in general, on Christianity.[98] Instead, she mouths post-Enlightenment platitudes: the line "What if we dared to look at the world just as it is" precedes her great scientific discovery in the final act, and she resists the well-meant pressure to convert from her Christian supporters by saying, "You do not question what you believe. Or cannot. I must." In response to the accusation that she does not believe in anything, she replies, "I believe in philosophy." This belief system ascribed to her has no basis in the historical record.

Over and over, elements are presented that cast Hypatia as a freethinking visionary in conflict with a rising tide of superstition. The destruction of the library, Cyril condemning her as a woman, her agnosticism or atheism, the heliocentric discovery—all these emphasize a clash between reason, and the forces of superstition that her views threatened. The interweaving of these narrative elements serves to link a celebration of the virtues of the classical tradition of "reason" with the negative, pejorative associations of the oncoming medieval and Christian world, with the Roman Empire "on the verge of collapse." The repeated symbolic shot of a revolving Planet Earth, half in light and half in darkness, buttresses this motif.

*Agora* positions itself as a film about reason as opposed to faith, and philosophy instead of violence. It is also a film deeply imbued with the characteristics of the decline and fall. In particular, it offers a simplistic rendering of Gibbon- and not Mann or Scott—in blaming religious superstition, in particular that of Christianity, for the loss of classical learning and wisdom, and the implicit arrival of a long Dark Age ushered in by Hypatia's death.

It should be noted that the film flopped internationally, grossing only $38 million on a $75 million budget. This may, however, have been the result of it only earning a very limited release in the USA, and the difficulty of finding a distributor due to its budget and length.[99] Furthermore, as a Spanish-produced film, it was that country's highest grossing release of 2009.[100] More notable than its earnings was the heated response it drew from many religious critics. In particular, it was openly attacked by the Religious Anti-Defamatory Observatory,[101] claiming the film was "reinforcing false clichés about the Catholic Church," and by a US Catholic bishop.[102] It was suggested in one review for the *Los Angeles Times*, however, that the film did not condemn specific Christian or Catholic religious dogma, but fundamentalism or religious ignorance in general.[103]

ROME, CIVILIZATION, AND THE MODERN AGE

The warnings of these contemporary authors and commentators about the possible, pending or imminent decline of the West strongly echo the bleak prognosticators of the first decades of the twentieth century. These very writers had helped coin the term "Western" to describe a faltering European civilization they believed was rapidly fading away, predominantly through its own internal degeneration. In doing so, they are reiterating Roman ruin and decline as *the* pivotal and iconic precedent.

These texts display two essential common traits. They claim to provide special, authoritative insight into the problems of the present day. However, while the specifics of the content and examples—such as the emphasis on Washington politics, mass culture, or a cosmic cyclical process—may vary, the principle and judgements evoked are almost precisely the same. There is little topicality or novelty in these declarations of decadence and decline; in their moral, cultural, and spiritual causes, and in the representation of their process with reference to Rome. The constant, universal myth of Rome's ending thereby serves its function as a prime precedent and analogy. It is a mythology in its own right, whether invoked solely and specifically, or in the broader purview of negative classicism. Such analyses of culture, mass culture, intellectual standards, and morals suggest that the present as a re-creation of the past, with the same ruinous repetitions.

Binding together these comparisons is this universal and constant theme: that the modern world has entered a stage of its history that is intimately comparable to the decline and fall of the Roman Empire. What a social scientist, or author, or filmmaker, or journalist offers as analysis of modern society, or mass culture, proves in fact to contain at its heart something else: a version of the same persistent, pervasive mythology that frames its subject in the context of the rise and fall of empires and civilizations that supposedly bookend the cycle of human affairs. This is the universal principle underlying our stated cultural myth, buried as it is within texts that carry the impression of genuine new analysis, but instead are better regarded as versions of the same act of mythologizing. In this process, the distinction between "high" and "mass" culture breaks down—it has little relevance as a contrast between meaning and approach.

However, it must be noted that the degree to which this fall—placed in secular, spiritual or more religious terms—is *directly* invoked varies. It is the central idea of Gibbon and Mann's version of *The Fall* (and the ideal case study for Tainter), one piece of a larger puzzle for Spengler, Toynbee, Kennedy—and only of incidental interest to many other pieces of work cited here. However, the *intention* of the inference is virtually always the same. In many cases, a passing allusion to Roman decline, or decadence, or the fall, or the "barbarians," the danger of the "masses," "mass culture," "bread and circuses," or such related notions, is meant to trigger a chain of associations pointing towards a secular implosion or reckoning: one comparable to the *proven* precedent of Rome's fall. Such analogies run into substantial problems. There was no equivalent in the ancient world for the mass media and its paraphernalia—network TV, centralized media, radio, television, cinema, or even mass literacy or a universal education system necessary to generate these processes. The mythology of negative classicism, however, tends to lump all these novel and unprecedented features of modern life into one category, with the maxim of "bread and circuses" the prime social and cultural marker; a means of equating the death of the ancient world with the doom of the modern.

It is also vital to observe here that in these accounts of history, both contemporary and modern, the comparative approach of the author is vital; with an analysis of the past, or allusion to it, deployed for the purpose of making subjective value judgements about the present. The value of the past is therefore directly informed by its relevance to the interpretation of the present. Such approaches deeply inform the representations of the decline and fall found in literature and cinema. Despite disagreement on the content and nature of these processes, all sides in these debates could and can draw upon an explicit *language* of decline; and, beneath this, a common latent set of assumptions and ideologies. Randolph Stern makes a point along these lines about Renaissance humanism: "Something like the decline of Rome was indispensable to the humanists' sense of their identity and cultural role. When it had occurred—with the subversion of the Roman Republic, as in Bruni, or with Biondo's barbarians—was an open question. But if there had been no decline, if Roman culture had passed directly and continuously to the moderns, there would have been little point in calling it back to life." Such was crucial to the concept of Renaissance, which harked back to a very particular classical ideal.[104]

NOTES

1. Leften S. Stavrianos, *The Promise of the Coming Dark Age* (New York: W.H. Freeman & Co, 1976), p. 66.
2. See Richard Romano and Melvin M. Leiman (eds.), *Views of Capitalism* (Glencoe: Illinois, 1970), p. 38, p. 316, and Gibbon (1993), I, p. 65.
3. Robert Sinai, *The Decadence of the Modern World* (Cambridge: Schenkelman, 1978), p. 5.

4. Robert Sinai, "What Ails us and why: On the Roots of Disaster and Decay," *Encounter* (April, 1979), pp. 8–17, quotes at pp. 15–16. See also Robert Sinai, "The Sinai Discussion," *Encounter* (February, 1980), pp. 87–93, which includes a number of critiques of this apocalyptic prophesying. With reference to the Roman model, Ronald Butt notably ponders "if it is the fate of all civilizations" to decline and fall, then "why should it disturb us intellectually, particularly if it is part of the process of natural death and rebirth?" For out of its decay came "the much higher, more spiritual and humane aspirations of Christian Europe." He also says, "Notably, this is not a criticism of the *idea* of the comparison ... simply an alternative attitude to its inevitability." See also Marshall McLuhan, *Understanding Media: The Extensions of Man* (London: McGraw-Hill, 1964).
5. Christopher Lasch, *The Culture of Narcissism: American Life in the Age of Diminishing Expectations* (New York: W.W. Norton and Co., 1978), p. 106.
6. Malcolm Muggerridge, "On the Threshold of the Eighties," *The American Spectator* (May 1980), p. 15.
7. Bernard J. James, *The Death of Progress* (New York: Alfred Knopt Incorporated, 1973), p. 38.
8. Op. cit., p. 39. See also Walter J. Ong, *The Barbarian Within* (New York: Macmillan, 1962).
9. Daniel Bell, *The Cultural Contradictions of Capitalism* (New York: Basic, 1976), p. 175, and p. 110 for the use of "demonic".
10. Op. cit., p. 168.
11. Richard Sennett, *The Fall of Public Man: On the Social Psychology of Capitalism* (London: Faber and Faber (ori. Pub. 1977), 2002), pp. 1–3.
12. Walter W. Wagar, *The City of Man: Prophecies of Civilization* (Baltimore: Penguin, 1967), p. 4. The title is, fittingly for my purpose here, an allusion to Augustine's (unfavourable) comparison between Rome and heaven.
13. Brantlinger, p. 297, quoting William I. Thompson, *Evil and the World Order* (New York: HarperCollins, 1976), p. 55. The opening chapter of that work is entitled "Meditations on the Dark Age."
14. As related in Cullen Murphy, *Are We Rome? The Fall of an Empire and the Fate of America* (New York: Mariner Books, 2007), p. 169.
15. Sinai, p. 5.
16. Hans Morgenthau, "Decline of the West," *Partisan Review*, XXII (1975), p. 514.
17. Gibbon (1993), IV, p. 117.
18. Marya Mannes, *They* (Garden City, New York: Doubleday Publishers, 1968), p. 32.

19. City of God, XIX. 6.
20. Rousseau, "A Discourse on the Arts and Sciences," in *The Social Contract and Discourses* (London: Everyman's Library, 1993).
21. George Braeur, *The Decadent Emperors: Power and Depravity in Third-Century Rome* (New York: Barnes and Noble (ori. Pub. 1967), 1995).
22. Transcript from his interview in the documentary by Adolfo Doring, *Blind Spot* (Woodstock, 2008), a film concerned with the consequences of a global dependency on fossil fuels.
23. Joseph A. Tainter, *The Collapse of Complex Societies* (New York: Cambridge University Press, (ori. Pub. 1988), 1990), in particular p. 11, p. 54, and pp. 63–86. He cites John B. Bury, *History of the Later Roman Empire from the Death of Theodosius I to the Death of Justinian* (AD 395 to AD 565) (London: Macmillan, 1923), I, pp. 311–2.
24. Tainter, pp. 63–86.
25. Op. cit., p. 86.
26. Op. cit., p. 124.
27. Bowersock (1996), pp. 29–43.
28. As an example see Max Boot, "The Case for American Empire," *The Weekly Standard* (15th October, 2001).
29. Paul Kennedy, *The Rise and Fall of the Great Powers: Economic Change and Military Conflict 1500–2000* (London: Fontana Press (ori. Pub. 1987), 1989), pp. xvi, xviii, xxiii. Imperial overstretch is summarized by Kennedy on pp. 438–9.
30. Arnold J. Toynbee, *America and the World Revolution and Other Lectures* (New York: Oxford University Press, 1962).
31. William L. Vance, *America's Rome, Volume 1: Classical Rome* (New Haven: Yale University Press, 1989), p. 387. On Eliot and the imperial frontier myth, see Edwards, p. 244, which discussed how *The Waste Land* has been viewed in part as a response to the crisis of the First World War, Western imperialism, and implicitly its Roman counterpart.
32. Kevin Philips, *Arrogant Capital: Washington, Wall Street, and the Frustration of American Politics* (New York: Back Bay Books, 1995) pp. xii-xiii. These failings and shortcomings include here "economic polarization", which has resulted in "a declining middle class."
33. Cornel West, *Race Matters* (New York: Vintage Books, 2001), p. 6, p. 18. For more books on this theme in recent years, see Edward Luttwak, *The Endangered American Dream* (New York, 1993), Daniel Lazare, *The Frozen Republic* (New York, 1996).
34. Knox, p. 305. This idea is also echoed in Allan Bloom, *The Closing of the American Mind* (New York: Simon & Schuster, 1987), p. 344. See also Russell Jacoby and Naomi Glauberman (eds.), *The Bell Curve Debate*

(New York: Random House, 1995), a compilation of 81 independently authored articles debating the issue.
35. Joseph Brodsky, "Homage to Marcus Aurelius," in Joseph Brodsky, *On Grief and Reason: Essays* (New York: Farrar Straus Giroux, 1995), pp. 267–298. For more on the presence of the Marcus Aurelius stereotype in popular culture see Martin M. Winkler, "*Star Wars* and the Roman Empire," in Martin M. Winkler (ed.), *Classical Myth and Culture in the Cinema* (New York: Oxford University Press, 2001), pp. 272–290.
36. Charles Murray and Richard Herrnstein, *The Bell Curve* (Free Press: New York, 1994), pp. 509–10.
37. Winkler (2009), p. xii.
38. Landau, pp. 19–20.
39. Richard Corliss, "*Gladiator*: The Empire Strikes Back," *Time* (8th May, 2000), p. 83.
40. Herbert Muschamp, "Throwing Our Anxieties to the Lions," *The New York Times* (30th April, 2000), p. 33.
41. Quoted from Paul M. Sammon, *Ridley Scott* (New York: Thunder's Mouth Press, 1999), p. 130.
42. Data is taken from IMDB at http://www.imdb.com/title/tt0172495/business?ref_=tt_dt_bus
43. Martin Arnold, "Making Books; Book Parties with Togas," *The New York Times* (11th July, 2002), http://web.archive.org/web/20080117055645/http:/query.nytimes.com/gst/fullpage.html?res=990CE2D61530F932A25754C0A9649C8B63
44. Bondanella (1987), p. 1.
45. Muschamp, p. 33. On the many tensions produced by the modern identification with Rome, see in particular William Fitzgerald, "Oppositions, Anxieties and Ambiguities in the Toga Movie," in Sandra R. Joshel, Margaret Malamud, and Donald T. McGuire, JR (eds.), *Imperial Projections: Ancient Rome in Modern Popular Culture* (New York: John Hopkins University Press, 2001), pp. 23–49.
46. In the "Gladiator: First Draft Revised" (4th April, 1998) of David Franzoni's screenplay for *Gladiator* the cultural supremacy of Rome is extolled in more explicit detail. Marcus says to the assembled soldiers: "For nine hundred years architects, mathematicians, poets, and philosophers have fled within her arms sheltered from superstition, prejudice, hate, and every form of human cruelty. We Romans have become a light in the barbarian night!" Marcus also calls Rome "this one heart of humankind." Quotation from www.hundland.com/scripts/Gladiator_FirstDraft.txt
47. For Scott's interest in the exactitude of his depiction see Corliss (2000), pp. 80–90.

48. Scott describes these influences in Ridley Scott, "Introduction", in Diane Landau (ed.), *Gladiator: The Making of the Ridley Scott Epic* (New York: Newmarket Press, 2000), pp. 7–9, and Gerome's painting is reproduced on pp. 23–4.
49. Ridley Scott explains this both in his director's audio commentary on the DVD release, and in Landau, p. 120.
50. Tacitus, *Agricola*, 2. 1, 3. 1.
51. Sandra Joshel, "*I, Claudius*: Projection and Imperial Soap Opera," in Joshel, Malamud, and McGuire, pp. 119–161.
52. David Franzoni, as quoted in James Russell, *The Historical Epic and Contemporary Hollywood: From Dances with Wolves to Gladiator* (London: Continuum International Publishing, 2007), p. 159, p. 172.
53. Solomon, p. 93.
54. Corliss (2000), p. 84 discusses the idea of Maximus as a "working-class hero." Additionally, Jon Solomon suggests a comparison with the general and former farmer Cincinnatus, "an early Roman exemplar of nobility," in Solomon, p. 94.
55. Op. cit., p. 95.
56. This also parallels the portrayal of the bisexual Crassus in Spartacus, for which see Alison Futrell, "Seeing Red: Spartacus as Domestic Economist," in Joshel, Malamud, and McGuire, pp. 77–118.
57. Monica S. Cyrino, "*Gladiator* and Contemporary American Society," in Martin M. Winkler (ed.), Gladiator: *Film and History* (Oxford: Blackwell, 2004), p. 145.
58. Richard Corliss, "Mann of the Hour," *Time* (4th August, 2006), available online at http://www.time.com/time/arts/article/0,8599,1223014,00.html, evoking the comparisons between George Bush Senior and Junior with respect to Iraq policy in the two Gulf Wars. For a contrasting attitude that also invokes imperialist comparison, David Frum and Richard Perle wrote in 2003, "America's vocation is not an imperial vocation. Our vocation is to support justice with power .... It is a vocation that has made us, at our best moments, the hope of the world," in David Frum and Richard Perle, *An End to Evil: How to Win the War on Terror* (New York: Random House, 2003), p. 275 and p. 279.
59. Chalmers A. Johnson, *The Sorrows of Empire: Militarism, Secrecy and the End of the Republic* (London: New Left Books, 2004), pp. 285–6. The overall analogy is supplied with this example on p. 285: "Militarism and imperialism always bring with them sorrows. The ubiquitous symbol of the Christian religion, the cross, is perhaps the world's most famous reminder of one sorrow that accompanied the Roman Empire." Other pejorative comparisons abound in the book—for instance, p. 28 refers to how "twentieth-century 'total war,' associated above all with air power, was known in medieval times as 'Roman war.'"

60. Patrick J. Buchanan, *State of Emergency: The Third World Invasion and Conquest of America* (New York: St Martin's, 2006), p. 3. His analysis quotes Peter Heather, specifically Heather (2005), p. 158.
61. Harold James, *The Roman Predicament: How the Rules of International Order Create the Politics of Empire* (Princeton: Princeton University Press, 2006), p. 6.
62. Murphy, p. 5.
63. Op. cit., p. 150.
64. Op. cit., p. 197.
65. Op. cit., pp. 155–6.
66. Op. cit., p. 158.
67. Op. cit., p. v.
68. Op. cit., p. 201.
69. Johnson (2004), pp. 285–6, as referenced in Murphy, p. 8. He also cites here Paul Kennedy's idea of "imperial overstretch." Changing circumstances are described with the slightly trite line: "Hadrian's wall would today have to be supplemented by Hadrian's firewall." Op. cit., p. 158.
70. Op. cit., p. 195.
71. Op. cit., p. 6
72. Goldsworthy, p. 21.
73. Op. cit., p. 7.
74. Op. cit., p. 16.
75. Op. cit., p. 413, p. 415.
76. Op. cit., pp. 408–9, also p. 120, p. 22 and p. 84.
77. Goldsworthy, p. 8, criticizes the "peaceful transition theory," and in particular the supposed strength of the later empire, saying that "a longer perspective is necessary to explain these shifts."
78. Op. cit., p. 5.
79. Op. cit., p. 6.
80. Charles Freeman, *The Closing Of The Western Mind: The Rise of Faith and the Fall of Reason* (London: Pimlico, 2003), back cover.
81. Peter Watson, "Money, Magic and Miracles," *Times Higher Education Supplement* (13th December, 2002), available online at http://www.timeshighereducation.co.uk/books/money-magic-and-miracles/173657.article
82. http://www.imdb.com/title/tt0349683/taglines
83. The literature on Arthur is far too vast and complicated to explore in any detail here, but for good summaries that have been used see Nicholas J. Higham, *King Arthur, Myth-Making and History* (London: Routledge, 2002), pp.11–37, which has a good summary of the debate on Arthur's existence, as does Thomas Green, *Arthuriana: Early Arthurian Tradition and the Origins of the Legend* (Lindes, 2009), at pp. 3–46. See also Frank

D. Reno, *The Historic King Arthur: Authenticating the Celtic Hero of Post-Roman Britain* (Jefferson, NC: McFarland, 1996).
84. Covington S. Littleton, "The Sarmatian Connection: New Light on the Origin of the Arthurian and Holy Grail Legends," *Journal of American Folklore*, XCI (1978), pp. 512–527.
85. Richard Wadge, "A British or Sarmatian Tradition," *Folklore*, XCVIII (1987), pp. 204–215. The Pelagian subplot in the film, involving the freethinking religious heretic whose execution inspired Arthur's final disillusionment with Rome, has very little historical veracity. Pelagius was not executed by the Romans, but most likely died of old age. See on this Charles G. Herbermann (ed.), *Catholic Encyclopedia*, XI (Robert Appleton Company: New York, 1911), p. 604.
86. The literature on Arthur is far too vast and complicated to explore in any detail here, but for good summaries that have been used here see Nicholas J. Higham, *King Arthur, Myth-Making and History* (London: Routledge, 2002), pp. 11–37 has a good summary of the debate on Arthur's existence.
87. For the life of Pelagius see Herbermann, p. 604.
88. While much of the legend originates with the accounts of Geoffrey of Monmouth in his Monmouth in his *Historia Regum Britanniae* (*History of the Kings of Britain*) written c. AD 1138, most modern Arthurian works are derivative of an adaption from the fifteenth century, written by Thomas Malory. See Geoffrey of Monmouth, "A History of the Kings of Britain," in Joseph Black (ed.), *The Broadview Anthology of British Literature: The Medieval Period* (Toronto: Broadview Press, 2009), pp. 157–179, and on Malory, Eugène Vinaver (ed.), *The Works of Sir Thomas Malory* (Oxford: Oxford University Press, 1990).
89. Doug Lefler, *The Last Legion* (The Weinstein Company, 2007).
90. This has echoes of the biblical story of Elijah competing with the prophets of Baal to perform a miracle. 1 Kings 18:20–24.
91. Gibbon (1993), V, p. 18. For the original source see Socrates Scholasticus, *Ecclesiastical History*, trans. Philip Schaff, Henry Wace (New York: Bohn, 1853), pp. 348–9.
92. Quote from an interview with the director, published in *The Guardian* (17th May, 2009). See http://www.theguardian.com/world/feedarticle/8512013
93. This statement is referred to in an open letter of protest by Antonis Alonso Marcus, the president of the Religious Anti-Defamatory Observatory, to Amenábar (7th October, 2009). See http://www.catholicnewsagency.com/news/civil_groups_protest_new_antichristian_film/

94. For an account of its destruction in the context of civic conflicts, see Peter Brown, *The Rise of Western Christendom: Triumph and Diversity 200–1000 AD* (London: Blackwell, 2003), pp. 73–4.
95. Antonio Mampaso, "The best legacy of Hypatia is its own history," interview with Enrique Sacristan (28th October, 2009). The entire interview is available online at http://www.oei.es/divulgacioncientifica/entrevistas_034.htm
96. "It is generally accepted that Greek astrologers, in either the 1st or 2nd centuries BC, invented the astrolabe," writes Robert E. Krebs, *Groundbreaking Scientific Experiments, Inventions, and Discoveries of the Middle Ages and the Renaissance* (New York: Greenwood, 2004), p. 196.
97. This letter "contains a detailed description of a hydroscope which Synesius asks Hypatia to order for him in Alexandria, requesting that she herself oversee its construction." Kari Vogt, "The Hierophant of Philosophy—Hypatia of Alexandria," in Kari E. Boerresen and Kari Vogt (eds.), *Women's studies of the Christian and Islamic traditions: ancient, medieval, and Renaissance foremothers* (Dordrecht: Kluwer Academic Publishers, 1993), p. 161.
98. Maria Dzielska and Christian Wildberg directly address these stereotypes and problems in an interview (preceding the release of *Agora* in October, and which does not mention the film at all); Maria Dzielska and Christian Wildberg, "Hypatia of Alexandria—a philosophical martyr," radio interview with Joe Gelonesi (4th April, 2009), transcript available online at http://www.abc.net.au/radionational/programs/philosopherszone/hypatia-of-alexandria—a-philosophical-martyr/3142424#transcript
99. Pamela McClintock and Sharon Swart, "Epic Bow for 'Agora'," *Daily Variety*, CCCV (New York, 2009), p. 8.
100. http://www.rottentomatoes.com/m/agora/
101. Anonymous, "Civil groups protest new anti-Christian film," *Catholic News Agency* (7th October, 2009), http://www.catholicnewsagency.com/news/civil_groups_protest_new_antichristian_film/
102. Robert Barron, "Christians must resist dangerous silliness of 'Agora'," *Catholic New World* (9th May, 2010), http://www.catholicnewworld.com/cnwonline/2010/0509/barron.aspx
103. Michael Ordoña, "Movie review: 'Agora' shows the true casualty of war," *Los Angeles Times* (4th June, 2010), http://articles.latimes.com/2010/jun/04/entertainment/la-et-capsules-20100604
104. Starn, p. 25. Much in fact has been written on the "humanist" and Renaissance literary conceptions of decline, with indirect, though not central, relevance to this study. Robert A. Nisbet, *Social Change and History: Aspects of the Western Theory of Development* (Oxford: Oxford

University Press (ori. Pub. 1969), 1992), John G. Pocock, *Politics, Language and Time: Essays on Political Thought and History* (New York: University of Chicago Press, 1989), Nancy S. Struever, *The Language of History in the Renaissance: Rhetoric and Historical Consciousness in Florentine Humanism* (New Jersey: Princeton University Press, 1970), and Skinner (1969), pp. 5–53.

CHAPTER 6

# Conclusion

In this book I set out to answer the question: What, within our time frame of the late nineteenth century to the present day, does the representation of the decline and fall of Rome tell us about the societies that produced these cultural texts? Exploring the ranging answers to this meant probing a second, and somewhat deeper, query: Are these representations of Rome transient and unique to their specific period, or do they possess universal qualities? Answering both these questions has required invoking two key conceptual models: a particular interpretation of the notion of myth, as the term is defined by Lévi-Strauss, and the metahistorical formulation of an integrated regime of representation found in Hayden White. Drawing on both of these ideas has been essential to coming to grips with the pervasive cultural presence of the decline and fall of Rome.[1] In an academic context, the word *myth* is clearly and demonstrably the most appropriate term to describe this, and I have demonstrated how the myth-model of Lévi-Strauss is a potent means to understand the peculiarities of this type of historical transmission. More broadly, one can see this as a case study of what one might term "historical reception," that displays how such work is integral to sensitive historical interpretation.

There is, however, an important sense in which our usage of his term deviates from the Straussian example. The myths outlined in that model describe, above all, their role as providing order and comfort in a chaotic universe.[2] What, then, about myths such as these, stories of the decline and decay and collapse of society? Do myths have to "affirm" or "confirm"? In these terms, the decline and fall functions as a powerful counter-myth, both to teleologies of progress, and the high and venerating ideals embodied in so much of the reception of the classical world. It is a critique or caveat of the social order, rather than an affirmation: structurally similar to the Straussian ideal of what myth truly *constitutes*, but embodying a whole other set of social and cultural tendencies.

This brings me to a defining feature of this myth: namely, that it maintains an atypically constant form. Acknowledging this fact reveals that both questions posed at the start of this conclusion are not indeed really separate, and must be answered together. The way in which the different authors and directors—from Gibbon to Amenábar—use the decline and fall reveals the overriding priorities of the universal components of this myth. It is one which can be given innumerable different causes, and related to an endless variety of later societies, states, and cultures; but for the myth to serve its function, the necessary characteristics of the story have to remain the same. In the literary and cinematic examples cited throughout this book, whether nineteenth-century or twenty-first, the story takes the same essential form. Rome fell because Rome first declined; she declined, because she was tainted from within; and the forces that corrupted her, with some local variation, are those that every society or civilization must hold in check if they are to be spared the consequences which befell the Roman example.

Without the utter clarity of this narrative, the story of Rome has no mythological meaning; and no comparative value for the authors who seek a tale about the present as much as the past. It would be only a specialist historical concern; with perhaps some wider, but largely symbolic significance as the "end of an era." But this is a myth far too grand in scope to be such a footnote; one which deploys a historical vision of human nature as a whole; and one which, while couched in universal moral and theological precepts, draws specifically on an idealized version of Late Roman history for its moral and intellectual force. The sweeping, comparative purpose of this invocation is what gives it a coherent meaning and visible identity, across the broad time frame of this study, and embodied in its varying textual forms.

The fall of Rome, the causes of its decline, and the universal relevance of the story, have occupied a unique place in the Western mind. As a society, we have shared a common obsession with this fall. It has been valued and exploited as an archetype for every perceived decline, from the political to the theological; and hence as a symbol for the multifari-

CONCLUSION 197

ous fears held about society, culture and civilization as a whole. There is a constant representation of Rome in this regard as "a world not unlike our own," engulfing the myth of Roman decline in a continuum with the current world of the author, and ancient history with perceptions of the present day. The decline and fall is a myth in which a mutually explored aspect of the contemporary world *is a recreation of the Roman Empire*, in some aspect or form, allowing the same moral force of judgement to apply.

An outline of this framework, and the manifestation of its recurring tropes and features, have been the basis for my description of this integrated regime of representation and its operation. The decline and fall proves to be a compelling enough narrative, bound up with a profound moral purpose, that it has featured substantially, in both overt and latent ways, not only in academic historiographies since Gibbon but also in the popular culture of the twentieth and twenty-first centuries. I have demonstrated how intimately the two have often been interlinked. In this manner, therefore, Gibbon provides the framework for the history of Durant; who shapes the historical representation of Anthony Mann; who in turn provides the cinematic precedent for *Gladiator*. Similarly, the literary and moral concepts of decline present in Augustine are repeated in twentieth-century criticism of modern empire, and the "bread and circuses" metaphor of Juvenal occurs as a prime example of the problems of modern mass culture and the industrialized world: features of society that would have been utterly alien to that poet of the ancient past.

Such, then, is the mythology at work here. It is constructed out of real history, and owes much of the description of the collapse of the Western Roman Empire to the accounts of its contemporaries and later historians. But it now has very little relationship remaining with any real history, and instead draws on a separate tradition of tropes and ideas for representing negative classicism, and the decline from the "high" classical to the medieval. From this, then, one can comprehend how the concept of the decline and fall can only be properly understood as a spatiotemporal construct, rather than a historical event—even when most of its popular and intellectual representations characterize and classify it as such, and indeed depend on the authority of so-called "history" to make their own point. In particular, I have highlighted the presence of the decline and fall as an ongoing cultural force by revealing how far and how much this subject has functioned as a metaphor for the concerns authors in Britain, Europe, and the USA have with the possibility of a similar decline, as they confront the perceived instability and pitfalls of the society to which they belong. These have, in the time frame of this book, been particularly centred on the threats and challenges to Western civilization from without and within; whether pre-Enlightenment superstition for Gibbon, spiritual decay for Toynbee and Spengler, the Cold War and the rise of television for those critics from the 1940s, late industrial decay and cultural collapse from the 1970s, or US foreign policy and its consequences in the new millennium.

Such criticisms have embraced a range of beliefs and ideologies. They all, however, demonstrate a form of negative classicism, in that they envisage a decline and fall that coheres to trends unfolding in their own time. In this way the fall of Rome is deemed a story that possesses universal significance, and one that can be related to the modern world as a moral tale. Occupying an arc of representational forms from Gibbon to *Gladiator*, it can pervade all levels of public consciousness, from the scholarly to the popular. It appeals to both Marxists and conservatives, Christian apologists and atheists, because its purpose and role is more expansive than such specific ideologies. This vision of the end of Roman civilization, an idea persisting in culture despite the intellectual onslaught of modern academic historiography, presents a uniquely powerful and pliable counter to a theory of progress: an eternally invoked warning of how and why such apparent progress can go wrong. I can lead this observation into an insight that the whole idea of cultural, political, or societal decay, specifically when tied to the Roman example, has *comparison* so deeply embedded in its meaning, origin, and continued usage, that the process has become fundamental to the very idea of the decline and fall of Rome. Virtually every social and cultural author and commentator who discusses the theme falls into a comparison with their own period, whether unconsciously or through explicit intent.

Furthermore, I have demonstrated how the very concept of the decline and fall is deeply *theological* in character, in its precepts and archetypes, whether wrapped up in a secular narrative or not. It is an idea and a description of history built on spiritual and religious notions of decadence and moral decline, and continues to bear the weight of their sanction. Yet, this detachment from a strictly providential theology, and its secularization by Gibbon, is critical to the formation of the myth; and a crucial reason for why these same ideas and judgements can maintain their relevance in the diverse array of history, literature, film and other cultural commentaries of the twentieth century onwards. Modern authors can transmit these ideas within a wholly secular context. Myth does not require religion in its function.

The exposure of the process of decline and fall carries the conviction of probing in depth and truth. This may explain why observers of historical deterioration have appeared so often in the mantles of either prophecy or of social science. With either analytical categories or evocative, artful demonstrations, these prophets believe themselves equipped to seek out the design and underlying meanings in history, and expose the worrisome deviations from a cultural or moral standard. For this approach, the fall of Rome proves to be an ideal candidate as the test-case for how society or civilization can apparently go wrong. The distillation of its history into a myth formula lends itself to being transposed to other time frames, where such values are deemed relevant; what Rome is thought to represent historically is also felt to be as authentically experienced elsewhere, whether it be Napoleon's Paris, or London at the zenith of the British Empire, or the USA as a sole superpower in the twenty-first century. By this means, the subjective experience and consideration of the past can be rendered as components of an "objective" system.

This historical idealisation of the decline and fall of Rome seeks to make itself synonymous with the order of history itself. Its end, in this sense, is not a fixed historical event, but an idea through time, a process of engagement between past and present. Within this definition of empire, an event such as the Sack of Rome by Alaric in AD 410, or the deposition of Romulus Augustulus in AD 476, marks not the demise of empire, but opens up the discursive opportunity to speak of Rome as an episode within the cyclical flux of empire and civilization as a whole. Rome, from being identified with that empire or point in time, becomes an archetype of rupture or discontinuity, of negative classicism and the slew of attached concepts of decline. In this book it became very clear that there is virtually no period when such assumptions about the contemporary world have not been made, across authors and genres and media, and where a common and continuous mythology about the imagined fall of Roman civilization was not present or invoked.

## Notes

1. Strauss (1968) and White (1973).
2. Strauss (1968), p. 224 and Cohen, pp. 337–53.

# Bibliography

## Classical and Medieval Texts in Translation and Latin

Ammianus. (1989). *Res Gestae* (trans: Rolfe, J.C.). London: Loeb Classical Library.
Anonymous. (1989). *Historia Augusta* (trans: Magie, D). London: Loeb Classical Library (ori. pub. 1924).
Augustine. (1997). *On Christian Teaching* (trans: Green, R.P.H.). Oxford: Oxford University Press.
Augustine. (2003). *The City of God* (trans: Bettenson, H.). Harmondsworth: Penguin Books (ori. pub. 1972).
Aurelius, M. (1992). *The Meditations* (trans: Farquharso, A.S.L.). New York: Everyman.
Cassius, D. (1921). *Roman History* (trans: Cary, E.). London: Loeb Classical Library.
Edwards, C. (trans.). (2010). *The Nibelungedlied: The Lay of the Nibelung*. New York: Oxford University Press.
Geoffrey of Monmouth. (2009). A history of the kings of Britain. In J. Black (Ed.), *The broadview anthology of British literature: The medieval period* (pp. 157–179). Toronto: Broadview Press.
Harries, J., & Woods, I. (1993). *Theodosian Code* (trans: Harries, J., & Woods, I.). New York: Cornell University Press.
Herodian. (1969). *The History of the Empire* (trans: Whittaker, C.R.). London: Loeb Classical Library.

Hesiod. (2006). *Hesiod: Theogony, Works and Days, Testimonia* (trans: Most, G.W., Loeb Classical Library). Harvard: Harvard University Press.
Jerome. (2009). *Commentary on Daniel* (trans: Archer, G.L.). Oregon: Wipf & Stock Publishers.
Juvenal. (1998). *The Sixteen Satires* (trans: Green, P.). London: Penguin Classics.
Libanius. (1977). *Selected Orations*, II (trans: Norman, A.F.). Harvard: Harvard University Press.
Plato. (2007). *The Republic* (trans: Lee, D.). London: Penguin.
Prudentius. (1989). *Prudentius* (trans: Thompson, H.J.). London: Loeb Classical Library.
Salvian of Marseilles. (1966). *De Gubernatione Dei* (trans: Sanford, E.M.). New York: Columbia University Press (ori. pub. 1930).
Scholasticus, S. (1853). *Ecclesiastical History* (trans: Schaff, P & Wace, H.). New York: Bohn, pp. 348–349.
Symmachus. (1973). Relationes. In R. H. Barrow (Ed.), *Prefect and emperor: The relationes of Symmachus, AD 384*. Oxford: Clarendon Press.
Tacitus. (1937). *Annals* (trans: Jackson, J.). London: Loeb Classical Library.
Tacitus. (1989). *Agricola, Germania, Dialogus* (trans: Hutton, M. & Peterson, W.). London: Loeb Classical Library.
Thucydides. (1973). *The History of the Peloponnesian War* (trans: Warner, R.). London: Penguin.

## Pre-twentieth Century Literature

Arnold, M. (1882). *Culture and anarchy*. New York: Macmillan.
Bentham, J. (1995). *Colonies, commerce, and constitutional law*. Oxford: Clarendon Press. ori. pub. 1820–22.
Berkeley, G. (1752). *A miscellany, containing several tracts on various subjects, by the Bishop of Cloyne*. London: J. and R. Tonson.
Burckhardt, C. J. (1965). *On History and Historians* (trans: Zohn, H.). New York: Harper and Row.
Burckhardt, C. J. (1983). *The age of Constantine the great*. Berkeley: University of California Press. ori. pub. 1852.
Burckhardt, C. J. (1990). *The Civilization of the Renaissance* (trans: Middlemore, S.G.C.). London: Penguin Classics (ori. pub 1860).
Gibbon, E. (1984). *Memoirs of my life and writings*. London: Penguin Classics. ori. pub. 1792–3.
Gibbon, E. (1993). *The history of the decline and fall of the Roman empire* (Vol. 6). London: Everyman Library. ori. pub. 1776–89.
Machiavelli, N. (2000). *Discourses on the First Decade of Titus Livy* (trans: Hill, T.N.). Gutenberg Project: Public Domain.

Mill, J. S. (1989). *On liberty and other writings.* Cambridge: Cambridge University Press. ori. pub. 1859.
Montesquieu. (1999). *Considerations on the causes of the greatness of the Romans and their decline* (trans: Lowenthal, D.). Indianapolis: Hackett (ori. pub. 1734).
Pater, W. (1985). *Marius the Epicurean.* London: Harmondsworth. ori. pub. 1885.
Rousseau, J-J. (1923). *The social contract and discourses by Jean-Jacques Rousseau* (trans: Cole, G.D.H.). London: J.M. Dent and Sons.
Sheffield, J. L. (Ed.). (1971). *The miscellaneous works of Edward Gibbon.* New York: Norton. ori. pub. 1814.
Smith, A. (1992). *The wealth of nations.* London: Penguin Classics. ori. pub. 1776.
Taylor, E. B. (1871). *Primitive culture.* London: John Murray.

## Modern Works

Aberth, J. (2003). *A knight at the movies: Medieval history on film.* New York: Routledge.
Adorno, T. W. (1941). Spengler today. *Studies in Philosophy and Social Sciences, IX,* 305–325.
Adorno, T. W. (1983). *Prisms: Studies in contemporary German thought* (trans: Nicholsen, S.W.). Massachusetts: MIT Press (ori. pub. 1967).
Adorno, T. W. (1991). In J. M. Bernstein (Ed.), *The culture industry: Selected essays on mass culture.* London: Routledge Classics.
Albrow, M. (1997). *The global age: State and society beyond modernity.* Cambridge: Stanford University Press.
Alexander, P. J. (1967). Medieval apocalypses as historical sources. *American Historical Review, LXXIII,* 997–1019.
Anderson, P. (1998). *The origins of postmodernity.* London: Verso.
Ankersmit, F. R. (1994). *History and tropology: The rise and fall of metaphor.* Oxford: University of California Press.
Anonymous. (2009, October 7). Civil groups protest new anti-Christian film. *Catholic News Agency.* http://www.catholicnewsagency.com/news/civil_groups_protest_new_antichristian_film/
Arnold, M. (2002, July 11). Making books; book parties with Togas. *The New York Times.* http://web.archive.org/web/20080117055645/http:/query.nytimes.com/gst/fullpage.html?res=990CE2D61530F932A25754C0A9649C8B63
Bachman, G. (1986). The name of the rose: Interview with Umberto Eco. *Sight and Sound, LV,* 129–131.
Baland, M., & Bryson, N. (1991). Semiotics and art history. *The Art Bulletin, LXXIII,* 174–298.

Baland, M., & Bryson, N. (Eds.). (2001). *Looking in: The art of viewing*. Amsterdam: Routledge.
Bandy, M. L., & Stoehr, K. (Eds.). (2012). *Ride, boldly ride: The evolution of the American western*. London: University of California Press.
Bann, S. (1984). *The clothing of Clio: A study of the representation of history in nineteenth-century Britain and France*. Cambridge: Cambridge University Press.
Bann, S. (1990). *The inventions of history: Essays on the representation of the past*. Manchester: Manchester University Press.
Baron, H. (1966). *The crisis of the early Italian Renaissance*. New York: Princeton.
Barra, A. (1989). The incredible shrinking Epic. *American Film, XIV*, 40–45.
Barron, R. (2010, May 9). Christians must resist dangerous silliness of 'Agora'. *Catholic New World*. http://www.catholicnewworld.com/cnwonline/2010/0509/barron.aspx
Barthes, R. (1981). The discourse of history. *Comparative Criticism, III*, 7–20.
Barthes, R. (2009). The Romans in films. In R. Barthes (Ed.), *Mythologies* (trans: Lavers, A.). London: Vintage Classics (ori. pub. 1972), pp. 26–28.
Bartlett, R. (2001). Introduction: Perspectives on the medieval world. In *Medieval Panorama* (pp. 1–27). London: Oxford University Press.
Bartlett, R. (2006). An introduction to Hesiod's work and days. *The Review of Politics, CXVIII*, 177–205.
Barzman, N. (2003). *The red and the blacklist: The intimate memoir of a Hollywood expatriate*. New York: Thunder's Mouth Press/Nation Books.
Basinger, J. (2007). *Anthony Mann*. Middletown: Wesleyan University Press.
Bazin, A (ed.). (1967). *What is cinema?* (trans: Gray, H), 2 vols. Los Angeles: University of California Press.
Bazin, A. (2005). The Western: Or the American film par excellence. In A. Bazin (Ed.), *What Is cinema?* (trans: Gray, H.). Berkeley: University of California Press (ori. pub. 1967), I, pp. 140–148.
Beard, M., & Henderson, J. (1995). *Classics: A very short introduction*. Oxford: Oxford University Press.
Bell, D. (1976). *The cultural contradictions of capitalism*. New York: Basic.
Benjamin, W. (1974). *On the concept of history* (trans: Redmond, D.). Frankfurt: Gesammelten Schriften, XIV.
Benjamin, W. (1999). The work of art in the age of mechanical reproduction. In Arendt, H. (ed.). *Illuminations* (trans: Zohn, H.). London: Pimlico (ori. pub. 1968), pp. 211–244.
Benjamin, W. (2003). *The origins of German tragic drama* (trans: Osborne, J.). London: Verso (ori. pub. 1972).
Berger, P. (2001). *The sacred Canopy*. New York: Anchor Books. ori. pub. 1969.
Besserman, L. (Ed.). (1996). *The challenge of periodization: Old paradigms and new perspectives*. London: Routledge.

Biddick, K. (1998). *The shock of medievalism*. Durham: Duke University Press.
Bildhaeur, B. (2011). *Filming the middle ages*. London: Reaktion Books.
Birchard, R. S. (2004). *Cecil B. DeMille's hollywood*. Lexington: University Press of Kentucky.
Bishop, M. (1961). Petrarch. In J. Plumb (Ed.), *The Italian Renaissance* (pp. 161–175). New York: American Heritage.
Black, J. B. (1965). *The art of history: A study of four great historians of the eighteenth century*. New York: Methuen and Co. Limited. ori. pub. 1926.
Bloch, M. (1973). *The Royal Touch: Monarchy and Miracles in France and England* (trans: Anderson, J.E.). London: Routledge.
Bloch, M. (1990). *Feudal society: The growth of ties of dependence*. London: Routledge.
Bloom, A. (1987). *The closing of the American mind*. New York: Simon & Schuster.
Bond, H. L. (1976). *The literary art of Edward Gibbon*. London: Greenwood Press. ori. pub. 1959.
Bondanella, P. (1987). *The eternal city: Roman images in the modern world*. Chapel Hill: University of North Carolina Press.
Bondanella, P. (1997). *Umberto Eco and the open text: Semiotics, fiction, and popular culture*. Cambridge: Cambridge University Press.
Boot, M. (2001). The case for American empire. *The Weekly Standard, 7*(5), 27–30. 15th October.
Bowersock, G. W. (1988). *Gibbon's historical imagination*. Stanford: Stanford University Press.
Bowersock, G. W. (1996). The vanishing paradigm of the fall of Rome. *Bulletin of the American Academy of Arts and Sciences, XLIX*, 29–43.
Braeur, G. (1995). *The decadent emperors: Power and depravity in third-century Rome*. New York: Barnes and Noble. ori. pub. 1967.
Brantlinger, P. (1986). *Bread and circuses: Theories of mass culture as social decay*. London: Cornell University Press.
Braudy, L. (1970). *Narrative form in history and fiction: Hume, Fielding and Gibbon*. Princeton: Princeton University Press.
Braudy, L., & Cohen, M. (Eds.). (2009). *Film theory and criticism*. London: Oxford University Press. ori. pub. 1974.
Brodsky, J. (1995). Homage to Marcus Aurelius. In J. Brodsky (Ed.), *On grief and reason: Essays* (pp. 267–298). New York: Farrar Straus Giroux.
Bronlow, K. (1968). *The Parade's gone by....* Berkeley: University of California Press.
Brown, P. (1967). The later Roman empire. *The Economic History Review, XX*, 327–343.
Brown, P. (1989). *The world of late antiquity: From Marcus Aurelius to Muhammad (AD 150–750)*. London: Thames and Hudson. ori. pub. 1971.

Brown, P. (2002). *The rise of western Christendom: Triumph and diversity 200–1000 AD.* Oxford: Wiley-Blackwell. ori. pub. 1973.
Brunt, P. A. (1974). Marcus Aurelius in his *meditations. The Journal of Roman Studies, LXIV,* 1–20.
Buchanan, P. J. (2006). *State of emergency: The third world invasion and conquest of America.* New York: St. Martin's.
Buck, W. R., Jr. (1980). Reading autobiography. *Genre, XIII,* 477–498.
Buckley, J. H. (1967). *The triumph of time: A study of Victorian concepts of time, history, progress, and decadence.* Cambridge: Harvard University Press.
Burke, P. (1976). Tradition and experience: The idea of decline from Bruni to Gibbon. *Daedalus: Edward Gibbon and the Decline and Fall of the Roman Empire, LV,* pp. 137–152.
Burke, P. (1989). History as social memory. In T. Butler (Ed.), *Memory: History, culture and the mind.* Oxford: Blackwell.
Burke, J. J. (1993). The romantic window and the postmodern mirror: The medieval worlds of Sir Walter Scott and Umberto Eco. In J. H. Alexander & D. Hewitt (Eds.), *Scot in carnival.* Aberdeen: Association for Scottish Literary Studies.
Bury, J. B. (1923). *History of the later Roman empire from the death of Theodosius I to the death of Justinian (AD 395 to AD 565).* London: Macmillan.
Bury, J. B. (2000). *The idea of progress: An inquiry into its origin and growth.* USA: Project Gutenberg. ori. pub. 1920.
Bush, R. (1991). *T.S. Eliot: The modernist in history.* Cambridge: Cambridge University Press.
Butterfield, A. (2002). *Poetry and music in medieval France.* Cambridge: Cambridge University Press.
Cameron, A. (1993). *The later Roman empire: AD 284–430.* Cambridge: Harvard University Press.
Cameron, A. (2008). A.H.M Jones and the end of the ancient world. In D. M. Gwynn (Ed.), *A.H.M Jones and the later Roman empire: Brill's series on the early middle ages* (Vol. 15, pp. 231–250). Leiden: Brill.
Cameron, A. (2011). *The last pagans of Rome.* Oxford: Oxford University Press.
Campbell, J. (1988). *The power of Myth.* New York: Doubleday.
Campbell, J. (1993). *The hero with a thousand faces.* California: Fontana. ori. pub. 1949.
Cantor, H. V. (1930). Venerable Bede and the Colosseum. *Transactions and Proceedings of the American Philological Association, LXI,* 150–164.
Cantor, N. F. (1991). *Inventing the middle ages: The lives, works, and ideas of the great medievalists of the twentieth century.* New York: William Morrow & Company.
Catholic Church. (2003). *Catechism of the catholic church: With modifications from the edition typica.* New York: Doubleday.

Cavallini, E. (2009). Was Commodus really that bad? In M. M. Winkler (Ed.), *The fall of the Roman empire: Film and history* (pp. 102–116). Oxford: Wiley-Blackwell.
Chadwick, H. (2010). *Augustine of Hippo: A life*. Oxford: Oxford University Press. ori. pub. 1986.
Chandler, J. (1990). Scott, Griffith, and film epic today. In G. W. Ruoff (Ed.), *The romantics and Us: Essays on literature and culture* (pp. 237–273). New Brunswick: Rutgers University Press.
Chaplin, E. (1994). *Sociology and visual representation*. London: Routledge.
Chase, G. (1972). The musicologist as historian: A matter of distinction. *Notes, XXIX*, 10–16.
Clark, K. (1972). *The Nude: A study in ideal form*. New Jersey: Princeton University Press. ori. pub. 1956.
Clark, M. (2005). *Mussolini: Profiles in power*. London: Pearson Longman.
Clay, D. (2009). Marcus Aurelius: The empire over himself. In M. M. Winkler (Ed.), *The fall of the Roman empire: Film and history* (pp. 89–101). Oxford: Wiley-Blackwell.
Cochrane, C. N. (1943). The mind of Edward Gibbon. *University of Toronto Quarterly, XII*, 1–17.
Cohen, P. S. (1969). Theories of Myth. *Man, IV*, 337–353.
Collins, R. (1991). *Early medieval Europe, 300–1000 AD*. London: Macmillan.
Corcoran, S. (2000). *The empire of the Tetrarchs: Imperial pronouncements and governments AD 284–324*. Oxford: Oxford University Press. ori. pub. 1996.
Corliss, R. (2000, May 8). Gladiator: The empire strikes back. *Time*, p. 83.
Corliss, R. (2006, August 4). Mann of the hour. *Time*, http://content.time.com/time/arts/article/0,8599,1223014,00.html
Craddock, P. B. (1989). *Edward Gibbon luminous historian 1772–1794*. Baltimore: Johns Hopkins University Press.
Csapo, E. (2004). *Theories of mythology*. London: Blackwell.
Curtis, E. R. (1990). *European literature in the later middle ages*. New Jersey: Princeton University Press. ori. pub. 1953.
Cyrino, M. S. (2004). Gladiator and contemporary American society. In Martin. M. Winkler (Ed.), *Gladiator: Film and history* (pp. 124–149). Oxford: Blackwell.
Davis, C. T. (1957). *Dante and the idea of Rome*. Oxford: Clarendon Press.
Dawson, C.. (1956). Edward Gibbon and the fall of Rome. In C. Dawson (Ed.), *The dynamics of world history*, ed. John J. Mulloy (pp. 326–353). New York: Sheed and Ward.
Dell, H. (2008). Past, present, future perfect: Paradigms of history in medievalism studies: Theorising modern medievalism. *Parergon, XXV*, 58–79.
Demandt, A. (1984). *Der Fall Roms: Die Aufl ösung des römischen Reiches im Urteil der Nachwelt*. Munich: Beck.

Denzin, N. K. (1995). *The cinematic society: The Voyeur's gaze*. London: Sage Publications Limited.
Derrida, J. (2001). Structure, sign, and play in the discourse of the human sciences. In J. Derrida (Ed.), *Writing and Difference* (trans: Bass, A.). London: Routledge (ori. pub. 1967), pp. 278–295.
Desai, G. G., & Nair, S. (Eds.). (2005). *Postcolonialisms: An anthropology of cultural theory and criticism*. Oxford: Rutgers University Press.
Doran, R. (Ed.). (2010). *The fiction of narrative: Essays on history, literature, and theory, 1957–2007*. Baltimore: The Johns Hopkins University Press.
Drew, W. (1986). *D. W. Griffith's intolerance: Its genesis and its vision*. Jefferson: McFarland & Company.
Drinkwater, J. F. (1984). Peasants and Bacaudae in Roman Gaul. *Classical Views, III*, 349–371.
Driver, M. W. (2004). What's accuracy got to do with it? Historicity and authenticity in medieval film. In M. Driver & S. Ray (Eds.), *The medieval hero on screen: Representations from Beowulf to Buffy* (pp. 19–22). North Carolina: McFarland and Co.
Dumphy, G. (2007). Literary transitions, 1300–1500: From late mediaeval to early modern. *The Camden House History of German Literature, IV*, 43–88.
Dundes, A. (Ed.). (1988). *The flood Myth*. Berkeley: University of California Press.
Dunn, J. (1985). *Rethinking modern political theory: Essays 1979–83*. Cambridge: Cambridge University Press.
Dunne, J. G. (1965, September 11). A Riot on TV. *New Republic*, p. 27.
Durant, W. (1980). *The story of civilization: Caesar and Christ*. New York: Simon & Schuster. ori. pub. 1944.
Durant, W., & Durant, A. (1977). *A dual autobiography*. New York: Simon and Schuster.
Dwyer, J. C. (1998). *Church history: Twenty centuries of catholic Christianity* (p. 155). New Jersey: Paulist Press.
Dzielska, M., & Wildberg, C. (2009, April 4). Hypatia of Alexandria—A philosophical martyr, transcript of a radio interview with Joe Gelonesi. http://www.abc.net.au/radionational/programs/philosopherszone/hypatia-of-alexandria---a-philosophical-martyr/3142424#transcript
Eagleton, T. (1996). *Literary theory*. Oxford: Blackwell.
Eckstein, A. M., & Lehman, P. (Eds.). (2004). *The searchers: Essays and reflections on John Ford's classic western*. Detroit: Wayne State University Press.
Eco, U. (1962). The myth of Superman. *Diacritics* (trans: Chilton, N.), II, pp. 14–22.
Eco, U. (1995). *Faith in fakes: Travels in hyper-reality* (trans: Weaver, W.). New York: Mariner Books (ori. pub. 1986).
Edwards, C. (Ed.). (1999). *Roman presences: Receptions of Rome in European culture, 1789–1945*. Cambridge: Cambridge University Press.

Eliot, T. S. (1945). *What is a classic?* London: Faber and Faber.
Eliot, T. S. (1973). *Notes towards the definition of culture.* London: Faber and Faber.
Elley, D. (1976). The fall of the Roman empire. *Films and Filming, XXII,* 18–24.
Elley, D. (1984). *The epic film: Myth in history.* London: Routledge Kegan and Paul.
Evans, R. (2001). *In defence of history.* London: Granta Books. ori. pub. 1997.
Fenwick, J. H., & Green-Armytage, J. (1965). Now you see it: Landscape and Anthony Mann. *Sight and Sound, XXXIV,* 186–189.
Ferguson, N. (2004). *Colossus: The rise and fall of the American empire.* New York: Penguin.
Ferro, M. (1988). *Cinema and history* (trans: Greene, N). Michigan: Wayne State University Press.
Finke, L., & Shichtman, M. B. (2009). *Cinematic illuminations: The middle ages on film.* Baltimore: The Johns Hopkins University Press.
Finlay, G. (1906). *History of the Byzantine empire from 716 to 1059.* New York: Dutton and Co.
Finley, M. I. (1965). Myth, memory and history. *History and Theory, IV,* 281–302.
Fitzgerald, W. (2001). Oppositions, anxieties and ambiguities in the Toga movie. In S. R. Joshel, M. Malamud, & D. T. McGuire Jr. (Eds.), *Imperial projections: Ancient Rome in modern popular culture* (pp. 23–49). New York: John Hopkins University Press.
Foucault, M. (2002). *The Archaeology of Knowledge* (trans: Smith, S.). New York: Routledge.
Franzoni, D. (1998, April 4). Gladiator: First draft revised, http://www.hundland.com/scripts/Gladiator_FirstDraft.txt
Frederick, B. C. (2005). *Hegel.* London: Routledge.
Freeman, C. (2003). *The closing of the western mind: The rise of faith and the fall of reason.* London: Pimlico.
Frum, D., & Perle, R. (2003). *An end to evil: How to win the war on terror.* New York: Random House.
Frye, N. (1974). The decline of the West by Oswald Spengler. *Daedalus, CIII,* 1–13.
Futrell, A. (2001). Seeing red: Spartacus as domestic economist. In S. R. Joshel, M. Malamud, & D. T. McGuire Jr. (Eds.), *Imperial projections: Ancient Rome in modern popular culture* (pp. 77–118). New York: John Hopkins University Press.
Garnsey, P. (2008). Writing the late Roman empire: Method and sources. In D. M. Gwynn (Ed.), *A.H.M Jones and the later Roman empire: Brill's series on the early middle ages* (Vol. 15, pp. 25–42). Leiden: Brill.

Gay, P. (1995). *The enlightenment: An interpretation.* New York: W.W. Norton & Co. ori. pub. 1968.
Geertz, C. (1964). Ideology as a cultural system. In D. E. Aptor (Ed.), *Ideology and discontent* (pp. 47–76). New York: Free Press.
Geertz, C. (1990). Religion as a cultural system. In M. Banton (Ed.), *Anthropological approaches to the study of religion* (pp. 1–46). London: Tavistock. ori. pub. 1966.
Geertz, C. (1993). Notes on a Balinese Cockfight. In C. Geertz (Ed.), *The interpretation of cultures* (pp. 412–453). New York: Basic Books. ori. pub. 1973.
Gerbi, A. (2010). *The dispute of the new world.* Pittsburugh: University of Pittsburough Press. ori. pub. 1955.
Giedion, S. (2008). *Space, time and architecture: The growth of a new tradition.* London: Harvard University Press. ori. pub. 1941.
Gilderhus, M. (2000). *History and historians: A historiographical introduction* (pp. 134–136). Upper Saddle River: Prentice-Hall.
Goffart, W. (1971). Zosimus, the first historian of Rome's fall. *American Historical Review, LXXVI*, 412–442.
Goffart, W. (1981). Rome, Constantinople, and the Barbarians. *American Historical Review, LXXXVI*, 275–306.
Goffart, W. (1988). *The narrators of Barbarian history (A.D. 550–800).* New Jersey: Princeton University Press.
Goffart, W. (2001). *Barbarians and Romans AD 418–54: The techniques of accommodation.* New Jersey: Princeton University Press. ori. pub. 1980.
Goldsworthy, A. (2009). *The fall of the west: The death of the Roman superpower.* London: Orion.
Gooch, G. P. (1913). *History and historians in the nineteenth century.* London: Longmans Green.
Gordon, B. J. (1975). *Economic analysis before Adam Smith: Hesiod to Lessius.* New York: Barnes and Noble.
Gossman, L. (1981). *The empire Unpossess'd: An essay on Gibbon's decline and fall.* Cambridge: Cambridge University Press.
Graves, R. (2006). *Count Belisarius.* London: Penguin. ori. pub. 1938.
Gunning, T. D. W. (1994). *Griffith and the origins of American narrative film: The early years at biograph.* Illinois: University of Illinois Press.
Gwynn, D. M. (2008). Idle mouths and solar haloes: A.H.M Jones and the conversion of Europe. In D. M. Gwynn (Ed.), *A.H.M Jones and the later Roman empire: Brill's series on the early middle ages* (Vol. 15, pp. 213–230). Leiden: Brill.
Hall, S. (1981). Notes on deconstructing the popular. In R. Samuel (Ed.), *People's history and socialist theory* (pp. 227–240). London: Routledge.
Hall, S. (1997). *Representation: Cultural representations and signifying practices.* London: Sage.

Halliday, J. (Ed.). (1997). *Sirk on Sirk: Conversations with John Halliday.* London: Faber and Faber. ori. pub. 1971.
Hardie, P. R. (1988). *Virgil's "Aeneid": Cosmos and Imperium.* London: Clarendon Press.
Hardwick, L., & Stray, C. (Eds.). (2007). *A companion to classical receptions.* Oxford: Wiley-Blackwell.
Harries, J. (1995). *Sidonius Apollinaris and the fall of Rome, AD 407–485.* Oxford: Clarendon Press.
Harris, M. (2001). *Cultural materialism: The struggle for a science of culture.* California: Altamira.
Harty, K. J. (2002). *The reel middle ages; American, Western and East European, Middle Eastern, and Asian films about medieval Europe.* Jefferson: McFarland.
Heather, P. (1991). *Goths and Romans 332–489.* Oxford: Clarendon Press.
Heather, P. (2005). *The fall of the Roman empire: A new history of Rome and the Barbarians.* Oxford: Oxford University Press.
Heather, P. (2008). Running the empire: Bureaucrats, curials, and senators. In D. M. Gwynn (Ed.), *A.H.M Jones and the later Roman empire: Brill's series on the early middle ages* (Vol. 15, pp. 97–120). Leiden: Brill.
Heidegger, M. (1984). *Nietzsche, Volume II: The Eternal Recurrence of the Same* (trans: Krell, D.F.). New York: Harper and Row (ori. pub. 1954).
Heinzelmann, M. (2001). *Gregory of Tours: History and Society in the Sixth Century* (trans: Carroll, C.). Cambridge: Cambridge University Press.
Henderson, R. M. D. W. (1972). *Griffith: His life and work.* New York: Oxford University Press.
Hepburn, R. W. (1955). George Hakewill: The virility of nature. *Journal of the History of Ideas, XVI*, 135–150.
Herbermann, C. G. (Ed.). (1911). *Catholic encyclopaedia* (Vol. XI, p. 604). New York: Robert Appleton Company.
Hermann, A. (1997). *The idea of decline in western history.* New York: Simon and Schuster.
Heyer, P. (2012). *Titanic century: Media, myth, and the making of a cultural icon.* California: Santa Barbara.
Higham, N. J. (2002). *King Arthur, Myth-making and history.* London: Routledge.
Highet, G. (1949). *The classical tradition: Greek and Roman influences on western literature.* Oxford: Oxford University Press.
Higson, A. (2011). *Film England, culturally English filmmaking since the 1990s.* New York: I. B. Tauris & Co.
Horkheimer, M. (2002). The concept of enlightenment. In T. Adorno, & M. Horkheimer (Eds.), *Dialectic of Enlightenment: Philosophical Fragments* (trans: Jephcott, E.). Stanford: Stanford University Press (ori. pub. 1944), pp. 1–34.

Howells, R. (1994). *The Interpretation of Popular Culture as Modern Myth* (PhD diss., Cambridge University).
Howells, R. (1998). Review of Titanic (1997). *Film and History, XXVIII*, 70–71.
Howells, R. (1999). *The Myth of the Titanic*. London: Palgrave Macmillan.
Inglis, F. (1990). *Media theory*. Oxford/Cambridge: Basil Blackwell.
James, B. J. (1973). *The death of progress*. New York: Alfred Knopt Incorporated.
James, H. (2006). *The Roman predicament: How the rules of international order create the politics of empire*. New Jersey: Princeton University Press.
Jauss, H.-R. (1970). Literary history as a challenge to literary theory. *New Literary History, II*, 7–37.
Joad, C. E. M. (1948). *Decadence: A philosophical inquiry*. London: Harthorpe.
Johnson, C. A. (2004). *The sorrows of empire: Militarism, secrecy and the end of the republic*. London: New Left Books.
Johnston, R. J. (2000). *The dictionary of human geography*. London: Wiley-Blackwell.
Jones, A. H. M. (1986). *The later Roman empire 284–602: A social, economic and administrative survey* (Vol. 2). Baltimore: John Hopkins. ori. pub. 1964.
Joshel, S. (2001). I, Claudius: Projection and imperial soap opera. In S. R. Joshel, M. Malamud, & D. T. McGuire (Eds.), *Imperial projections: Ancient Rome in modern popular culture* (pp. 119–161). New York: John Hopkins University Press.
Kallendorf, C. W. (Ed.). (2007). *A companion to the classical tradition*. Oxford: Blackwell Publishing.
Kennedy, P. (1989). *The rise and fall of the great powers: Economic change and military conflict 1500–2000*. London: Fontana Press. ori. pub. 1987.
Kennedy, D. (1999). A sense of place: Rome, history and empire revisited. In C. Edwards (Ed.), *Roman presences: Receptions of Rome in European culture, 1789–1945* (pp. 19–34). Cambridge: Cambridge University Press.
Kinney, D. (1995). Rape or restitution of the past? Interpreting Spolia. In S. C. Scott (Ed.), *The art of interpreting* (pp. 53–67). Pennsylvania: University Park.
Knox, B. (1994). *Backing into the future: The classical tradition and its renewal*. New York: W.W. Norton & Co.
Kopecek, T. A. (1974). Curial displacements and flight in later fourth-century Cappadocia. *Historia, XXIII*, 319–342.
Koszarski, R. (Ed.). (1977). *Hollywood directors 1941–76*. New York: Oxford University Press.
Kracauer, S. (1995a). *History: The last things before the last*. New York: Marcus Weiner. ori. pub. 1969.
Kracauer, S. (1995b). *The Mass Ornament* (trans: Levin, T.Y.). Massachusetts: Harvard University Press (ori. pub. 1927).
Kracauer, S. (1997). *Theory of film: The redemption of physical reality*. Chichester: Princeton University Press. ori. pub. 1960.

Krebs, R. E. (2004). *Groundbreaking scientific experiments, inventions, and discoveries of the middle ages and the renaissance.* New York: Greenwood.
Landau, D. (Ed.). (2000). *Gladiator: The making of the Ridley Scott epic.* New York: Newmarket Press.
Lang, A. (2005). *Myth, ritual and religion.* New York: Cosimo Classics. ori. pub. 1887.
Lasch, C. (1978). *The culture of narcissism: American life in the age of diminishing expectations.* New York: W.W. Norton and Co.
Lavan, L. (2008). A.H.M Jones and 'The Cities' 1964–2004. In D. M. Gwynn (Ed.), *A.H.M Jones and the later Roman empire: Brill's series on the early middle ages* (Vol. 15, pp. 167–192). Leiden: Brill.
Leach, E. (1969). *Genesis as Myth and other essays.* London: Random House.
Leach, E. (Ed.). (2004). *The structural study of myth and totemism.* London: Tavistock. ori. pub. 1967.
Leavis, Q. D. (2000). *Fiction and the reading public.* London: Pimlico. ori. pub. 1932.
Leotard, J.-F. (1984). *The postmodern condition: A report on knowledge.* Manchester: Manchester University Press. ori. pub. 1979.
Levin, T. (1996). Iconography at the movies: Panofsky's film theory. *Yale Journal of Criticism, IX,* 27–55.
Lévi-Strauss, C. (1966). *The Savage Mind* (trans: Weidenfield, G.). Chicago: University of Chicago Press.
Lévi-Strauss, C. (1968). *Structural anthropology I* (trans: Jacobson, C.). London: Penguin.
Lévi-Strauss, C. (1978). *Structural anthropology II* (trans: Layton). London: Penguin.
Lévi-Strauss, C. (1983). *Mythologiques* (Vol. 4). Chicago: University of Chicago Press. ori. pub. 1969.
Liebeschuetz, J. H. W. G. (2001). *The decline and fall of the Roman city.* Oxford: Oxford University Press. ori, pub. 1972.
Lindley, A. (1999). The ahistoricism of medieval film. *Screening the Past,* VI. http://tlweb.latrobe.edu.au/humanities/screeningthepast/firstrelease/fir598/ALfr3a.htm
Littleton, C. S. (1978). The Sarmatian connection: New light on the origin of the Arthurian and Holy Grail Legends. *Journal of American Folklore, XCI,* 512–527.
Livingstone, E. A. (2005). Original sin. *The Oxford dictionary of the Christian church* (pp. 1202–1204). Oxford: Oxford University Press,
Lowenthal, D. (1995). *The past is a foreign country.* Cambridge: Cambridge University Press. ori. pub. 1985.
MacMullen, R. (1984). *Christianizing the Roman empire (A.D. 100–400).* New Haven: Yale University Press.

Maier, C. S. (2006). *Among empires: American ascendancy and its predecessors.* Cambridge: Harvard University Press.
Malinowski, B. (1992). *Magic, science and religion and other essays.* Illinois: Waveland Press. ori. pub. 1954.
Mampaso, A. (2009, October 28). The best legacy of Hypatia is its own history, interview with Enrique Sacristan, http://www.oei.es/divulgacioncientifica/entrevistas_034.htm
Mann, A. (1977). Empire demolition. In R. Koszarski (Ed.), *Hollywood directors 1941–76* (pp. 332–338). New York: Oxford University Press.
Mannes, M. (1968). *They.* New York: Doubleday Publishers.
Manuel, F. E. (1967). *The eighteenth century confronts the gods.* Cambridge: Harvard University Press.
Marwick, A. (2001). *The new nature of history: Knowledge, evidence, language.* London: Palgrave Macmillan.
Massie, A. (2006, November 19). Return of the Roman. *Prospect,* CXXVIII, http://www.prospectmagazine.co.uk/features/returnoftheroman
Mathisen, R. W. (1993). *Roman aristocrats in Barbarian Gaul: Strategies for survival in an age of transition.* Austin: University of Texas Press.
Matson, L. D. (2010). *Re-presentations of Dante Gabriel Rossetti: Portrayals in fiction, drama, music, and film.* New York: Cambria Press.
McCabe, C. (1986). Defining popular culture. In C. McCabe (Ed.), *High theory/low culture: Analysing popular television and film* (pp. 1–36). Manchester: St Martin's Press.
McClintock, P., & Swart, S. (2009). Epic bow for 'Agora'. *Daily Variety,* CCCV. p. 8. New York: Silverman.
McKinnon, K. (1986). *Greek tragedy in film.* Rutherford: Fairleigh Dickinson University Press.
McLuhan, M. (1964). *Understanding media: The extensions of Man.* London: McGraw-Hill.
Missiaen, J.-C. (1967). A lesson in cinema. *Cahiers du Cinéma in English,* XII, 44–51.
Mitchell, T. C. (2004). *The Bible in the British museum: Interpreting the evidence.* London: British Museum Press. ori. pub. 1988.
Mitchell, S. (2006). *A history of the later Roman empire.* AD 284–641. London: Blackwell.
Momigliano, A. (1969). Review: Ammianus and the Historia Augusta by Ronald Syme. *The English Historical Review,* XXIII, 566–569.
Momigliano, A. (1973). Review: Emperors and biography. Studies in the Historia Augusta by Ronald Syme. *The English Historical Review,* LXXXVIII, 114–115.
Mommsen, T. (1909). *The province of the Roman empire.* London: Macmillan.

Mommsen, T. (1942). Petrarch's conception of the 'Dark Ages'. *Speculum, XVII*, 226–242.
Monaco, J. (2000). *How to read a film*. New York: Oxford University Press. ori. pub. 1981.
Morgan, D. (1998). *Visual piety: A history and theory of popular religious images*. London: University of California Press.
Morgenthau, H. (1975). Decline of the West. *Partisan Review, XXII*, 508–516.
Muggerridge, M. (1980, May). On the threshold of the eighties. *The American spectator*, p. 15.
Muller, M. F. (1899). *Three lectures on the science of language*. Chicago: Open Court Publishing.
Murphy, C. (2007). *Are we Rome?* Boston: Houghton Mifflin Harcourt.
Murray, C., & Herrnstein, R. (1994). *The bell curve*. New York: Free Press.
Muschamp, H. (2000, April 30). Throwing our anxieties to the lions. *The New York Times*, p. 33.
Neilson, F. (1945). The decline of civilizations. *American Journal of Economics and Sociology, IV*, 479–497.
Nicolls, J. H. (Ed.). (1955). *Force and freedom: An interpretation of history by Jacob Burckhardt*. New York: Meridian Books.
Nisbet, R. A. (1992). *Social change and history: Aspects of the western theory of development*. Oxford: Oxford University Press. ori. pub. 1969.
Northup, L. (2006). Myth-placed priorities: Religion and the study of myth. *Religious Studies Review, XXXII*, 5–10.
Norwich, J. J. (1991). *Byzantium: The apogee*. London: Viking Press.
Novick, P. (1988). *That noble dream: The objectivity question and the American historical profession*. Cambridge: Cambridge University Press.
O'Donnell, J. J. (2005). *Augustine: A new biography*. New York: ECCO.
Oertel, F. (1939). The economic life of the empire. In *The Cambridge ancient history* (Vol. XII, pp. 232–282). Cambridge: Cambridge University Press.
Ong, W. J. (1962). *The Barbarian within*. New York: Macmillan.
Ordoña, M. (2010, June 4). Movie review: 'Agora' shows the true casualty of war. *Los Angeles Times*. http://articles.latimes.com/2010/jun/04/entertainment/la-et-capsules-20100604
Orrison, K. (1990). *Written in stone: Making Cecil B. DeMille's epic, the Ten Commandments*. New York: Vestal Press.
Philips, K. (1995). *Arrogant capital: Washington, wall street, and the frustration of American politics*. New York: Back Bay Books.
Pirenne, H. (2001). *Mohammed and Charlemagne*. Massachusetts: Courier Dover Publications. ori. pub. 1937.
Plumb, J. H. (Ed.). (1961). *The Italian Renaissance* (pp. 161–175). New York: American Heritage.

Pocock, J. G. (1989). *Politics, language and time: Essays on political thought and history*. New York: University of Chicago Press.
Pocock, J. G. (2000). Gibbon and the primitive church. In S. Collini, R. Whatmore, & B. Young (Eds.), *History, religion and culture: British intellectual history, 1750–1950* (pp. 48–68). Cambridge: Cambridge University Press.
Pocock, J. G. (2002). The Ironist. *London Review of Books, XXII*, 13–17.
Pocock, J. G. (2003). *Barbarism and religion: The first decline and fall*. Cambridge: Cambridge University Press.
Popper, K. (2002). *The poverty of historicism*. London: Routledge. ori. pub. 1957.
Powell, A. (1999). *Jesus as a figure in history: How modern historians view the Man from Galilee*. Westminster: John Knox Press.
Power, E. (2004). *Medieval People* (pp. 1–17). Gutenberg Project: Public Domain (ori. pub. 1924).
Pratt, K. J. (1965). Rome as eternal. *Journal of the History of Ideas, XXVI*, 25–44.
Pulver, A. (2005, February 5). Adaptation of the week no. 44: The name of the rose. *The Guardian*.
Quinton, A. (1993, April 30). Clash of symbols. *Times Higher Education Supplement*, pp. 15–16.
Rehm, W. (1966). *Der Untergang Roms im abendländischen Denken*. Darmstadt: Buchgesellschaft. ori. pub. 1930.
Reinhold, M. (2002). Historian of the classic world: A critique of Rostovtzeff. In M. Reinhold (Ed.), *Studies in classical history and society* (pp. 83–91). New York: Oxford University Press.
Renan, E. (1890). *The history of the origins of Christianity VII: Marcus Aurelius*. London: Mathieson.
Reno, F. D. (1996). *The historic king Arthur: Authenticating the Celtic hero of post-roman Britain*. Jefferson, NC: McFarland.
Richards, G. (2008). *Hollywood's ancient worlds*. Winchester: Hambledon Continuum.
Robertson, J. (1997). Gibbon's Roman empire as a universal monarchy: The decline and fall and the imperial idea in early modern Europe. In R. McKitterick & R. Quinault (Eds.), *Edward Gibbon and empire* (pp. 247–270). Cambridge: Cambridge University Press.
Robin, D. (2010). *This holy seed: Faith, hope and love in the early churches of North Africa*. Chester: Tamarisk Publications.
Romano, R., & Leiman, M. M. (Eds.). (1970). *Views of capitalism*. Illinois: Glencoe.
Romilly, J. (1977). *The rise and fall of states according to Greek authors*. Ann Arbor: University of Michigan Press.
Rose, P. W. (1991). Teaching Greek myth and confronting contemporary myths. In M. M. Winkler (Ed.), *Classics and cinema* (pp. 17–39). Lewisburg: Bucknell University Press.

Rose, P. W. (2009). The politics of *the fall of the Roman empire*. In M. M. Winkler (Ed.), *The fall of the Roman empire: Film and history* (pp. 241–261). Oxford: Wiley-Blackwell.
Rosenstone, R. A. (1995a). The historical film as real history. *Film-Historia, V*, 5–23.
Rosenstone, R. A. (1995b). *Visions of the past: The challenge of film to our idea of history*. Massachusetts: Harvard University Press.
Rosenstone, R. A. (2000). Oliver stone as historian. In R. Toplin (Ed.), *Oliver Stone's USA* (pp. 26–39). Lawrence: University of Kansas.
Rosenstone, R. A. (2003). The reel Joan of Arc: Reflections on the theory and practice of the historical film. *The Public Historian, XXV*, 61–77.
Rosenstone, R. A. (2006). *History on film/film on history*. London: Longman.
Rosser, J. H. (2011). *Historical dictionary of Byzantium*. Massachussets: Scarecrow Press.
Rostovzeff, M. I. (1957). *The social and economic history of the Roman empire*. Oxford: Oxford University Press. ori. pub. 1926.
Russell, J. (2007). *The historical epic and contemporary hollywood: From dances with wolves to gladiator*. London: Continuum International Publishing.
Said, E. W. (2003). *Orientalism*. London: Penguin. ori. pub. 1979.
Salo, D. (2004). Heroism and alienation through language in *the lord of the rings*. In M. Driver & S. Ray (Eds.), *The medieval hero on screen: Representations from Beowulf to Buffy* (pp. 23–37). Jefferson: McFarland.
Sarris, A. (1968). *The American cinema, director and directions 1929–68*. New York: Dutton.
Schlesinger, A. M. (2004). *The imperial presidency*. Boston: Houghton Mifflin. ori. pub. 1973.
Scorsese, M., & Wilson, M. H. (1997). *A personal journey with Martin Scorsese through American movies*. New York: Miramax Books/Hyperion.
Scott, G. (1973). *The rise and fall of the league of nations*. New York: Macmillan.
Scott, R. (2000a). Introduction. In D. Landau (Ed.), *Gladiator: The making of the Ridley Scott epic* (pp. 2–9). New York: Newmarket Press.
Seed, D. (2009). *Cinematic fictions: The impact of the cinema on the American novel*. Liverpool: Liverpool University Press.
Segal, R. (2004). *Myth: A very short introduction*. Oxford: Oxford University Press.
Sennett, R. (2002). *The fall of public Man: On the social psychology of capitalism*. London: Faber and Faber. ori. pub. 1977.
Seydor, P. S. (1997). *Peckinpah: The western films: Reconsideration*. Urbana: University of Illinois Press.
Seznec, J. (1992). *The Survival of the Pagan Gods: The Mythological Tradition and its Place in Renaissance Humanism and Art* (trans: Sessions, B.F.). New Jersey: Princeton University Press (ori. pub. 1953).

Shackleton, R. (1977). The impact of French literature on Gibbon. In G. W. Bowersock, J. Clive, & S. R. Graubard (Eds.), *Edward Gibbon and the decline and fall of the Roman empire* (pp. 207–218). Cambridge: Harvard University Press.

Shulman, M. (1973). *The Ravenous eye: The impact of the fifth factor.* London: Collins.

Sinai, R. (1978). *The decadence of the modern world.* Cambridge: Schenkelman.

Sinai, R. (1979, April). What Ails us and why: On the roots of disaster and decay. *Encounter,* pp. 8–17.

Sinai, R. (1980, February). The Sinai discussion. *Encounter,* pp. 87–93.

Skinner, Q. (1969). Meaning and understanding in the history of ideas. *History and Theory, VIII,* 5–53.

Slotkin, R. (1998). *Gunfighter nation: The myth of the frontier in twentieth-century America.* Norman: University of Oklahoma Press.

Sobchack, V. (1990). Surge and splendor: A phenomenology of the Hollywood historical epic. *Representations, XXIX,* 24–49.

Solomon, J. S. (2001). *The ancient world and the cinema.* New York: Yale University Press. ori. pub. 1978.

Sorkal, A. (2008). *Beyond the Hoax: Science, philosophy and culture.* Oxford: Oxford University Press.

Sorlin, P. (1980). *The film in history: Restaging the past.* Oxford: Barnes and Noble.

Southern, P., & Dixon, K. R. (2000). *The late Roman army.* London: Routledge.

Southgate, B. (2003). *Postmodernism in history: Fear or freedom?* London: Routledge.

Spengler, O. S. (1991). *Decline of the West* (trans: Atkinson, C.F.). New York: Oxford University Press (ori. pub. 1932).

Spring, D., & Taylor, R. (Eds.). (1993). *Stalinism and Soviet cinema.* London: Routledge.

Starn, R. (1975). Meaning-levels in the theme of historical decline. *History and Theory, XIV,* 1–31.

Stavrianos, L. S. (1976). *The promise of the coming dark age.* New York: W.H. Freeman & Co.

Stone, J. R. (Ed.). (2002). *The essential Max Müller: On language, mythology, and religion.* New York: St Martin's Press.

Stoneman, R. S. (1992). *Palmyra and its empire: Zenobia's revolt against Rome.* Ann Arbor: University of Michigan Press.

Storey, J. S. (2000). *Cultural theory and popular culture: An introduction.* New Jersey: Prentice Hall.

Strinati, D. (2004). *An introduction to theories of popular culture.* London: Routledge.

Struever, N. S. (1970). *The language of history in the renaissance: Rhetoric and historical consciousness in Florentine humanism.* New Jersey: Princeton University Press.

Swain, S., & Edwards, M. (Eds.). (2006). *Approaching late antiquity: The transformation from early to late empire.* Oxford: Oxford University Press.
Syme, R. (1971). *Emperors and biography.* Oxford: Oxford University Press.
Tainter, J. A. (1990). *The collapse of complex societies.* New York: Cambridge University Press. ori. pub. 1988.
Thompson, W. I. (1976). *Evil and the world order.* New York: Harpercollins.
Thompson, E. A. (2002). *Romans and Barbarians: The decline of the western empire.* Madison: University of Wisconsin Press. ori. pub. 1982.
Toynbee, A. J. (1962). *America and the world revolution and other lectures.* New York: Oxford University Press.
Toynbee, A. J. (1973). *A study of history* (Vol. 1). New York: Oxford University Press. ori. pub. 1946.
Trevelyan, G. M. (1913). *Clio, a muse: and other essays.* London: Longmans Green. ori. pub. 1904.
Tuekolsky, R. (2009). *The literate eye: Victorian art writing and modernist aesthetics.* Oxford: Oxford University Press.
Tuveson, E. L. (1972). *Millenium and Utopia: A study in the background of the idea of progress.* Berkeley: University of California Press. ori. pub. 1949.
Vachel, L. (1919). *The art of the motion picture.* New York: Macmillan.
Vance, W. L. (1989). *America's Rome.* New Haven: Yale University Press.
Vaughan, J. C. (1973). *Soviet socialist realism: Origins and theory.* London: Macmillan.
Vidal, G. (2006). *Point to point navigation: A memoir, 1964–2006.* London: Little Brown.
Vinaver, E. (Ed.). (1990). *The works of Sir Thomas Malory.* Oxford: Oxford University Press.
Vogt, K. (1993). The Hierophant of philosophy—Hypatia of Alexandria. In K. E. Boerresen & K. Vogt (Eds.), *Women's studies of the Christian and Islamic traditions: Ancient, medieval, and renaissance foremothers* (pp. 155–174). Dordrecht: Kluwer Academic Publishers.
Wadge, R. (1987). A British or Sarmatian tradition. *Folklore, CXVIII,* 204–215.
Wagar, W. W. (1967). *The city of man: Prophecies of civilization.* Baltimore: Penguin.
Wallace, L. (1998). *Ben-Hur: A tale of the Christ.* Oxford: Oxford World's Classics.
Ward, A. M. (2009). History, ancient and modern. In M. M. Winkler (Ed.), *The fall of the Roman empire: Film and history* (pp. 51–88). Oxford: Wiley-Blackwell.
Ward-Perkins, B. (2000). Specialized production and exchange. *Cambridge Ancient History, XIV,* 350–361.
Ward-Perkins, B. (2005). *The fall of Rome and the end of civilization.* Oxford: Oxford University Press.

Ward-Perkins, B. (2008a). Jones and the late Roman economy. In D. M. Gwynn (Ed.), *A.H.M Jones and the later Roman empire: Brill's series on the early middle ages* (Vol. 15, pp. 193–212). Leiden: Brill.
Warshow, R. (2002). The Westerner. In R. Warshow (Ed.), *The immediate experience: Movies, comics, theatre, and other aspects of popular culture* (pp. 434–450). London: Harvard University Press. ori. pub. 1962.
Watson, P. (2002, December 13). Money, magic and miracles. *Times Higher Education.* http://www.timeshighereducation.co.uk/books/money-magic-and-miracles/173657.article
Watson, A. (2004). *Aurelian and the third century* (pp. 52–53). London: Taylor & Francis.
Ward-Perkins, B. (2008). Jones and the late Roman economy. In D. M. Gwynn (Ed.), *A.H.M Jones and the later Roman empire: Brill's series on the early middle ages* (Vol. 15, pp. 193–212). Leiden: Brill.
Weiss, R. (1969). *The renaissance discovery of classical antiquity.* Oxford: Blackwell.
West, C. (2001). *Race matters.* New York: Vintage Books.
White, H. (1978). The historical text as literary artifact. In H. White (Ed.), *Tropics of discourse: Essays in cultural criticism* (pp. 81–100). Baltimore: John Hopkins.
White, H. (1988). Historiography and historicity. *The American Historical Review,* XCIII, 1193–1199.
White, H. (1995). Response to Arthur Marwick. *Journal of Contemporary History,* XXX (London: Sage), pp. 233–246.
White, D. M., & Rosenberg, B. (Eds.). (1971). *Mass culture revisited.* New York: Van Nostrand Reinhold.
Whittaker, C. R. (1976). Agri Deserti. In M. I. Finley (Ed.), *Studies in Roman property* (pp. 137–165). Cambridge: Cambridge University Press.
Whittington, H. (1964). *The fall of the Roman empire.* New York: Gold Medal Books.
Wickham, C. (2009). *The inheritance of Rome: A history of Europe from 400 to 1000 AD* (p. 3). London: Penguin.
Wicking, C., & Patterson, B. (1969). Interview with Anthony Mann. *Screen,* X, 32–54.
Williams, D. (1991). Medieval movies. *Yearbook of English Studies,* XX, 1–31.
Winkler, M. M. (1985). Classical mythology and the western film. *Comparative Literature Studies,* XXII, 516–540.
Winkler, M. M. (Ed.). (1991a). *Classics and cinema.* Lewisburg: Bucknell University Press.
Winkler, M. M. (1991b). Introduction. In M. M. Winkler (Ed.), *Classics and cinema* (pp. 9–16). Lewisburg: Bucknell University Press.
Winkler, M. M. (1995). Cinema and the fall of Rome. *Transactions of the American Philological Association,* CXXV, 135–154.

Winkler, M. M. (1996). Homeric *kleos* and the western film. *Syllecta Classica, VII,* 43–54.
Winkler, M. M. (2001). Star Wars and the Roman empire. In M. M. Winkler (Ed.), *Classical myth and culture in the cinema* (pp. 272–290). New York: Oxford University Press. ori. pub. 1991.
Winkler, M. M. (2009a). A critical appreciation of the fall of the Roman empire. In M. M. Winkler (Ed.), *The fall of the roman empire: Film and history* (pp. 1–52). Oxford: Wiley-Blackwell.
Winkler, M. M. (2009b). Edward Gibbon and *the fall of the Roman empire*. In M. M. Winkler (Ed.), *The fall of the Roman empire: Film and history* (pp. 145–173). Oxford: Wiley-Blackwell.
Winthrop, H. (1971). Variety of meaning in the concept of decadence. *Philosophy and Phenomenological Research, XXXI,* 510–526.
Witonski, P. P. (Ed.). (1974). *Gibbon for moderns: The history of the decline and fall of the Roman empire with lessons for America today.* New Rochelle: Arlington House.
Woods, W. F. (2004). Authenticating realism in medieval film. In M. W. Driver & S. Ray (Eds.), *Medieval hero on screen* (pp. 38–52). North Carolina: McFarland & Company.
Wootton, D. (1994). Narrative, irony, and faith in Gibbon's decline and fall. *History and Theory, XXXIII,* 77–105.
Wyke, M. (1997). *Projecting the past: Ancient Rome, cinema and history.* London: Routledge.
Wyke, M. (1999). Ancient Rome and the traditions of film history. *Screening the Past,* VI, http://tlweb.latrobe.edu.au/humanities/screeningthepast/firstrelease/fr0499/mwfr6b.htm
Ziolkowski, T. (1993). *Virgil and the moderns.* Princeton: Princeton University Press.

## Filmography

Amenábar, A. (2009). *Agora* (Newmarket).
Annuand, J-J. (1986). *The Name of the Rose* (Twentieth Century Fox).
Cameron, J. (1997). *Titanic* (Twentieth Century Fox).
DeMille, C. B. (1922). *Manslaughter* (Paramount Pictures).
DeMille, C. B. (1932). *The Ten Commandments* (Paramount Pictures, remade 1956).
Doring, A. (2008). *Blind Spot* (Woodstock).
Eastwood, C. (1992). *Unforgiven* (Warner Bros).
Ford, J. (1964). *Cheyenne Autumn* (Warner Bros).
Griffith, D. W. (1915). *Birth of a Nation* (Epoch).
Griffith, D. W. (1916). *Intolerance* (Triangle Film Corporation).

Klingler, W. (1943). *Titanic* (Universum Film AG).
Kubrick, S. (1960). *Spartacus* (Universal Pictures).
Lefler, Douglas. (1967). *The Last Legion* (The Weinstein Company).
LeRoy, M. (1951). *Quo Vadis* (MGM).
Macdonald, K. (2011). *The Eagle* (Universal Pictures).
Mann, A. (1950). *The Furies* (Paramount Pictures).
Mann, A. (1964). *The Fall of the Roman Empire* (Paramount Pictures).
Mann, A. (1969). *El Cid* (Allied Artists).
Marshall, N. (2010). *Centurion* (Pathe).
Peckinpah, S. (1969). *The Wild Bunch* (Warner Bros).
Ray, N. (1963). *55 Days at Peking* (Allied Artists).
Scott, R. (2000). *Gladiator* (Universal Pictures).
Sirk, D. (1954). *Sign of the Pagan* (Universal International).
Vidor, K. (1940). *Northwest Passage* (MGM).
Wyler, W. (1959). *Ben Hur* (MGM).
Zinnemann, F. (1952). *High Noon* (United Artists).

# INDEX

**A**
Adorno, T.W., 79n174, 84, 104n4, 111n104, 115, 142n9, 143n15
*Agora*, 179, 181, 182, 184
agri deserti, 23, 25
Alexander, P.J., 105n28
*The American Spectator*, 152
anthropological
  approaches, 14
  treatment, 60
antiquity, 1–3, 8, 9, 11, 12, 15, 22–4, 34, 36, 41, 42, 59, 61–5, 89, 90, 115, 174–5
Arnold Hugh Martin (A.H.M) Jones, 21, 68n1, 189n43
Arnold, M., 58, 79n169, 117
arrogant capital, 159
assassination, 31
authenticity, 51, 66, 67, 135, 177

**B**
Babylon, 9
Bachman, G., 82n216

Bal, M., 52, 78n143
Bann, S., 18n29, 54, 78n151
Baron, H., 104n15, 143n21
Barron, R., 193n102
Barthes, R., 53, 67, 75n91, 78n149, 82n223
Bartlett, R., 73n65, 92, 108n48, 109n63
Beard, M., 61, 73n66, 80n192
Bell, D., 153, 187n9
Benjamin, W., 6, 17n10, 59, 80n183
binary oppositions, 47
Black, J.B., 110n78, 192n88
Bowersock, G.W., 3, 9, 16n7, 91, 99, 107n38, 107n44, 136, 158
Braeur, G., 188n21
Brantlinger, P., 37, 73n70, 154, 187n13
bricolage, 46
Brodsky, J., 160, 189n35
Brown, P., 8, 23, 69n3, 71n35
Bryson, N., 52, 78n143
Buchanan, P.J., 171, 191n60
Buckley, J.H., 143n24

Note: Page numbers with "n" denote notes.

© The Editor(s) (if applicable) and The Author(s) 2016
J. Theodore, *The Modern Cultural Myth of the Decline and Fall of the Roman Empire*, DOI 10.1057/978-1-137-56997-4

Burckhardt, C.J., 54, 100–2, 110n91, 111n92, 111n97, 111n102
Burke, P., 74n90, 104n3
Bury, J.B., 33, 103n2, 157, 175, 176, 188n23
Byzantium, 10, 21, 37, 98

C
Cameron, A., 17n18, 24, 33, 70n19
Cameron, J., 38, 74n78, 162
Cantor, N.F., 17n11, 56
Cavallini, E., 128, 130, 145n51, 146n64
Chandler, J., 148n89
Chaplin, E., 41, 74n83
Chase, G., 18n30
Chinese whispers, 12
Christian Church, 22, 23, 26–8, 51, 91, 102
Christianity, 8, 27, 28, 33, 45, 88, 90, 94, 96, 97, 124–6, 131, 136–9, 153, 176, 177, 180–4
cinematic representations, 5, 11, 40, 58–68, 86, 120, 122–5, 127, 128, 130–2, 139, 141, 161, 177, 186, 196, 197
classical tradition, 36, 39, 59, 61, 62, 99, 121, 128, 160, 181, 184
classicism, 36–7, 59, 61, 63, 119, 185, 186, 197–9
*The Closing of the Western Mind—The Rise of Faith and the Fall of Reason*, 176
Cohen, P., 43, 44, 46
*The Collapse of Complex Societies*, 156
*coloni*, 23, 25
comparative inquiry, 36
complaints of moral decay, 160
Corliss, R., 170, 189n39, 190n54, 190n58
crisis of the third century, 157

Csapo, E., 75n97
*The Cultural Contradictions of Capitalism*, 153
*The Culture of Narcissism*, 152
Cyrino, M.S., 169, 190n57

D
Dark Ages, 31, 35, 61, 68, 89, 92, 121, 152, 154, 155, 184
Davis, C.T., 18n25
decadence, 10, 86–7, 100–3, 119, 120, 151, 154
decline of civilizations, 1, 34–9, 83–90, 98, 118, 155
Demandt, A., 16n6
DeMille, C.B., 10, 67, 82n222, 119, 122, 132, 140, 144n39
Dixon, K.R., 71n45
Dunne, J.G., 120, 144n29
Durant, A., 146n59
Durant, W., 129–31, 138, 140, 143n16, 145n56, 146n59, 170, 175, 197
Dwyer, J.C., 107n46
Dzielska, M., 193n98

E
*The Eagle*, 178
Eagleton, T., 13, 49, 53, 74n88
Eco, U., 60, 66, 76n109, 77n132, 80n189, 82n216
Edwards, C., 17n22, 80n194, 188n31
Elley, D., 16n5, 82n225, 127, 137, 141, 145n46, 149n105, 149n113, 150n113
Evans, R., 78n144

F
faddish practices, 152, 153
fall of empires, 6, 155, 185

INDEX    225

*The Fall of Public Man: On the Social Psychology of Capitalism*, 153–4
*Fall of the Roman Empire*, 126–41, 163, 166, 170, 196–7
*The Fall of the West: The Death of the Roman Superpower*, 174–6
False Consciousness, 58
Ferguson, N., 144n40, 171
Ferro, M., 17n15
Frankfurt school, 58, 60, 115
Franzoni, D., 167, 190n52
Frederick, B.C., 76n117
Freeman, C., 177, 191n80
Frye, N., 116, 142n11

G
Gay, P., 110n89, 110n90
Geertz, C., 5, 13, 14, 16n9, 77n121
general observations, 93, 95, 142n1
German Democratic Republic (GDP), 38
Gibbon, E., 8, 18n24, 21, 22, 28, 88, 91, 105n16, 108n52, 109n67, 125, 129, 130, 134, 136, 182, 192n91
  decadence, 100–3
  decline and fall, 90–9
Gilderhus, M., 79n161
*Gladiator*, 161–70, 197, 198
Goffart, W., 31, 32, 72n54, 72n58, 107n39
Goldsworthy, A., 174–6, 191n77
great instauration, 153
Greco-Roman heritage, 9
Gwynn, D.M., 28, 69n2, 71n41

H
Halliday, J., 145n42
Hall, S., 41, 42, 74n82
Heather, P., 29, 70n29, 71n48, 71n50

Henderson, J., 61, 73n66
Hepburn, R.W., 104n7
hermeneutics
  approach, 4–5
  methodology, 13–16
Herrnstein, R., 189n36
Heyer, P., 74n77
Highet, G., 99, 103, 104n11, 110n81, 121, 122, 144n35
*Historia Augusta*, 130, 134, 135
historical myopia, 67
historiography, 2, 5, 6, 11–13, 15, 24, 28, 29, 33, 34, 49, 54, 55, 66, 68, 83, 90
Horkheimer, M., 84, 104n4
Howells, R., 7, 16n2, 17n17, 19n45, 38, 50, 77n134
humanity, 9, 44, 48
Hypatia, 179, 180, 183, 184

I
impression, 7, 22, 119, 138, 168, 176, 185
intellectual armoury, 13

J
James, B.J., 152, 155, 187n7
James, H., 191n61
Jauss, H.-R., 53, 78n146
Johnson, C.A., 170, 171, 173, 190n59, 191n69
Jones, A.H.M., 21–3, 25, 26, 28, 33, 68n1
Joshel, S., 190n51

K
Kennedy, P., 159, 160, 185, 188n29
Klingler, W., 74n76
Knox, B., 59, 80n180, 160, 188n34

Kracauer, S., 7, 17n16, 48, 58, 64,
    77n122, 79n175

**L**
Lang, A., 75n95
Lasch, C., 152, 187n5
*The Last Legion*, 178
Late Antiquity, 8, 9, 22, 24
Leach, E., 76n112
Leavis, Q.D., 59, 80n184
Lefler, D., 178, 192n89
Leotard, J.-F., 78n140
LeRoy, M., 122, 125
Levey, M., 149n100
Lévi-Strauss, C., 2, 3, 5, 14, 16n3, 38,
    43, 46–50, 55, 76n111, 76n114,
    77n119, 84, 117, 120, 195, 196
Liebeschuetz, J.H.W.G., 70n28
limitations, 28–30, 33, 34, 44, 48
Lindley, A., 60, 68, 80n185
Lindsay, V., 60, 80n188
Littleton, C.S., 192n84
Livingstone, E.A., 104n12
Lowenthal, D., 53, 78n150
Lukacs, J., 151
luxuria, 10

**M**
Macdonald, K., 178
Machiavelli, N., 85, 91, 94, 95, 102,
    107n43
Malinowski, B., 43–6, 51, 75n100
Mampaso, A., 183, 193n95
manifold weaknesses, 28
Mann, A., 129, 134–5, 138, 145n54
Mannes, M., 155, 187n18
*Manslaughter*, 119
*Marius the Epicurean*, 137
Marwick, A., 57, 18n38
mass culture, 151–61

Mathisen, R.W., 72n51
McClintock, P., 193n99
mentalities, 2
modernity, 2, 68
modern mind, 45, 64, 83
Mommsen, T., 11, 103, 106n29,
    111n105
Monaco, J., 81n210
moral judgements, 93, 126
Morgan, D., 12, 18n33
Morgenthau, H., 155, 187n16
*Motion Picture Herald*, 140
Muggerridge, M., 152, 187n6
Muller, M.F., 44, 45, 75n96
Murphy, 173
Murray, C., 160, 189n36
Muschamp, H., 162, 189n40
myth, 2–4, 6–7, 195–6
    anthropological approaches, 14
    atypical model, 34–9
    interdisciplinary study, 39–40
    theory, 41–50

**N**
Neilson, F., 118, 119, 144n27
*New York Herald Tribune*, 141
Nicolls, J.H., 111n93
9/11, 170–7
Novick, P., 78n137

**O**
Ordoña, M., 193n103

**P**
pax deorum, 27
Philips, K., 159, 188n32
physical degeneration, 101
Piganiol, A., 32, 72n57
pliable period, 15

Pocock, J.G., 99, 110n84
Popper, K., 53, 55, 78n145
postmodernism, 52
Power, E., 32, 72n56
Pratt, K.J., 17n20
prehistory, 67
professional history, 11, 55, 57, 61, 157
propaganda, 5, 38, 57, 58, 117
proper history, 54, 55
Pulver, A., 82n215

**Q**
Quinton, A., 120, 144n30
*Quo Vadis*, 122, 124, 125, 131, 136, 140

**R**
reception theory, 1, 42
*recreation of the Roman Empire*, 197
Rehm, W., 114
Renaissance, 2, 9, 36, 89, 91, 92, 98, 100, 101, 103, 121, 181, 182, 186
representation, 1
Richards, G., 65, 81n211
Riefenstahl, L., 166
Roman
　narratives and cold war, 121–6
　twentieth-century society, 113–20
Rosenberg, B., 144n31
Rosenstone, R.A., 61, 80n191
Rose, P.W., 36, 73n67
Rousseau, J.-J., 96, 109n66, 155, 188n20

**S**
Scott, R., 136, 161, 167, 190n48, 190n49
The Senate and people of Rome (SPQR), 169

Sennett, R., 154, 187n11
Shulman, M., 120, 144n28
*Sign of the Pagan*, 123, 125
Sinai, R., 151, 152, 155, 186n3, 187n4
Smith, A., 96, 109n65
social constructionist, 42
Solomon, J., 16n5, 81n195, 145n47, 167, 168
Southern, P., 71n45
Spengler, O., 24, 35, 85, 114–9, 138, 142n3, 198
Spolia, 41, 42
Starn, R., 84, 193n104
Stavrianos, L.S., 151, 186n1, 187n4
Storey, J., 58, 79n163
story-telling natives, 48
*Study of History*, 117
Swart, S., 193n99

**T**
Tainter, J.A., 35, 156–58, 185, 188n23
Theodosian Code, 23, 25, 26
*Times Literary Supplement*, 177
Toynbee, A.J., 117, 143n19, 143n20, 152, 188n30
tradition, 12
*Triumph of the Will*, 166

**V**
Vance, W.L., 159, 188n31
Vidal, G., 122, 144n40

**W**
Wadge, R., 192n85
Wagar, W.W., 154, 187n12
Wallace, L., 148n94
Ward, A.M., 128, 145n53

Ward-Perkins, B., 21, 23, 24, 28, 31, 69n2, 69n6, 70n18, 71n50, 72n53, 72n55
Watson, P., 191n81
West, C., 160, 188n33
Western Roman Empire, 21–34
White, D.M., 120, 144n31
White, H., 4, 16n8, 18n29, 54, 78n152, 78n153, 78n156, 79n158, 195
Whittington, H., 149n99
Wickham, C., 30, 72n52
Wildberg, C., 193n98
Williams, D., 66, 82n220
Winkler, M.M., 18n31, 18n34, 61, 62, 80n193, 81n197, 81n198, 81n209, 127, 145n48, 161
Wootton, D., 110n83
Wyke, M., 11, 62, 64, 80n179

**Z**
Ziolkowski, T., 143n18

The manufacturer's authorised representative in the EU is Springer Nature Customer Service Centre GmbH, Europaplatz 3, 69115 Heidelberg, Germany. If you have any concerns regarding our products, please contact ProductSafety@springernature.com

Printed and bound by CPI Group (UK) Ltd, Croydon, CR0 4YY
23/03/2026
02076682-0002